The Essential Guide

to

Nutrition

and the

Foods We Eat

Everything You Need to Know About the Foods You Eat

THE ESSENTIAL GUIDE

to

Nutrition

and the

Foods We Eat

The American Dietetic Association
with
Jean Pennington, PhD, RD

Quill

A *HarperResource* Book
An Imprint of HarperCollinsPublishers

HarperCollins books may be purchased for educational, business, or sales promotional use. For information, please write to: Special Markets Department, HarperCollins Publishers, Inc., 10 East 53rd Street, New York, New York 10022.

Designed by Jessica Shatan

Library of Congress Cataloging-in-Publication Data

The essential guide to nutrition and the foods we eat : everything you need to know about the foods you eat / The American Dietetic Association with Jean Pennington, editor. — 1st ed.
   p.   cm.
   ISBN 0–06–271595-X (hc). — ISBN 0–06–273346-X (pb)
   1. Nutrition—Tables. 2. Food—Composition—Tables. I. Pennington, Jean A. Thompson. II. American Dietetic Association.
   TX551.E87 1999   98–41937
   613.2′8—dc21   CIP

03 CC/RRD 10 9 8 7 6 5 4

Contents

INTRODUCTION   1

For Starters   2
Can the foods I eat today really affect my health? • Can I really eat any food I want?

The Meat of the Matter   6
A Guide to Your Food Choices • What do people really know about food and nutrition? • How do I make the Food Guide Pyramid work for me? • What about vegetarians? • Do all foods fit in the Pyramid? • Where does my cheeseburger (and other mixed dishes) fit? • Do alcoholic beverages fit? • How many servings from each group are right for me (and my family)? • Is it okay to eat the same foods every day? • Do I need to follow the Pyramid every day? • What should my meal look like? • Where do I begin to make changes in my diet?

About the American Dietetic Association

The American Dietetic Association is the world's largest organization of food and nutrition professionals. Founded in 1917, The American Dietetic Association promotes optimal nutrition to improve public health and well-being. The Association has nearly 70,000 members, of whom approximately 75 percent are registered dietitians (RD). The membership also includes dietetic technicians (DTR) and others holding advanced degrees in nutrition and dietetics. As the public education center of the Association, the National Center for Nutrition and Dietetics provides programs and services to inform and educate the public about food and nutrition issues. The Center and The American Dietetic Association are located at 216 W. Jackson Boulevard, Chicago, IL 60606.

Registered dietitians offer preventive and therapeutic nutrition services in a variety of settings, including health care, business, research, and educational organizations, as well as private practice. Registered dietitians working in the health-care field serve as vital members of medical teams, three-quarters providing medical nutrition therapy to treat illnesses, injuries, and chronic conditions such as diabetes.

The credentials "RD" signify that a practitioner has completed a rigorous program of education and training. The registered dietitian must have at least a baccalaureate degree in an approved program of dietetics or a related field from an accredited U.S. college or university. In addition, he or she must complete an internship or similar experience and pass a national credentialing exam. To retain RD status, dietitians must fulfill continuing education requirements to update and enhance their knowledge and skills.

To find a registered dietitian, the expert in diet, health, and nutrition, ask your physician or call your local hospital. You can also access The American Dietetic Association's toll-free dietitian referral service by calling 800-366-1655 or visiting the web site at www.eatright.org.

Acknowledgments

We acknowledge and thank the many food companies and restaurants that responded to our request and provided food label nutrition information for this book. We also offer our thanks to Michele Tuttle, MPH, RD, for patiently entering and organizing the data; to Sally Schakel, RD, for her thorough review of the data tables; to George Alexander for his computer assistance; and to Betsy Hornick, MS, RD, for her editorial guidance and assistance.

Foods included in this book were chosen to be representative of the many categories and types of foods available in today's grocery stores. The actual nutrient information came from several different sources: food manufacturers, directly from food labels, and from FDA and USDA databases for fresh fruit, vegetables, meat, poultry, and fish. Be aware that the nutrition information on labels of specific food products that you buy may be different from the values reported here because of changes in product formulations (recipes), sizes of packages, or serving sizes.

Introduction

Over the past several decades, our understanding of the relationship between food (and the nutrients it contains) and health has grown tremendously. For instance, we now know that our chances of developing certain chronic diseases, including type 2 diabetes, cancer, osteoporosis, hypertension, obesity, and diseases of the heart, cardiovascular system, and kidney may be linked to what we eat. With this increased knowledge, dietary recommendations now emphasize including protective nutrients, like fiber and calcium, and limiting intake of nutrients such as fat, saturated fat, cholesterol, and sodium, which are associated with chronic diseases. To help put these dietary recommendations into practice, two important tools are available to help consumers make wise food choices: the Food Guide Pyramid and the Nutrition Facts panel (found on food labels).

If you are like most Americans, you probably rush through the grocery store without taking time to carefully examine food labels. Maybe you glance at the Nutrition Facts on food labels, but also wonder what the numbers really mean and how to use them. Chances are you are aware of the Food Guide Pyramid, but don't necessarily put the recommendations into practice. You're not alone. With the busy pace of life today, these are challenges for many people. To help you tackle these challenges, we've compiled nutrition information from the food labels of many of the foods you'll find in your grocery store, and grouped these according to the Food Guide Pyramid for your use at home. You now have the information gathered together in one place to use as a reference and to examine at your leisure.

This book is designed for anyone who wants to learn how to eat well. It will help you think about foods and the nutrients they supply as you make your selections in grocery stores and restaurants, and as you prepare foods to eat at home. You may have picked up this book for the nutrient information, but you'll also want to take some time to read through these introductory pages. You'll learn just how easy it is to make the Food Guide Pyramid work for you and your family. Recommended serving portions for foods from each food group are described along with the number of servings you need each day and how to count servings in mixed dishes. Useful tips are provided for how to use the nutrition information on food labels to make "every food fit" in your eating plan. If you're interested in understanding how nutrient information in foods is determined, you can read about how food scientists measure the amounts of nutrients in foods.

We encourage you to be open-minded and adventurous about foods. There's no doubt that eating is one of life's greatest pleasures. Everyone deserves an opportunity to achieve good health without sacrificing the enjoyment of great-tasting food. The health benefits that come from eating well and being physically active are tremendous. What is most important is that you make healthy choices that fit your lifestyle so you can do the things you want to do. Good luck in achieving your goals and the best of health to you!

FOR STARTERS

Can the foods I eat today really affect my health?
Absolutely, although the effects may not be immediate. Many health problems related to the foods we eat take time to develop. For example, osteoporosis, obesity, cardiovascular disease, type 2

diabetes, hypertension, and certain types of cancer are diseases that may be related to the foods we eat and to our lifestyles. These health problems often develop slowly over time, with few or no apparent symptoms until the disease is diagnosed. When symptoms of these diseases do become apparent, it may be too late to fully repair the damage done to your body.

Foods are composed of many hundreds of different chemical compounds. Some of these chemical compounds are called nutrients because they are known to nourish our bodies and perform important life functions, such as providing energy, promoting growth and healing, maintaining the health of body tissues, or facilitating important chemical reactions in body tissues. The main nutrients in foods are:

water

carbohydrate (including starch, dietary fiber, and sugars)

protein

fat

vitamins

minerals

While much is known about the nutrients and other compounds in foods and their relationships to disease, much remains to be learned about the complex interactions between nutrients and many other compounds in foods. Here are some key associations known about food intake and health. You may see statements referring to these associations on certain food labels:

- Eating enough calcium may reduce your risk for osteoporosis (thin, fragile bones).

- Limiting the amount of sodium you eat may reduce your risk for hypertension (high blood pressure).

- Limiting the amount of saturated fat and cholesterol you eat may reduce your risk for heart disease.

- Eating fruits, vegetables, and grain products that contain fiber may reduce your risk for heart disease.

- Limiting the amount of total fat you eat may help reduce your risk for cancer.

- Eating fiber-containing grain products, fruits, and vegetables may reduce your risk for cancer.

- Eating fruits and vegetables that are "low in fat" and "good sources" of dietary fiber, vitamin A, or vitamin C may reduce your risk for cancer.

- Women eating adequate amounts of folic acid, one of the B vitamins, throughout their childbearing years may reduce their risk of having a child with a neural tube defect.

- Eating soluble fiber from whole oats as part of a diet low in saturated fat and cholesterol may reduce your risk for heart disease.

- Eating foods with soluble fiber from psyllium seed husk (in certain breakfast cereals) as part of a diet low in saturated fat and cholesterol may reduce your risk for heart disease.

- Eating foods with sugar alcohols does not promote tooth decay.

Can I really eat any food I want?
Basically, yes. But be sensible. You can enjoy *all* foods, just don't overdo it. If you have favorite foods that you want to eat frequently (even daily), you can learn how to build them into your eating plan. The keys to healthy eating are balance, variety, and moderation. *Balance* means eating foods from different food groups, *variety* means eating different types of foods each day

DISEASE DEFINITIONS

Osteoporosis: bone thinning, which increases risk of fractures; more common in women and the elderly. Osteoporosis may result from inadequate calcium intake. It is also related to inadequate vitamin D intake or insufficient exposure to sunshine, lack of physical activity, lowered estrogen levels, and genetics.

Cardiovascular Disease: diseases of the heart and blood vessels, which may cause heart attacks and strokes. Cardiovascular disease may be caused by hardening of the arteries and/or by the buildup of fat (especially cholesterol) in the artery walls.

Type 2 Diabetes: adult-onset diabetes usually associated with being overweight. Type 1 diabetes usually begins in childhood and requires treatment with insulin as well as diet. Diabetes is a complicated disease, but basically it means that the body has difficulty moving glucose (the breakdown product of the carbohydrates we eat) from the blood to body tissues. This results in a high blood-glucose level and sugar (glucose) in the urine.

Hyptertension: high blood pressure; associated with a higher risk for stroke and heart attack.

Cancer: a disease in which cells multiply out of control and disrupt the normal functioning of one or more of the body's organs. About one-third of cancers are related to what we eat. For example, breast cancer is associated with a high fat intake, and colon cancer is associated with a low intake of fruits and vegetables.

from each food group, and *moderation* means eating reasonable portions of foods. The nutrition information on the labels of foods (some of which is reproduced for you in this book) can help you by identifying a reasonable serving portion and tell you how a serving of food contributes to your recommended daily intake of nutrients.

Of course, there are some exceptions to the "all foods can fit" concept. If you, a friend, or a family member are on a therapeutic diet, then some foods may not fit into your eating pattern. For example, some people need to limit foods with large amounts of sodium, fat, saturated fat, or cholesterol because of a medical condition, such as heart disease. If certain foods make you sick or worsen a medical condition, you will need to make careful food choices. If you have special dietary concerns, consult with a registered dietitian to help you choose foods and plan your meals. (A registered dietitian will have the initials R.D. after her/his name.)

THE MEAT OF THE MATTER

A Guide to Your Food Choices

Because of the known relationships between the foods we eat and our health, nutrition and health experts offer general advice, referred to as the Dietary Guidelines for Americans. These guidelines are developed by nutrition and health experts who examine research related to food and health. The first set of guidelines was published in 1980. They were revised in 1985, 1990 and again in 1995 to reflect the most current knowledge about diet and health. The guidelines are published jointly by the U.S. Department of Health and Human Services (DHHS) and U.S. Department of Agriculture (USDA). The current *Dietary Guidelines for Americans* (3rd ed., 1995) are:

- Eat a variety of foods.

- Balance the food you eat with physical activity. Maintain or improve your weight.

- Choose a diet with plenty of grain products, vegetables, and fruit.

- Choose a diet low in fat, saturated fat, and cholesterol.

- Choose a diet moderate in sugars.

- Choose a diet moderate in salt and sodium.

- If you drink alcoholic beverages, do so in moderation.

What do people really know about food and nutrition?

The American Dietetic Association (ADA) conducted a survey in 1997 asking adults about food and health knowledge and behavior. Here are some of the results from that survey:

67% knew about the Food Guide Pyramid

34% said they are careful in selecting what they eat to
achieve a balanced diet

40% don't want to give up the foods they like

43% said they make an effort to get regular physical activity

It appears from the ADA survey that many people are quite knowledgeable about food and health. The question remains, how do we really eat? The current state of American eating resembles a top-heavy pyramid. A recent USDA evaluation of American eating habits indicates that we're eating more than we should from the tip of the pyramid (fats, oils, and sweets) and less than we should from the fruit, dairy, and meat groups. On average, servings from the grain and vegetable groups are at the low end of the recommended ranges. We could improve our eating patterns (and our health) by planning our meals using the Pyramid below as our guide. This means focusing more on grains, vegetables, and fruits, ensuring adequate intakes of dairy products and meat, and eating less from the tip of the Pyramid.

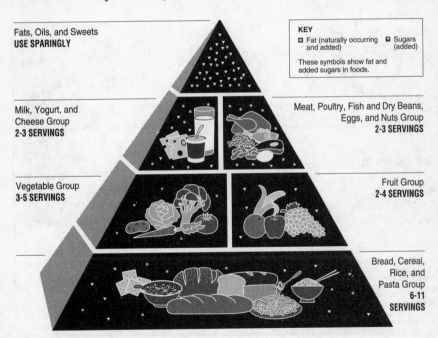

Fats, Oils, and Sweets
USE SPARINGLY

KEY
☐ Fat (naturally occurring   ☑ Sugars
and added)   (added)

These symbols show fat and
added sugars in foods.

Milk, Yogurt, and
Cheese Group
2-3 SERVINGS

Meat, Poultry, Fish and Dry Beans,
Eggs, and Nuts Group
2-3 SERVINGS

Vegetable Group
3-5 SERVINGS

Fruit Group
2-4 SERVINGS

Bread, Cereal,
Rice, and
Pasta Group
**6-11
SERVINGS**

EVOLUTION OF U.S. FOOD GUIDES

Have you ever wondered what happened to the Basic 7 or the Basic 4 Food Guides? If you were born before 1950, you probably remember learning about a circle with seven food groups represented as slices of a pie.

BASIC 7 FOOD GUIDE (1946–58)

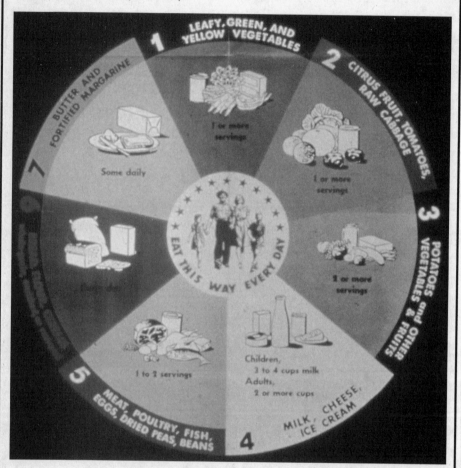

This graphic was developed by the USDA in the mid-1940s, and was used during and after World War II. It was the first national food guide used in the U.S.

In 1958, USDA simplified the Basic 7 to the Basic 4. The Basic 4 Food Guide consisted of four food groups represented by squares within a larger rectangle:

BASIC 4 FOOD GUIDE (1958–79)

Milk Group

Children under 9 years	2–3 cups/day
Children 9–12 years	3 or more cups/day
Teenagers	4 or more cups/day
Adults	2 or more cups/day

Meat Group
2 or more servings/day
> Beef, veal, pork, lamb, poultry, fish, eggs
> Alternatives: dry beans, dry peas, nuts

Vegetable & Fruit Group
4 or more servings/day including:
1. 1 citrus fruit or other source of vitamin C
2. 1 dark green or deep-yellow vegetable for vitamin A at least every other day

Bread & Cereal Group
4 or more servings/day
> Whole grain, enriched, or restored products

The emphasis of both the Basic 7 and the Basic 4 was to provide adequate energy and enough of the "protective" nutrients (protein, vitamins, and minerals) to prevent nutrient deficiencies. It was not uncommon in those years for people in certain areas of the U.S. to have diseases like pellagra from too little niacin, rickets from too little vitamin D, and even poor growth from too little protein and calories. That's why the meat group was emphasized for protein and iron; the dairy group for protein, calcium, phosphorus, riboflavin, and vitamin A; the grain group for thiamin, riboflavin, niacin, and iron; and the fruit and vegetable groups for vitamins A and C.

In 1979, the USDA issued a modified version of the Basic 4 Food Guide which included a fifth food group— the fats, sweets, and alcohol group. The guidance for this new group was "to be moderate in the consumption of foods containing fat and sugar and to consume alcoholic beverages moderately or not at all."

In 1992, the Food Guide Pyramid was introduced. Unlike the Basic 7, which illustrates "pie" slices for seven food groups and the Basic 4, which puts equal emphasis on all four food groups, the Pyramid shows a decreasing emphasis on foods from the base to the tip. The Food Guide Pyramid is actually a visual representation of the Dietary Guidelines for Americans, with emphasis on adequate intake of grain products, fruits, and vegetables, and moderate intakes of fat, saturated fat, cholesterol, and sugar.

How do I make the Food Guide Pyramid work for me?

The Food Guide Pyramid is constructed in the shape of a pyramid to emphasize proportions of foods from each group. While the number of recommended servings differs for each food group, all five of the main food groups are important. Each of the five food groups make important contributions to your overall diet. The tip of the Pyramid is not considered a food group because these "extras" provide primarily calories with few nutrients. Your daily food plan should be individualized to meet your personal energy and nutrient needs (more on this to come).

Bread, Cereal, Rice, and Pasta Group (6 to 11 servings each day). The grain group makes up the largest section at the base of the Pyramid. So the largest number of servings should be from this group. In addition to bread, cereals, rice, and pasta, other foods in this group include tortillas, crackers, rolls, bagels, buns, muffins, waffles, pancakes, and many other foods made from wheat, rice, oats, corn, and barley. Grain products are sources of carbohydrates, B vitamins (thiamin, riboflavin, and niacin), and iron. In addition, if you select whole-grain products or products made from whole-grain flour, you will also obtain dietary fiber and other important vitamins (vitamin B_6, pantothenic acid, folic acid) and minerals (zinc, copper, magnesium, and manganese). Since January 1998, refined grain products have also been fortified with the B vitamin folic acid, because low intakes of folic acid during pregnancy have been associated with birth defects.

Vegetable Group (3 to 5 servings each day) and Fruit Group (2 to 4 servings each day).
The next level up on the Pyramid contains the vegetable group and the fruit group. An easy way to remember how many servings to include from this level is to think "five a day" for a minimum of five servings per day of vegetables and fruits combined. There are many important nutrients and food components in vegetables and fruits that help us stay healthy and reduce our risks for cancer and other diseases. Some of these components (dietary

fiber, antioxidants, and other food chemicals, such as phyto-chemicals) have been identified and others have not. Keep in mind that health benefits of vegetables and fruits come from eating them as foods, and that you probably can't get all the same effects if you try to replace these nutrient-rich foods with dietary supplements (such as vitamin and/or mineral pills).

Milk, Yogurt, and Cheese Group (2 to 3 servings each day) and Meat, Poultry, Fish, Dry Beans, Eggs, and Nuts Group (2 to 3 servings each day).
The third level of the Pyramid includes the "milk" group and the "meat" group. Milk, yogurt, and cheese provide protein, calcium, phosphorus, magnesium, and riboflavin along with other essential nutrients. Meat, poultry, and fish provide protein, iron, zinc, vitamin B_6, vitamin B_{12}, other B vitamins, and trace elements. Legumes (beans and peas) can serve as meat alternatives and provide protein and iron as well as carbohydrate, dietary fiber, B vitamins, and various minerals.

Tip of the Pyramid (use sparingly).
The tip of the Pyramid includes foods that are high in fat (such as butter, cream, margarine, and vegetable oils) or sugar (such as table sugar, honey, molasses, and syrups). These foods provide calories, but few other nutrients. The foods in the tip add pleasure to eating because they contribute flavor to foods from the other groups. The advice of the Pyramid is to use them "sparingly," so as not to overdo calories and fat.

What about vegetarians?
Vegetarians can also use the Food Guide Pyramid. Within the meat group of the Food Guide Pyramid, there are quite a few nonmeat foods that provide protein and other nutrients found in meat, including eggs, beans, peas, soybeans, lentils, peanuts, peanut butter, other legumes, nuts, and seeds. Vegetarians can obtain adequate protein and other nutrients from these other foods, of which most are plant-based. Vegetarians do not need to combine specific foods

within a meal. The body makes its own complete proteins if a variety of plant foods—vegetables, grains, legumes, nuts, and seeds—and enough calories are eaten during the day.

If dairy products are not eaten, other foods rich in calcium should be selected, such as legumes, fortified soy foods, certain vegetables (bok choy, broccoli, kale, collard, mustard, and turnip greens), dried figs, and calcium-fortified orange juice and grain products. Vegans (vegetarians who do not eat any animal products, including eggs or dairy products) need to pay attention to obtaining adequate amounts of vitamin B_{12}, calcium, iron, zinc, and other trace elements. Children, teenagers, pregnant women, and breast-feeding women who follow a vegan diet should be sure that their nutrient and energy intakes are sufficient to provide for adequate growth, development, and/or milk production. A registered dietitian (RD) can help plan vegetarian diets that meet individual needs.

A Food Guide Pyramid for vegetarian meal planning follows:

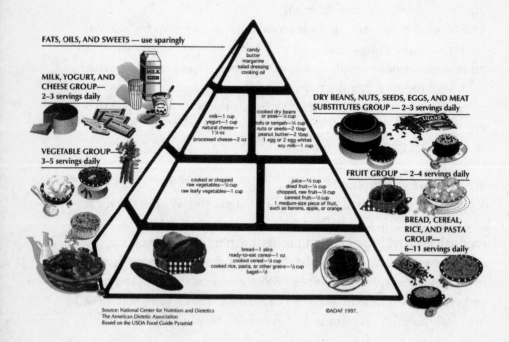

FATS, OILS, AND SWEETS — use sparingly

candy
butter
margarine
salad dressing
cooking oil

MILK, YOGURT, AND CHEESE GROUP—
2–3 servings daily

milk—1 cup
yogurt—1 cup
natural cheese—
1½ oz
processed cheese—2 oz

DRY BEANS, NUTS, SEEDS, EGGS, AND MEAT SUBSTITUTES GROUP — 2–3 servings daily

cooked dry beans
or peas—½ cup
tofu or tempeh—¼ cup
nuts or seeds—2 tbsp
peanut butter—2 tbsp
1 egg or 2 egg whites
soy milk—1 cup

VEGETABLE GROUP—
3–5 servings daily

cooked or chopped
raw vegetables—½ cup
raw leafy vegetables—1 cup

juice—¾ cup
dried fruit—¼ cup
chopped, raw fruit—½ cup
canned fruit—½ cup
1 medium-size piece of fruit,
such as banana, apple, or orange

FRUIT GROUP — 2–4 servings daily

BREAD, CEREAL, RICE, AND PASTA GROUP—
6–11 servings daily

bread—1 slice
ready-to-eat cereal—1 oz
cooked cereal—½ cup
cooked rice, pasta, or other grains—½ cup
bagel—½

Source: National Center for Nutrition and Dietetics
The American Dietetic Association
Based on the USDA Food Guide Pyramid

©ADAF 1997.

Do all foods fit in the Pyramid?
Some foods may not seem to "fit" in any one food group. Foods
are wonderfully complex mixtures of ingredients and nutrients.
While it is probably quite clear to you where most foods fit in the
Pyramid groupings, for some foods, it may not be so obvious. For
other foods, changes to nutrient composition that occur during
processing or preparation may alter their Pyramid grouping. Here
are some examples and guidelines to help you think about where
some "confusing" foods fit in the Food Guide Pyramid:

- Legumes (beans, peas, and lentils) are included in the
  meat group because they are sources of protein, one of
  the major nutrients contributed by this group. Choices
  include pinto beans, kidney beans, pink beans, cowpeas
  (also known as black-eyed peas), lentils, black beans, red
  beans, soybeans, lima beans (mature and immature), and
  split peas. Legumes are actually quite versatile as they fit
  into more than one group. A serving of legumes (about ½
  cup cooked) can be counted as a serving from the meat
  group or from the vegetable group, but not both. Legumes
  also fit in the vegetable group because, like vegetables,
  they are good sources of fiber and other important
  nutrients.

- Other beans and peas, like green beans, Italian beans,
  string beans, snap beans, wax beans, and snow peas (the
  long flat peas commonly used in Chinese cooking) belong
  in the vegetable group. They do not serve as protein
  sources, although they contain other important nutrients
  that vegetables provide.

- Meat substitutes and analogues, such as vegetarian
  patties, are usually made from soybeans or other legumes
  and constitute servings from the meat group.

- Peanuts are actually legumes. Peanuts and peanut butter
  are sources of protein, but contain more fat than other

legumes in the meat group. Compared to other nuts (pecans, cashews, walnuts) and seeds, however, peanuts contain less fat.

- Bacon generally counts as a fat rather than a meat, although Canadian bacon is lower in fat and fits in the meat group.

- Creams of various kinds, such as whipped cream, half & half, sour cream, and cream cheese, do contain some calcium and other nutrients, but are higher in fat than other dairy products and are considered fats rather than servings from the milk, yogurt, and cheese group.

- Tomato sauce and tomato paste carry many of the same nutrients as tomatoes and count as vegetable servings. Ketchup doesn't count as a vegetable serving because it loses much of its nutrients during processing. The same holds true for cucumbers and pickles; cucumbers count as vegetables, but pickles don't. Ketchup and sweet pickles actually belong in the tip of the Pyramid because of the sugar added to them. Dill pickles are "extra" foods because they contain very few calories or nutrients.

- Preserves and jams are fruit products that are high in sugar and don't supply all of the nutrients of the fruits from which they were derived, so they fit in the Pyramid tip.

- Potato chips actually count as a vegetable serving, but when they're fried, they also contain a hefty amount of fat. Compared to a medium baked potato (3 ounces), which contains about 70 calories and virtually no fat, 1 ounce of potato chips contains about 150 calories and almost 10 grams of fat. Of course, potato chips that are baked or made with fat substitutes contain less fat and fewer calories.

- Regular salad dressings, margarine, butter, cooking oil, mayonnaise, syrups, candy, and regular soft drinks belong in the tip of the Pyramid because they provide primarily fat and/or sugar.

- Beverages such as coffee, tea, cereal coffee, spring/mineral/tap waters, and artificially sweetened beverages contain few calories and are considered "extra" foods.

Where does my cheeseburger (and other mixed dishes) fit?
Many of the foods we eat are mixed-dish entrees or desserts, such as sandwiches, pizza, lasagna, stews, carrot cake, and puddings. Mixed-dish foods contain foods from more than one food group, and therefore "count" as servings from more than one group. Let's look at two examples:
Large cheeseburger:

Ingredients	Pyramid Groups
Bun	2 grain group servings
Lettuce, tomato, and onion (about ½ cup combined)	1 vegetable group serving
1½ oz processed cheese	1 milk group serving
4 oz cooked ground beef	2 meat group servings
Mayonnaise	tip of the pyramid

Large slice of thick crust cheese pizza with vegetable toppings:

Ingredients	Pyramid Groups
Pizza crust	3 bread group servings
Tomato sauce, mushrooms, and green pepper (about ½ cup combined)	1 vegetable group serving
2 oz mozzarella cheese	2 milk group servings

With a little bit of thought, you can "break down" your mixed dish entrees and desserts into their component foods and fit the foods into the groups of the pyramid. For some foods such as soups, you'll need to do a bit of investigative work to determine how to group them. Soups may have a grain base (such as pasta or rice), a vegetable base (such as tomato, potato, or corn), a milk base (such as cream soups), or a water base (such as bouillon or broth), and they may contain a variety of ingredients (including cream, butter, or oils). If you think there is enough of a grain, vegetable, meat, and/or milk in a soup (compared to a Pyramid serving portion), count it as a serving or half a serving from one or more of these groups. If the soup is primarily broth, classify it as an extra food.

Do alcoholic beverages fit?

Many people enjoy wine, beer, liqueurs, cocktails, and various distilled spirits. While the Food Group Pyramid does not provide a group for alcoholic beverages, the Dietary Guidelines for Americans recommend that if you consume these beverages, you should do so in moderation. This means no more than one alcoholic beverage per day for women and no more than two alcoholic beverages for men.

How many servings from each group are right for me (and my family)?

Each Pyramid group has a recommended range of servings to account for individual differences in how many calories people need each day. Your needs will depend on your age, sex, and how active you are. Children in growth spurts and women who are pregnant or nursing their babies need extra calories and nutrients. Teenage boys and young men (18–24 years) probably have the highest calorie and nutrient requirements of all. Men generally have higher calorie needs than women because men (on average) are bigger than women and have more muscle mass. However, larger or more physically active women may have similar (or higher) calorie needs than smaller or less active men. Our calorie needs tend to decrease gradually with age, and our calorie needs in our older years are largely dependent on how active we remain.

Use the table shown here to get an idea of how many servings from each food group are right for you and members of your family.

	MANY WOMEN OLDER ADULTS	CHILDREN TEEN GIRLS ACTIVE WOMEN MOST MEN	TEEN BOYS ACTIVE MEN
Calorie level*	about 1,600	about 2,200	about 2,800
Bread servings	6	9	11
Vegetable servings	3	4	5
Fruit servings	2	3	4
Milk servings	2–3+	2–3+	2–3+
Meat servings	2 (about 5 oz total)	2 (about 6 oz total)	3 (7 oz total)

These are approximate calorie totals if you choose low-fat, lean foods from the five major groups and use foods from the fats, oils, and sweets group sparingly.

+ *Women who are pregnant or breast-feeding, teenagers, children, and young adults (up to age 24) need at least three servings per day to help meet their calcium requirements.*

The calorie levels of 1,600, 2,200, and 2,800 are average requirements. Actual energy needs vary from person to person depending on body size and shape, resting metabolic rate, physical activity, and rate of growth (for children and teenagers). If you need more calories, you can choose extra servings of foods from the various groups and/or add foods from the tip of the Pyramid (fats, oils, and sweets) to your current food selections. An option for adding more food to your meal plan without getting too many extra calories is to select more items from the fruit and vegetable groups. Many of these foods are low in calories, and they provide dietary fiber and various vitamins and minerals.

Here are some guidelines on how to measure a serving.

FOOD GROUP AND SERVING SIZES	HINTS FOR ESTIMATING PORTION SIZE
BREAD, CEREAL, RICE, AND PASTA GROUP	
A serving is:	
1 slice bread	a cassette tape
½ bagel	whole bagel (2 servings) = a hockey puck
1 oz (about 1 cup) ready-to-eat cereal	a large handful
½ cup cooked cereal, rice, or pasta	a cupcake wrapper
1 small tortilla	6 inches, or the size of a small plate
1 pancake	a compact disk
VEGETABLE GROUP	
A serving is:	
1 cup raw, leafy vegetables	4 outer romaine or iceberg lettuce leaves
½ cup other vegetables, cooked or raw	a small fist
1 medium potato (2 servings)	a computer mouse
¾ cup vegetable juice	
FRUIT GROUP	
A serving is:	
1 medium apple, orange, pear, or peach	a tennis ball
½ cup chopped, cooked, or canned fruit	1 cup fruit (2 servings) = a baseball
¾ cup fruit juice	
MILK, YOGURT, AND CHEESE GROUP	
A serving is:	
1 cup milk	
1½ oz natural cheese	6 dice, 3 dominoes, or a 9-volt battery
2 oz processed cheese	8 dice
MEAT, POULTRY, FISH, LEGUME, EGG, NUT, AND SEED GROUP	
A serving is:	
2–3 oz cooked lean meat, fish, or poultry	a deck of cards, bar of soap, or palm of your hand

1 oz (½ serving)	a matchbox or computer diskette
8 oz (3–4 servings)	thin paperback book

Count as 1 ounce of meat:

½ cup cooked beans or peas	
1 egg or ¼ cup egg substitute	
2 tablespoons peanut butter	a ping pong ball
⅓ cup nuts or seeds	a handful

Most of us tend to underestimate the quantities of food that we actually eat. Using recommended portion sizes, you'll see that it's actually quite easy to reach the recommended 11 grain servings per day (if that's right for you). Consider the following daily intake, which easily adds up to 11 grain servings:

Grain servings:

- 1 cup of ready-to-eat cereal and a bagel for breakfast   3
- sandwich with 2 slices of bread for lunch   2
- 4 rye crackers for an afternoon snack   2
- 1 cup of rice and a roll with dinner   3
- 2 medium cookies   1

Products that are made with flour such as cakes, muffins, and cookies count as grain servings; the fat and sugar they contain count in the tip of the Pyramid.

Eating at least five servings of fruits and vegetables is quite easy. Consider the following daily intake, which adds up to six servings of vegetables and fruits:

Fruit/vegetable servings:

- 6 fluid oz (¾ cup) of orange juice   1 fruit
  for breakfast
- 1 cup of tossed salad and an   1 vegetable and 1 fruit
  apple for lunch

- ½ cup of broccoli and ½ cup of   2 vegetables
  mashed potatoes with dinner

- ½ cup grapes as an evening snack   1 fruit

The selection of orange juice is an excellent source of vitamin C, and the broccoli contains both vitamins A and C. Other good sources of vitamin C include grapefruit, tangerines, cantaloupe, and spinach, and sources of vitamin A include cantaloupe, spinach, and other dark green leafy vegetables.

Is it okay to eat the same foods every day?
Remember that variety is a cornerstone to healthy eating. Every food carries its own unique combination of nutrients. There's nothing wrong with eating the foods you like every day, but when you eat a variety of foods both within and among the food groups, you are more likely to get the right amounts of the many different nutrients you require. Likewise, eating a single food, like a large serving of French fries to meet several of your vegetable servings, is okay occasionally, but remember that most French fries are also deep fried, making them high in fat and calories. To include French fries in your food plan, enjoy one serving and select other vegetables for your remaining servings. Besides, eating the same foods day after day is boring. Be adventurous! Expand your tastes to enjoy a variety of foods!

Do I need to follow the Pyramid every day?
Not necessarily. It's okay to be flexible—just balance your food intake over several days. Life is hectic and on some days, it may be hard to meet your recommended servings from each food group. Don't worry if you (or your children) stray away from the Food Guide Pyramid occasionally. Try to eat well most days, and don't worry about the days when it doesn't happen. At the minimum, focus on grains, vegetables, and fruits. For example, on those hectic days, carry a bagel, pretzels, carrots, apples, or dried fruit

(things that carry well and won't spoil quickly). This may help get you through until you can sit down to a real meal with grains, vegetables, a dairy source, and a protein source.

The more often you eat "Pyramid style," the more natural it will feel. Soon, you probably won't have to think about selecting a balanced meal or daily menu. You will just do it! Encourage children to use the Food Guide Pyramid to learn about foods, serving portions, and daily meal plans. Help them develop some balanced meal plans that offer variety and moderation and meet the number of servings from the food groups.

What should my meal look like?

When you plan meals for yourself and your family, think about the proportions of the Food Guide Pyramid and ask, "Does my meal follow Pyramid guidelines?" The following example compares a top-heavy meal, where most of the foods come from the upper food groups, to a broad-based meal that includes foods in proportions that more closely resemble the Food Guide Pyramid.

TOP-HEAVY MEAL	BROAD-BASED MEAL
Gelatin salad with canned peaches	Romaine with mandarin oranges, almond slices, and poppy seed dressing
Meatloaf (beef & pork) with gravy, baked potato with sour cream	Pasta and marinara sauce with slices of chicken breast, zucchini, onions, tomato pieces, and grated mozzarella cheese
Green beans with butter sauce	Broccoli and cauliflower with basil and parsley
Dinner roll with butter	Whole grain roll
Cola	Sparkling water
Chocolate creme pie with whipped topping	Low-fat frozen yogurt with fresh raspberries

COMPARISONS

Pyramid tip

gelatin salad, gravy, sour cream,   poppy seed dressing
   butter sauce, butter, chocolate creme
   pie, whipped topping

Meat group

meat loaf   chicken breast, almond slivers

Milk group

no servings   mozzarella cheese, low-fat frozen
                                        yogurt

Fruit group

canned peaches   mandarin oranges, raspberries

Vegetable group

potato, green beans   marinara sauce, zucchini, onions,
                                        tomato, broccoli, cauliflower,
                                        romaine

Grain group

dinner roll   pasta, whole grain roll

Where do I begin to make changes in my diet?

You may be wondering how you can make changes to your diet that you can stick with. Start by being realistic. Make small changes over time, say over a few months. For most people, small steps work better than giant leaps. Don't try to make too many changes at the same time. Start slowly and master one small change at a time. For example, if you fall short of meeting your fruit and vegetable needs, you may want to start by adding a serving of a vegetable or fruit each day. Later on, you can try substituting a fruit or vegetable for a high-fat snack a couple of days each week. This advice also works for physical activity. Try making small changes, such as walking more each day (maybe at lunchtime or in the evening) or taking the stairs. Later you can add a weekly dance or aerobics class or a long walk on weekends.

To help you follow the Food Guide Pyramid, think about your daily food plan priorities in the following order:

- Think first of the Pyramid base—grains, vegetables, and fruits. Include these foods in each meal and choose them for snacks. Think of grains and vegetables as the basis of your main dishes (rather than only as side dishes).

- Include the 2–3 servings of milk, yogurt, or cheese somewhere in your meals or snacks. These dairy products are easy to include in mixed dishes, salads, desserts, and baked or cooked grain products.

- Include the 2–3 servings from the meat, poultry, fish, legume, nuts, and seeds group. Remember it doesn't take much to make a serving. Be creative with mixed dishes that include products from the meat group with grains and vegetables.

- Go easy on the extras (fats, oils, sugars, and sweets) from the tip of the Pyramid.

- Be creative with desserts to incorporate foods from the other groups such as low-fat yogurt with fruit, peach or strawberry shortcake, carrot cake, or pumpkin/sweet potato pie.

To help you get started, draw an empty Food Guide Pyramid on a sheet of paper. As you go through the day, record the number of servings you eat from each food group. Remember to calculate your servings based on the recommended serving sizes. Do this several times throughout your week to help you to think about what you're eating and to remind you to choose enough servings from each food group. Soon you'll be able to do this in your mind without drawing the Pyramid.

COUNT UP FIVE A DAY

Americans typically fall short of the recommended five daily servings of fruits and vegetables. Here are a few hints that may help you and your children increase vegetable and fruit intake during the day:

• Pack several fruits and vegetables to take to work or school and eat them for breakfast, lunch, or snacks.

• Serve sliced or cut pieces of vegetables and fruits with meals and as snacks. Children and teenagers (and adults too) may eat more fruit and vegetables and get more variety if they don't have to commit to eating a whole apple, banana, carrot, etc.

• Add cut up or pureed vegetables to your tomato sauce. (The pureed vegetables also make your sauce thicker and tastier!)

• Add grated raw vegetables (such as carrots or zucchini), grated fruits (such as apples), mashed bananas, mashed pumpkin, and/or dried fruit to your bread, pancake, cake, and cookie batters.

• Increase (double or triple) the amount of vegetables in recipes.

• Use chopped fruit to replace jam, jelly, or preserves on bread, rolls, and peanut butter sandwiches.

• Substitute fruit juice for soda or iced tea, or mix fruit juice into your iced tea or sparkling water.

A GUIDE TO LABEL READING

Anatomy of a food label

You've learned about the *Dietary Guidelines for Americans* and the Food Guide Pyramid. The last piece of information you need to build healthy eating patterns is how to read and use information on food labels—the Nutrition Facts panel.

Food labels vary in their size, shape, color, and content. Some labels provide a picture of the food they contain or a picture of the food as prepared. For foods that require preparation, the label usually provides preparation directions, such as stove top and microwave cooking. Labels may also provide information about food safety. Ingredients in foods are listed on the label in decreasing order by weight. The list of ingredients includes both food names and chemical names (usually food additives).

Food labels also list the manufacturer's name and address, and on some food labels you may find a guarantee from the manufacturer and a more detailed address or a toll-free phone number so that you can contact the manufacturer if you have questions about a food. Nearly all labels contain a Nutrition Facts panel. This is the part of the label that tells you about the nutrients in a serving portion of the food.

Nutrition Facts

Serving Size 1 cup (228g)
Servings Per Container 2

Amount Per Serving

Calories 260   Calories from Fat 120

	% Daily Value*
Total Fat 13g	**20%**
Saturated Fat 5g	**25%**
Cholesterol 30mg	**10%**
Sodium 660mg	**28%**
Total Carbohydrate 31g	**10%**
Dietary Fiber 0g	**0%**
Sugars 5g	
Protein 5g	

Vitamin A	4%	Vitamin C	2%
Calcium	15%	Iron	4%

* Percent Daily Values are based on a 2,000 calorie diet. Your daily values may be higher or lower depending on your calorie needs:

	Calories	2,000	2,500
Total Fat	Less than	65g	80g
Sat Fat	Less than	20g	25g
Cholesterol	Less than	300mg	300mg
Sodium	Less than	2,400mg	2,400mg
Total Carbohydrate		300g	375g
Dietary Fiber		25g	30g

Calories per gram:
Fat 9   •   Carbohydrates 4   •   Protein 4

Nutrition Facts Panel

Let's spend a little time looking at the various components of the Nutrition Facts panel. These panels provide information about the nutrients that are of greatest concern to health. Look back at the sample label on page 25. The first thing the Nutrition Facts panel tells you is the serving size and the number of servings per container. All of the nutrition information is based on the stated serving size. The label then provides the total calories and fat calories per serving. Next, there is a listing that provides the amounts and percent Daily Values (% DV) for total fat, saturated fat, cholesterol, sodium, total carbohydrate, and dietary fiber. The amounts of sugars and protein are provided as grams only. The amounts of vitamin A, vitamin C, calcium, and iron are provided as % DV only. All of these nutrients are required to be listed on the Nutrition Facts panel.

The nutrition information is provided for products *as sold*. This is important to remember, because some foods, such as soups or mixes for cakes and breads, will have other ingredients added during the preparation stage. For example, the preparation directions for condensed corn soup call for the addition of milk. The nutrient values that you will see on the Nutrition Facts panel are for the product *without* the milk added. However, some product labels will have "dual" labeling with one set of values for the product as sold and another set of values for the food as prepared.

Daily Values

Daily Values (DVs) are reference numbers for nutrients that are based on what health experts know about nutrition and health. Some DVs, which are listed on the bottom of most labels, are recommended maximums for the day (such as 65 grams or less of total fat if you eat 2,000 calories per day), while others are minimums (such as 300 milligrams or more of total carbohydrate if you eat 2,000 calories per day). The DVs for the nutrients listed on the Nutrition Facts panel are:

Nutrient	Daily Value
Calories	2,000
Total fat	less than 65 grams (30% of total calories)
Saturated fat	less than 20 grams (10% of total calories)
Cholesterol	less than 300 milligrams
Sodium	less than 2,400 milligrams (2.4 grams)
Total carbohydrate	300 grams (60% of total calories)
Dietary fiber	25 grams (11.5 grams per 1,000 calories)
Protein	50 grams (10% of total calories)
Vitamin A	5,000 IU (international units)
Vitamin C	60 milligrams
Calcium	1 gram (1,000 milligrams)
Iron	18 milligrams

Most people are interested in how a food contributes to the total daily nutrient intakes or how one food compares with another. The % DVs are designed for this purpose. The % DVs, which are based on an average diet of 2,000 calories per day, allow you to determine how a food contributes to your total daily intake of nutrients. For example, a serving of corn soup provides 5% DV for total fat and saturated fat. It also provides 1% DV for cholesterol, 30% DV for sodium, 7% DV for total carbohydrate, 8% DV for fiber, 10% DV for vitamin A, 0% DV for vitamin C, and 2%

DV each for calcium and iron. The higher the percentage, the more of that nutrient the food serving contributes.

Most people eat 10 to 20 different foods during a day. For most nutrients, the goal is to be around 100% of the DV for each nutrient on most days—if your calorie needs are around 2,000. For some nutrients, such as vitamin A, vitamin C, iron, calcium, and fiber, aim for 100% or more of the DV. For other nutrients like fat, saturated fat, cholesterol, and sodium, it's wise to eat no more than 100% of the DV. If your needs are higher or lower than 2,000 calories per day, you can still use the % DV information, but you'll need to adjust your % DV goal. If your calorie needs are less than 2,000, you actually need less than 100% DV for each nutrient. Likewise, if your calorie needs are greater than 2,000, you may need more than 100% DV for each nutrient. Find your approximate daily calorie needs in the following chart. The corresponding value listed is the % DV for each nutrient that you should aim for.

Calories	% DV
1,600	80
2,000	100
2,200	110
2,500	125
2,800	140

Calories

Calories are a measure of the energy supplied by food when it is used by the body. Calories (energy) are supplied by carbohydrate, fat, protein, and alcohol. Carbohydrate and protein provide 4 calories per gram; alcohol provides 7 calories per gram; and fat provides 9 calories per gram. If you consistently eat more calories than your body can use, you will gain weight. Regardless of the source—carbohydrate, protein, fat, or alcohol—your body converts extra calories to fat and stores it as body fat.

Calories from fat

Calories from fat is the number of calories that are supplied by fat in a serving of food. This number is obtained by multiplying the grams of fat by 9 calories per gram. It is rounded for labeling. The calories from fat are less than or equal to total calories. Most foods contain a mixture of fat, carbohydrate, and protein. Total calories includes calories from protein and carbohydrate as well as fat.

Total fat

Fat is a concentrated source of calories for your body. Fat provides energy, and it helps you absorb the fat-soluble vitamins (vitamins A, D, E, and K). When stored in your body, fat provides warmth and padding to protect your bones, muscles, and internal organs. Fat in foods contributes to our eating pleasure as many of the flavors that we enjoy are contributed by fat. (Think of the flavors of steak, French fries, butter, avocado, and sour cream.)

The amount of total fat in a serving of food is listed in grams (g) and as % DV on the Nutrition Facts panel. The % DV for fat gives you an idea of how much fat a serving contributes to the total recommended fat in a 2,000-calorie diet. The % DV for fat on the Nutrition Facts panel is based on a 2,000-calorie reference diet that has no more than 30% of calories from fat (65 grams or less fat per day). Keep in mind that this goal of no more than 30% of calories from fat applies to your *total* diet over time, not to a single food or meal.

Saturated fat

The fat in foods can be classified as saturated, monounsaturated, or polyunsaturated. Most foods contain a combination of these three types of fat. Nutrition experts emphasize reducing your intake of saturated fat because this type of fat can raise blood cholesterol levels more than any other dietary component, even more than dietary cholesterol.

The amount of saturated fat in a serving of food is listed in grams (g) and % DV on the Nutrition Facts panel. The % DV for saturated fat tells you how much saturated fat a serving of food contributes to a 2,000-calorie diet. The % DV for saturated fat on the nutrition label is based on a DV of no more than 20 grams of saturated fat per day. This number is based on a 2,000-calorie reference diet that has no more than 10% of calories from saturated fat.

Cholesterol
Cholesterol is a fatlike substance, necessary for making cell membranes (the outer coverings of all body cells), vitamin D, and some hormones and digestive enzymes. We obtain cholesterol in two different ways: one is to eat foods that contain it, and the other is to make it inside our bodies. Dietary cholesterol is the cholesterol found in foods. Only animal foods contain cholesterol. Blood cholesterol is the cholesterol in your bloodstream. It comes from foods you have eaten and your body's ability to manufacture this compound.

The amount of cholesterol in a serving of food is listed in milligrams (mg) and as % DV on the Nutrition Facts panel. The % DV for cholesterol is 300 milligrams, and is the same for all calorie levels.

Sodium
We need sodium to control blood pressure and blood volume and to help our nerves and muscles work properly. Sodium chloride (NaCl) is the chemical name for salt. Salt is the most common source of sodium in the diet and is abundant in our foods.

The amount of sodium in a serving of food is listed in milligrams (mg) and as % DV on the Nutrition Facts panel. The % DV gives you an idea of how much sodium a serving of food contributes to your total daily intake. The % DV for sodium is based on the recommended level of no more than 2,400 mg of sodium per day.

Total carbohydrate
Carbohydrate is the main energy source for our body's cells. Eating enough carbohydrate also keeps protein from being used for

energy and helps the body to use fat properly. Carbohydrates include sugars, starches, and dietary fiber. The amount of total carbohydrate in a serving of food is listed in grams (g) and as % DV on the Nutrition Facts panel. Nutrition experts recommend that at about 55–60% of your total calories come from carbohydrates. The % DV for total carbohydrate on the Nutrition Facts panel is based on 60% of calories from carbohydrate in a 2,000-calorie diet, or about 300 grams of carbohydrate per day.

Dietary fiber
As mentioned above, dietary fiber is a type of carbohydrate. Dietary fiber is found only in plant foods, and is the part of plant foods that human bodies cannot digest.

The amount of dietary fiber in a serving of food is listed in grams (g) and as % DV on the Nutrition Facts panel. The % DV for dietary fiber tells you how much fiber a serving contributes to a 2,000 calorie diet. Nutrition experts recommend that you aim for 20 to 30 grams of dietary fiber a day. The % DV for dietary fiber on the Nutrition Facts panel is based on the goal of 25 grams of fiber per day.

Sugars
As mentioned above, sugars are a type of carbohydrate. Sugars include sucrose (table sugar), fructose, galactose, glucose, lactose, and maltose. The amount of sugars in a serving of food is listed on the label in grams only. A goal for intake of sugars is not listed because sugars serve primarily to add flavor and calories to foods.

Protein
Protein is essential for growth and maintenance of our body cells, tissues, and organs. Protein is listed on the Nutrition Facts panel in grams (g) per serving. The % DV is not required to be listed. Daily needs for protein are about 50 grams per day for women and 63 grams per day for men. Protein requirements for infants, children, and teenagers range from 13 to 59 grams per day depending upon age and gender. These levels are easily achieved in diets that contain the recommended number of servings from the meat and

dairy food groups. Plant-based foods also contain protein, but in smaller amounts. The extra protein we eat is used by our bodies as fuel, or if we eat more than we can use for fuel, protein is converted to fat and stored in our bodies.

Vitamins and Minerals

The Nutrition Facts panel lists % DVs for vitamin A, vitamin C, calcium, and iron. Food manufacturers may also list other vitamins and minerals such as thiamin, riboflavin, folic acid, niacin, zinc, and magnesium. If a vitamin or mineral claim is made on a food label or if a food is fortified with a vitamin or mineral, then

---

MORE ABOUT FOOD LABELS

• If a manufacturer has added a nutrient to a food product or makes a claim about a nutrient on the label, that nutrient must be listed on the Nutrition Facts panel.

•Some food packages are too small to include the Nutrition Facts panel (for example, a package of gum). Instead, a phone number is provided so you can call to request information from the manufacturer. On other small packages, you may see a modified version of the Nutrition Facts panel.

• Manufacturers are permitted to use a modified Nutrition Facts panel if the food does not contain many of the nutrients usually listed. The modified label lists only calories, total fat, sodium, total carbohydrate, and protein.

• Some manufacturers provide information about additional nutrients on food labels. The following is a list of "voluntary" nutrients that manufacturers may include on Nutrition Facts panels:

Potassium	Folate (Folic acid)
Polyunsaturated fat	Vitamin B_{12}
Monounsaturated fat	Biotin
Vitamin D	Pantothenic acid
Vitamin E	Phosphorus
Thiamin	Iodine
Riboflavin	Magnesium
Niacin	Zinc
Vitamin B_6	Copper

DESCRIPTIVE TERMS ON FOOD LABELS

Manufacturers may use descriptive terms (or claims) on food labels if the nutrient content of their products meets the definitions set by FDA or USDA.

CALORIE TERMS

Calorie-free means a food has less than 5 calories per serving.

Low calorie means a food has 40 calories or less per serving.

Reduced calorie means that a food has at least 25% fewer calories than a comparable product.

Light or *Lite* means that a food has at least ⅓ fewer calories or 50% less fat. If more than half of the calories are from fat, the fat content must be reduced by 50% or more.

FAT TERMS

Fat-free means a serving of food has less than 0.5 grams of fat.

Low fat mean a serving of food has 3 grams or less fat.

Reduced fat means a food has at least 25% less fat than a comparable product. For example, reduced-fat oatmeal cookies would have at least 25% less fat than regular oatmeal cookies.

SATURATED FAT TERMS

Saturated fat-free means that a serving of food has less than 0.5 grams of saturated fat.

Low saturated fat means that a serving of food contains 1 gram or less of saturated fat and no more than 15% of calories from saturated fat.

Reduced saturated fat or *Less saturated fat* means a food has at least 25% less saturated fat than a comparable product.

CHOLESTEROL TERMS

Claims describing cholesterol content on food labels must meet nutrient requirements for both cholesterol and saturated fat. This is because both dietary cholesterol and saturated fat can raise blood cholesterol. This dual requirement helps us because cholesterol-free foods that are also high in saturated fat cannot use the descriptive terms.

Cholesterol-free means a serving of food has less than 2 mg of cholesterol and 2 grams or less of saturated fat.

Low cholesterol means a serving of food has 20 milligrams or less of cholesterol and 2 grams or less of saturated fat.

Reduced cholesterol or *Less cholesterol* means that a serving of food has at least 25% less cholesterol (than a comparable product) and 2 grams or less of saturated fat.

(cont'd)

Descriptive Terms (cont'd)

SODIUM TERMS

Sodium-free or *Salt-free* means less than 5 mg sodium per serving.

Very low sodium means 35 mg or less of sodium per serving.

Low sodium means 140 mg or less sodium per serving.

Reduced sodium or *Less sodium* means at least 25% less sodium than a comparable product.

Unsalted, Without added salt, or *No salt added* means that no salt was added during processing. Check the label carefully as this does not necessarily mean that the product is sodium-free. (It may have contained sodium prior to processing.)

FIBER TERMS

Good source of fiber, Contains fiber, or *Provides fiber* means that a food contains 10–19% DV (2.5 to less than 5 grams) of dietary fiber per serving.

High fiber, Rich in fiber, or *Excellent source of fiber* means that a food contains 20% DV or more (5 grams or more) of dietary fiber per serving.

SUGAR TERMS

Sugar-free mean less than 0.5 gram sugar per serving.

Reduced sugar or *Less sugar* means at least 25% less sugar than a comparable product.

VITAMIN AND MINERAL TERMS

Good Source of . . . , Contains . . . , Provides . . . means that a serving of food contains 10–19% DV of the nutrient.

High in . . . , Rich in . . . , Excellent Source of . . . means that a serving of food contains 20% DV or more of the nutrient.

More . . . , Fortified with . . . , Enriched with . . . , Added . . . means that a serving of food contains at least 10% more of the DV than a comparable product.

the manufacturer must list the % DV for that vitamin or mineral on the Nutrition Facts panel.

Daily Values for a day's intake

To illustrate how you can use % DVs in your daily meal planning, let's try adding up % DVs for a day of meals. You don't need to do this every day, but you may want to try it periodically to monitor how you're doing. If you aim for your optimal number of servings from each food group, your daily % DV totals should be just fine, and over a few days or a week, they will probably average out to balance your days of heavy food intake with your days of lighter intake. Percent DVs are especially useful for comparison shopping in the grocery store. Note: When you're doing comparative shopping, be sure you are comparing % DVs for foods with the same serving size.

SAMPLE DAILY INTAKE								% DAILY VALUES			
FOODS & SERVING PORTIONS	CAL	FAT	SAT FAT	CHOL	SOD	CARB	FIBER	VIT A	VIT C	CALC	IRON
Breakfast											
raisin bran cereal, 1 cup	170	2	0	0	13	14	28	15	0	4	25
2% fat milk, 1 cup	130	8	15	7	5	4	0	10	4	30	0
banana, 1 medium	110	0	0	0	0	7	20	2	8	0	2
orange-cranberry juice, 8 fluid oz	130	0	0	0	1	11	—	—	6	—	—
herb tea, 8 fluid oz	0	0	0	0	0	0	0	0	0	0	0
Breakfast totals	540	10	15	7	19	36	48	27	18	34	27
Lunch											
tuna sandwich											
multigrain bagel, 1 medium	170	2	3	0	13	12	4	0	0	6	10
tuna, canned in water, 2 oz	70	1	0	12	10	0	0	0	0	0	0
lettuce, ¾ cup	7	0	0	0	1	1	4	20	3	2	0
tomato, ½ medium	17	1	0	0	0	1	2	10	20	1	1
celery, ½ stalk	5	0	0	0	1	1	2	1	4	1	1
mayonnaise, 2 tbsp	200	34	18	4	6	0	0	0	0	0	0
peach, 1 medium	40	0	0	0	0	3	8	2	10	0	0
seltzer water, 8 fluid oz	0	0	0	0	0	0	0	0	0	0	0
Lunch totals	509	38	21	16	31	18	20	33	37	10	12

FOODS & SERVING PORTIONS	CAL	FAT	SAT FAT	CHOL	SOD	CARB	FIBER	VIT A	VIT C	CALC	IRON
Dinner											
spinach salad											
spinach, 1 cup	30	0	0	0	—	1	8	50	40	10	6
cucumber, ⅓ medium	15	0	0	0	0	1	4	4	10	2	2
grated carrot, ½ medium	35	0	0	0	1	1	4	135	5	1	0
mozzarella cheese, grated, 1 oz	70	9	20	5	6	0	0	4	0	15	0
ranch dressing, 2 tbsp	190	31	15	5	7	1	0	0	0	0	0
white rice casserole											
rice, 1 cup	50	0	0	0	0	24	0	0	0	0	16
baked chicken breast slices, 2 oz	90	5	5	12	8	1	0	0	0	0	2
green beans, ½ cup	12	0	0	0	0	1	3	1	1	1	0
onions, ½ cup	30	0	0	0	0	2	6	0	10	2	1
green peppers, ½ cup	15	0	0	0	0	1	4	4	80	1	1
white sauce, ½ cup	130	12	15	3	37	4	4	10	0	2	2
nonfat plain yogurt, 1 cup	160	5	10	7	6	7	0	0	0	35	0
sweetened red cherries, ½ cup	140	0	0	0	0	11	4	0	2	0	2
mineral water, 8 fluid oz	0	0	0	0	0	0	0	0	0	0	0
Dinner totals	967	62	65	32	65	55	37	208	148	70	32

FOODS & SERVING PORTIONS	CAL	FAT	SAT FAT	CHOL	SOD	CARB	FIBER	VIT A	VIT C	CALC	IRON
Snack											
oatmeal raisin cookies, 2 medium	220	12	10	2	10	12	6	0	0	0	12
herb tea, 8 fluid oz	0	0	0	0	0	0	0	0	0	0	0
Snack totals	220	12	10	2	10	12	6	0	0	0	12
Calorie & % Daily Value totals	2,236	122	111	57	125	121	111	268	203	114	83

Cal—calories; Sat fat—saturated fat; Chol—cholesterol; Sod—sodium; Carbo—carbohydrate; Vit A—vitamin A; Vit C—vitamin C; Calc—calcium

This daily intake of foods was close to the reference intake of 2,000 calories. It exceeded 100% DV for fiber, vitamin A, vitamin C, and calcium, but it did not meet 100% DV for iron. It exceeded 100% DV for fat and saturated fat. Remember, you don't need to have a perfect diet every day. The higher and lower nutrient intakes can be balanced out over several days.

TO FOLLOW

Food composition

Food companies generally keep very accurate information about the ingredient and nutrient content of the foods that they manufacture and sell. The nutrient values that manufacturers include on nutrition labels must follow regulations (laws) developed by the USDA (for meat and poultry products) and the FDA (for all other foods).

The science of food composition began about 100 years ago in government laboratories in the United States, when food chemists analyzed foods for the very basic elements of water, protein, and fat. In subsequent years, chemists developed analytical methods for vitamins, minerals, and other food components. More recently, technology and equipment have evolved, making food chemistry a very sophisticated science.

Just to give you an idea of the process, think about the nutrient content of a fast-food cheeseburger. How does the chemist determine which nutrients and how much of each are in this cheeseburger? First, cheeseburgers from franchises across the country are purchased based on a sophisticated sampling design. They are frozen and sent air freight from the cities where they were purchased to the laboratory. The chemist logs them in and checks to be sure that they are in good condition (no thawing or signs of spoilage). The chemist homogenizes the cheeseburgers by placing them in a large blender and mixing them until they are a uniform (no lumps), liquid mixture. For some foods it is necessary to add a measured amount of distilled water to liquify the food. Next, small samples of the mixture are subjected to chemical tests for those nutrients listed on the food label. The nutrient values that result are usually rounded to be in compliance with government regulations. For foods with added nutrients, such as bread made with enriched flour or a breakfast cereal with added vitamins and minerals, the food chemists must also analyze the foods for the added nutrients since these must also be listed on the food label.

Labeling regulations require that nutrient values be rounded in certain ways (different for each nutrient). This provides uniformity to the labels and, hopefully, makes it easier for consumers to use. Government regulations also specify that the numbers on the label must be within 10% of the actual values (the values that would result if the food in a package were actually analyzed). Because food companies cannot assure that every food package has exactly the same nutrient values, food companies tend to be conservative when putting nutrient values on their labels. In general, nutrient values on labels of processed foods tend to underestimate vitamins, minerals, protein, fiber, and carbohydrate and overestimate calories, fat, saturated fat, cholesterol, and sodium. Nutrient values may differ for different brands of the same food due to variations in the formulation (or recipe), processing methods, or analytical methods. Labels values are good guides to the nutrient content of foods, but you shouldn't let a small difference in a % DV value between two foods alter your decision about which to purchase. If the % DVs are close, select the product that tastes better to you and/or is less expensive.

How to Use the Tables in this Book

There are thousands of foods available from U.S. grocery stores and restaurants. This book contains nutrient information from the Nutrition Facts panel of some of the more commonly available food products. They are mostly brand-name, packaged products. Currently, nutrition labeling information is available for only a few raw fruits, vegetables, fish, poultry, and meats. The sources of information in the following tables include: food companies from whom we requested the information; food labels from products purchased in grocery stores; and FDA and USDA values for raw fruit, vegetables, fish, poultry, and meat. Some foods, such as various milks and cheeses, are listed generically (without brand names) because the nutrient labeling values are very similar among the different brands. The nutrient values on the labels of some products may be different from the values reported here because of new or different product formulations by the manufacturers or because of changes in the size of packaging. Values listed as "Not significant" on food labels are listed as zeros in the tables.

The table presents the foods in sections that correspond to Pyramid food groups. There are many foods that contain ingredients from two or more of the food groups. These foods are presented in the food group that represents the main ingredient. For example, pasta dishes are located in the grain group. The foods are also listed alphabetically in the index if you have difficulty locating them. And there is a group for those "extra" foods that contain few calories or nutrients. Foods included in this book were chosen to be representative of the many categories and types of foods available in today's grocery stores. If you're looking for a particular product, and it is not listed, you might try looking at the nutrient values for a similar product (or the same product with a different brand name). Here's how foods are grouped in the tables that follow.

Bread, Cereal, Pasta, Rice, and Other Grain Products

Breads
   Bread and Bread Products
   Bread-based Entrees[1]
   Bread-based Meals/dinners[2]

Cereals
   Cereals, Ready-to-eat
   Cereals Served Warm

Crackers

Grain-based Desserts
   Brownies, Cakes, and Snack Cakes
   Cereal/granola Bars
   Cookies
   Pastry
   Pies and Snack Pies

Grain-based Snack Foods

Pasta
   Pasta
   Pasta-based Entrees
   Pasta-based Meals/dinners
   Pasta-based Soups

Rice
   Rice and Rice-based Entree
   Rice-based Soups

Vegetables

Vegetables and Vegetable Juices

Vegetable-based Entrees

Vegetable-based Soups

Vegetable Products
　　Pickles and Pickle Relishes
　　Potato-based Chips and Snacks
　　Tomato-based Dips, Pastes, Salsas, and Sauces

Fruit

Fruit

Fruit Juices and Juice Drinks

Fruit Spreads

Milk, Cheese, Yogurt, and Other Dairy Products

Cheese and Cheese Products

Dairy-based Desserts

Milk, Milk Beverages, and Soymilk

Yogurt

Meat, Poultry, Fish, Beans, Eggs, and Nuts

Beans[3]
　　Beans, Bean Dips, and Bean Entrees
　　Bean-based Soups

Eggs, Egg Entrees, and Egg Substitutes

Fish
　　Fish
　　Fish-based Entrees

Fish-based Meals/dinners
Fish-based Chowders, Soups, and Stews

Frankfurters, Luncheon Meats, and Meat Snacks

Meat
Meat
Meat-based Entrees
Meat-based Meals/dinners
Meat-based Soups

Meat Substitutes

Nut Butters/pastes, Nuts, and Seeds

Poultry
Poultry
Poultry-based Entrees
Poultry-based Meals/dinners
Poultry-based Chowders and Soups

Fats, Oils, and Sweets (and Alcohol)

Alcoholic Beverages

Fat- and Oil-based Products

Sweets
Beverages, Sweetened
Candy
Gelatin Desserts, Sugars, Syrups, and Toppings

Extra Foods[4]

Nutrients
in
Serving
Portions
of
Foods[5]

Bread, Cereal, Pasta, Rice,

and other

Grain Products

BREADS: BREAD AND BREAD PRODUCTS

Food Name	Serving Size	gm	mL	Calories	Calories from Fat	Total Fat (g)	%DV	Saturated Fat (g)	%DV	Cholesterol (mg)	%DV	Sodium (mg)	%DV	Total Carbohydrates (g)	%DV	Fiber (g)	%DV	Sugars (g)	Protein (g)	Vitamin A (%DV)	Vitamin C (%DV)	Calcium (%DV)	Iron (%DV)
bagel, cinn raisin, Lender's Big 'n Crusty	1 bagel	85		240	20	2.5	4	0	0	0	0	330	14	47	16	2	9	13	8	0	0	0	15
bagel, cinn raisin, Singer's	1 bagel	78		220	5	1	1	0	0	0	0	260	11	44	15	2	8	6	8	0	0	6	15
bagel, egg, Thomas	1bagel	61		170	10	1.5	2	0.5	3	15	5	280	12	35	12	2	8	4	7	0	0	6	10
bagel, multi-grain, Thomas	1 bagel	61		170	15	1.5	2	0.5	3	0	0	310	13	35	12	1	4	4	6	0	0	6	10
bagel, onion, Thomas	1 bagel	61		170	10	1.5	2	0.5	3	0	0	300	13	35	12	2	8	4	6	0	0	6	10
bread, Bran'nola, Arnold	1 slice	38		90	20	2	3	0	0	0	0	125	5	18	6	3	12	3	4	0	0	0	6
bread, brown, S&W	½ slice	46		90	5	1	1	0	0	0	0	220	9	21	7	2	8	12	3	0	15	4	4
bread, honey wheat berry, Arnold	1 slice	32		70	10	1	2	0	0	0	0	160	7	16	5	3	12	2	3	0	0	0	4
bread, oatmeal, Brownberry	1 slice	27		70	10	1	2	0	0	0	0	135	6	13	4	1	4	<1	2	0	0	0	4
bread, pita, white, Thomas Sahara	1 pita	57		150	10	1	2	0	0	0	0	290	12	31	10	1	4	3	6	0	0	10	10
bread, pita, whole wheat, Sunberry	1 pita	45		110	5	1	1	0	0	0	0	200	8	22	7	2	7	1	4	0	0	8	8
bread, pita, whole wheat, Thomas Sahara	1 pita	57		130	10	1	2	0	0	0	0	310	13	28	9	5	20	2	7	0	0	6	6
bread, raisin cinn, Arnold	1 slice	27		70	10	1	2	0	0	0	0	90	4	14	5	0	0	3	2	0	0	0	4
bread, Roman Meal Round Top	1 slice	28		70	10	1	2	0	0	0	0	140	6	13	4	1	4	2	3	0	0	4	6
bread, rye, Arnold	1 slice	32		70	5	1	2	0	0	0	0	150	6	16	5	1	4	>1	3	0	0	4	4
bread, rye, caraway, Brownberry	1 slice	30		70	5	1	2	0	0	0	0	160	7	15	5	1	4	>1	3	0	0	4	4
bread, rye, dark, Mrs. Wright's	1 slice	32		80	10	1	2	0	0	0	0	180	8	15	5	2	7	1	3	0	0	6	8
bread, rye, Jewish seeded, Arnold	1 slice	32		70	5	1	2	0	0	0	0	150	6	16	5	1	4	>1	3	0	0	4	4
bread, rye, pumpernickel, Brownberry	1 slice	28		70	5	0.5	1	0	0	0	0	150	6	14	5	1	4	1	2	0	0	0	4
breadsticks, cheese, Lance	4 pieces	13		50	10	1	2	0	0	0	0	120	5	8	3	0	0	0	2	0	0	4	2
breadsticks, garlic, Lance	4 pieces	13		50	10	1	2	0	0	0	0	180	8	10	3	0	0	0	2	0	0	0	2
breadsticks, Lance	4 pieces	13		50	10	1	2	0	0	0	0	130	5	9	3	0	0	0	2	0	0	4	2
breadsticks, sesame, Lance	4 pieces	13		60	20	2	3	0.5	2	0	0	95	4	8	3	1	4	0	2	0	0	2	2
bread stuffing mix, seasoned, Arnold	2 cups mix	67		250	30	3.5	5	0.5	2	0	0	820	34	49	16	2	8	3	9	0	0	4	15
bread stuffing mix, herb seasoned, Arnold	2 cups mix	67		240	30	3.5	5	0.5	2	0	0	740	31	48	16	4	16	3	9	4	0	6	25

Food Name	Serving Size	gm	mL	Calories	Calories from Fat	Total Fat (g)	%DV	Saturated Fat (g)	%DV	Cholesterol (mg)	%DV	Sodium (mg)	%DV	Total Carbohydrates (g)	%DV	Fiber (g)	%DV	Sugars (g)	Protein (g)	Vitamin A (%DV)	Vitamin C (%DV)	Calcium (%DV)	Iron (%DV)
bread, wheat, Arnold Brick Oven	2 slices	48		110	25	3	5	0	0	0	0	170	7	21	7	3	12	3	5	0	0	0	4
bread, wheat, Brownberry	1 slice	36		80	10	1	2	0	0	0	0	210	9	17	6	2	8	2	3	0	0	0	4
bread, white, Arnold Brick Oven	2 slices	48		130	20	2.5	4	0	0	0	0	250	10	24	8	1	4	4	3	0	0	4	8
bread, white, Brownberry	2 slices	48		120	15	1.5	2	0	0	0	0	160	7	24	8	1	4	2	4	0	0	2	10
bread, whole bran, Brownberry	1 slice	25		60	10	1	2	0	0	0	0	140	6	12	4	2	8	<1	2	0	0	0	4
bread, whole wheat, stoneground, Arnold	1 slice	27		60	10	1	2	0	0	0	0	115	5	12	4	2	8	2	3	0	0	0	2
bun, wheat, Brownberry	1 bun	50		130	20	3.5	3	0	0	0	0	210	9	24	8	2	8	3	5	0	0	2	8
bun, white, Arnold	1 bun	47		130	25	3	5	0.5	3	0	0	190	8	24	8	1	4	3	4	0	0	4	8
bun, white, Brownberry	1 bun	50		140	30	3.5	5	0.5	2	0	0	210	9	25	8	1	4	3	4	0	0	4	10
croutons, cheese & garlic, Arnold	2 Tbsp	7		30	10	1	2	0	0	0	0	50	2	5	2	0	0	0	1	0	0	0	2
croutons, Ital, Arnold	2 Tbsp	7		30	10	1	2	0	0	0	0	65	3	4	1	0	0	0	1	0	0	0	2
croutons, seasoned, Arnold	2 Tbsp	7		30	10	1	2	0	0	0	0	60	3	5	2	0	0	0	1	0	0	0	2
English muffin, honey wheat, Thomas	1 muffin	57		110	10	1	2	0	0	0	0	190	8	24	8	3	12	2	5	0	0	8	6
English muffin, sourdough, Thomas	1 muffin	57		120	10	1	2	0	0	0	0	190	8	25	8	1	4	2	4	0	0	8	10
English muffin, Thomas	1 muffin	57		120	10	1	2	0	0	0	0	200	8	25	8	1	4	2	4	0	0	8	8
French toast, cinn swirl, frzn, Swanson	1 package	156		440	250	28	43	12	60	150	50	580	24	34	11	2	8	11	14	6	0	8	10
French toast sticks, frzn, Swanson Kids	1 package	106		310	130	14	22	4	20	45	15	300	13	41	14	2	8	17	7	10	0	8	4
pancakes, mini, frzn, Swanson Kids	1 package	120		320	70	8	12	4	20	45	15	640	27	54	18	2	8	24	7	0	0	6	4
roll, white dinner, Arnold	2 rolls	38		110	20	2	3	0	0	0	0	150	6	20	7	<1	3	4	3	0	0	2	6
taco shell, corn, Ortega	2 shells	30		140	60	7	10	1	6	0	0	200	8	20	7	2	10	0	2	2	0	6	4
taco shell, corn, white, Ortega	2 shells	30		140	60	7	10	1	6	0	0	200	8	18	6	2	10	1	2	2	0	6	4
tortilla, flour, fajita style, Pinata	1 tortilla	64		200	40	5	7	0.5	3	0	0	300	13	35	12	2	8	1	6	0	0	8	10
tostada shell, corn, Ortega,	2 shells	30		150	70	8	12	1.5	7	0	0	190	8	18	6	2	9	0	2	0	0	4	4
waffle, blueberry, frzn, Eggo	2 waffles	78		220	70	8	12	1.5	8	20	7	450	19	33	11	0	0	7	5	20	0	4	20
waffle, buttermilk, frzn, Eggo	2 waffles	78		220	70	8	12	1.5	8	25	8	480	20	30	10	0	0	3	5	20	0	4	20

Consult a similar product for brand names not listed.

Food Name	Serving Size	gm	mL	Calories	Calories from Fat	Total Fat (g)	%DV	Saturated Fat (g)	%DV	Cholesterol (mg)	%DV	Sodium (mg)	%DV	Total Carbohydrates[8] (g)	%DV	Fiber[8] (g)	%DV	Sugars[8] (g)	Protein (g)	Vitamin A (%DV)	Vitamin C[7] (%DV)	Calcium (%DV)	Iron (%DV)
waffle, homestyle, frzn, Eggo	2 waffles	78		220	70	8	12	1.5	8	25	8	470	20	30	10	0	0	3	5	20	0	4	20
waffle, nutri-grain, frzn, Eggo	2 waffles	78		190	60	6	9	1	5	0	0	430	18	30	10	4	16	4	5	20	0	4	20
waffle, oat bran, frzn, Common Sense	2 waffles	78		200	60	7	11	1.5	8	0	0	350	15	27	9	3	12	3	6	20	0	4	20
waffle sticks, frzn, Swanson Kids	1 serving	78		330	150	17	26	7	35	75	25	250	10	39	13	1	4	32	4	0	0	2	6

BREADS: BREAD-BASED ENTREES[1]

Food Name	Serving Size	gm	mL	Calories	Calories from Fat	Total Fat (g)	%DV	Saturated Fat (g)	%DV	Cholesterol (mg)	%DV	Sodium (mg)	%DV	Total Carbohydrates[6] (g)	%DV	Fiber[6] (g)	%DV	Sugars[5] (g)	Protein (g)	Vitamin A (%DV)	Vitamin C[7] (%DV)	Calcium (%DV)	Iron (%DV)
biscuit, bacon, egg, & cheese, Hardee's	1 biscuit	169		610	330	37	57	13	65	280	93	1630	68	45	15	NA	NA	NA	24	NA	NA	NA	NA
biscuit, ham, egg, & cheese, Hardee's	1 biscuit	185		540	270	30	46	11	55	285	95	1660	69	48	16	NA	NA	NA	20	NA	NA	NA	NA
biscuit, omelet, Hardee's	1 biscuit	164		570	270	33	51	12	60	290	97	1370	57	45	15	NA	NA	NA	22	NA	NA	NA	NA
biscuit, sausage, & egg, Hardee's	1 biscuit	179		630	360	40	62	22	110	285	95	1480	62	45	15	NA	NA	NA	23	NA	NA	NA	NA
biscuit, sausage, egg, & cheese, frzn, Swanson	1 biscuit	156		490	270	30	46	12	60	145	48	1110	46	36	12	3	12	4	18	0	0	15	15
britos, beef & bean, frzn, Patio	10 britos	168		420	170	19	29	7	33	20	6	800	33	51	17	7	28	2	11	10	4	4	8
britos, beef nacho, frzn, Patio	10 britos	168		410	170	18	28	18	92	20	7	1050	44	48	16	5	20	3	13	2	2	6	8
britos, cheese nacho, frzn, Patio	10 britos	168		360	110	13	19	4	19	15	4	500	21	52	17	3	11	8	10	0	4	15	6
britos, chicken spicy, frzn, Patio	10 britos	168		400	150	16	25	4	19	25	9	640	27	52	17	3	13	2	13	0	0	10	10
burrito, bacon & scrambled eggs, frzn, Swanson	1 burrito	99		250	100	11	17	4	20	90	30	540	23	27	9	1	4	3	10	2	2	8	10
burrito, bean & cheese, frzn, Patio	1 burrito	140		270	50	5	8	2.5	13	5	2	530	22	46	15	7	29	2	9	4	6	6	6
burrito, beef & bean, Patio	1 burrito	140		280	60	7	10	3	17	15	4	860	36	45	15	7	27	5	10	6	2	0	0
burrito, beef, bean, & red chili, frzn, Patio	1 burrito	142		260	45	5	8	2	10	10	3	640	27	42	14	7	28	3	11	4	8	2	10
burrito, Big Beef Supreme, Taco Bell	1 burrito	291		520	210	23	35	10	50	70	23	1450	60	52	17	9	36	3	26	30	8	15	15
burrito, cheese & pepperoni, frzn, Swanson	1 burrito	99		240	81	9	14	3	15	60	20	410	17	28	9	2	8	3	9	2	0	6	20
burrito, chicken con queso, frzn, Healthy Choice	1 entree	299		355	50	6	9	2.5	13	35	12	590	25	60	20	6	24	11	14	30	25	10	10
burrito, chicken, frzn, Patio	1 burrito	140		260	35	4	6	1.5	7	15	5	740	31	44	15	3	13	5	12	0	2	6	4
burrito, chili cheese, Taco Bell	1 burrito	142		330	120	13	20	6	30	35	12	880	37	37	12	4	16	2	14	60	0	15	8
burrito, ham & cheese, frzn, Swanson	1 burrito	99		210	50	6	9	2	10	60	20	440	18	29	10	2	8	3	9	0	2	6	10
burrito, hot & spicy, frzn, Swanson	1 burrito	99		220	65	7	11	3	15	55	18	490	20	30	10	3	12	3	9	2	2	8	15
burrito, red chili, frzn, Patio	1 burrito	142		270	60	6	9	2	10	10	3	850	35	42	14	6	24	4	11	8	6	2	15
burrito, sausage, frzn, Swanson	1 burrito	99		240	110	12	18	4	20	90	30	500	21	24	8	1	4	2	9	2	2	6	8

Consult a similar product for brand names not listed.

Food Name	Serving Size	gm	mL	Calories	Calories from Fat	Total Fat (g)	%DV	Saturated Fat (g)	%DV	Cholesterol (mg)	%DV	Sodium (mg)	%DV	Total Carbohydrates[8] (g)	%DV	Fiber[8] (g)	%DV	Sugars[8] (g)	Protein (g)	Vitamin A (%DV)	Vitamin C[7] (%DV)	Calcium (%DV)	Iron (%DV)
burrito, scrambled eggs, frzn, Swanson	1 burrito	99		200	70	8	12	3	15	60	20	510	21	25	8	2	8	2	8	2	4	8	8
eggrolls, chicken, frzn, Chun King	6 eggrolls	102		210	60	7	11	1.5	8	10	3	260	11	30	10	3	12	2	6	2	2	2	2
eggrolls, chicken, frzn, LaChoy	1 eggroll	85		210	80	9	14	4.5	21	15	5	550	23	25	9	2	8	4	6	10	2	2	6
eggrolls, chicken, mini, frzn, LaChoy	6 eggrolls	85		210	80	9	14	2.5	11	15	5	650	27	25	8	2	10	3	6	2	0	2	6
eggrolls, mu shu pork, frzn, LaChoy	1 eggroll	170		190	60	7	11	1.5	8	15	5	330	14	25	8	2	8	8	6	6	0	2	6
eggrolls, pork & shrimp, bite size, frzn, LaChoy	12 eggrolls	85		210	90	10	15	2.5	12	10	3	540	23	25	8	2	8	3	6	2	0	2	4
eggrolls, pork & shrimp, frzn, Chun King	6 eggrolls	85		220	80	8	12	2	10	10	3	260	11	29	10	3	12	2	6	2	6	2	2
eggrolls, pork & shrimp, mini, frzn, LaChoy	6 eggrolls	85		210	80	9	14	2.5	12	15	5	540	23	27	9	2	8	4	6	2	0	2	6
eggrolls, pork, frzn, LaChoy	1 eggroll	85		220	100	11	17	2.5	13	10	3	390	16	24	8	2	8	6	5	6	0	2	6
eggrolls, shrimp, frzn, Chun King	6 eggrolls	98		190	50	6	9	1	5	10	3	360	15	29	10	3	12	2	5	2	6	2	2
eggrolls, shrimp, frzn, LaChoy	1 eggroll	85		180	60	7	11	1.5	7	15	5	490	21	25	8	2	8	6	5	2	0	4	6
eggrolls, shrimp, mini, frzn, LaChoy	6 eggrolls	85		190	60	6	9	1.5	7	10	3	730	31	28	9	2	8	3	5	10	0	2	6
eggrolls, sweet & sour chicken, frzn, LaChoy	1 eggroll	85		220	80	9	14	2	9	15	5	550	23	29	10	2	8	10	6	2	4	2	6
eggrolls, veg & lobster, mini, frzn, LaChoy	6 eggrolls	206		190	60	7	11	1.5	7	5	2	440	18	27	9	2	8	3	5	0	2	0	4
enchanadas,[8] beef & bean, frzn, Stouffer's	1 enchanada	156		150	50	6	9	2	9	15	5	550	23	18	6	3	13	3	7	10	30	8	8
enchanadas,[8] chicken & veg, frzn, Stouffer's	1 enchanada	135		230	110	13	20	5	25	50	16	490	20	17	5	1	5	5	10	4	0	10	4
enchilada, beef & cheese, frzn, Banquet Family	1 enchilada	104		130	40	4	6	1.5	8	5	2	690	29	19	6	3	12	4	4	10	2	10	6
enchilada, beef, frzn, Patio Family	2 enchiladas	161		210	70	8	12	3	15	20	7	940	39	29	10	5	18	1	5	6	0	10	6
enchilada, cheese, frzn, Patio Family	2 enchiladas	161		210	60	7	11	3.5	17	20	7	880	37	30	10	2	8	4	6	8	0	10	4
enchilada, chicken, sour crm sauce, & rice, frzn, Lean Cuisine	1 entree	255		290	40	5	7	2	10	25	7	530	22	48	16	5	20	5	12	6	6	15	4

Food Name	Serving Size	gm	mL	Calories	Calories from Fat	Total Fat (g)	%DV	Saturated Fat (g)	%DV	Cholesterol (mg)	%DV	Sodium (mg)	%DV	Total Carbohydrates[6] (g)	%DV	Fiber[6] (g)	%DV	Sugars[6] (g)	Protein (g)	Vitamin A (%DV)	Vitamin C[7] (%DV)	Calcium (%DV)	Iron (%DV)
French bread pizza, cheese, frzn, Healthy Choice	1 pizza	170		340	45	5	8	1.5	8	15	5	480	20	51	17	7	27	4	22	4	0	40	25
French bread pizza, pepperoni, frzn, Healthy Choice	1 pizza	170		340	45	5	8	1.5	8	20	7	580	24	49	17	8	32	5	24	6	0	30	30
French bread pizza, sausage, frzn, Healthy Choice	1 pizza	170		320	45	5	8	1.5	8	25	8	580	24	48	16	5	21	5	21	4	0	15	15
French bread pizza, supreme, frzn, Healthy Choice	1 pizza	180		330	45	5	8	1.5	8	20	6	580	24	51	17	6	22	5	21	8	0	15	20
French toast & sausage, frzn, Swanson	1 package	156		410	230	26	40	9	45	110	37	580	24	33	11	3	12	8	13	8	0	10	10
McMuffin, egg, McDonald's	1 muffin	137		290	110	12	19	4.5	23	235	78	710	30	27	9	1	6	3	17	10	2	15	15
McMuffin, sausage, & egg, McDonald's	1 muffin	163		440	250	28	44	10	50	255	86	810	34	27	9	1	6	3	19	10	0	15	15
muffin w/egg, bacon, & cheese, frzn, Swanson	1 muffin	116		290	140	15	23	6	30	95	32	750	31	25	8	2	8	2	14	0	0	15	10
Nachos, Big Beef Supreme, Taco Bell	1 order	195		430	210	24	37	7	35	40	13	720	30	43	14	9	36	3	12	4	6	10	10
pancakes & bacon, frzn, Swanson	1 entree	128		400	180	20	31	7	35	100	33	1030	43	42	14	1	4	13	12	0	0	6	6
pancakes & sausage, frzn, Swanson	1 entree	170		490	230	25	38	11	55	90	30	950	40	52	17	3	12	15	14	0	0	8	10
pancakes, silver dollar & sausage, frzn, Swanson	1 entree	106		340	160	18	28	9	45	70	23	670	28	36	12	1	4	11	9	0	0	6	8
pizza, frzn, Celentano	2 ¼ slices	158		340	100	11	17	5	25	25	8	440	18	46	15	4	16	6	14	6	0	20	15
pot pie, beef, frzn, Banquet	1 pot pie	198		400	210	23	35	11	55	30	10	1000	42	38	13	1	4	8	9	15	0	2	6
pot pie, beef, frzn, Morton	1 pot pie	198		310	150	17	26	8	40	15	5	1380	58	34	11	2	8	NA	7	10	0	2	6
pot pie, beef, frzn, Swanson	1 pot pie	198		400	210	23	35	10	50	30	10	830	35	39	13	3	12	5	10	25	0	2	8
pot pie, beef, frzn, Swanson Hungry Man	1 pot pie	397		710	340	38	58	16	80	55	18	1440	60	71	24	6	24	11	22	50	0	4	15
pot pie, chicken, frzn, Banquet	1 pot pie	198		380	200	22	34	9	45	40	13	950	40	36	12	1	4	6	10	20	0	2	6
pot pie, chicken, frzn, Morton	1 pot pie	198		320	160	18	28	7	35	25	8	1020	43	32	11	3	12	NA	8	10	0	4	6
pot pie, chicken, frzn, Swanson	1 pot pie	198		410	200	22	34	8	40	30	10	810	34	45	15	3	12	5	9	35	2	4	10

Consult a similar product for brand names not listed.

Food Name	Serving Size gm	mL	Calories	Calories from Fat	Total Fat (g)	%DV	Saturated Fat (g)	%DV	Cholesterol (mg)	%DV	Sodium (mg)	%DV	Total Carbohydrates (g)	%DV	Fiber (g)	%DV	Sugars (g)	Protein (g)	Vitamin A (%DV)	Vitamin C (%DV)	Calcium (%DV)	Iron (%DV)
pot pie, chicken, frzn, Swanson Entree Deluxe	255		470	190	21	32	7	35	20	7	950	40	56	19	7	28	6	14	50	10	4	8
pot pie, chicken, frzn, Swanson Hungry Man	397		650	320	35	54	14	70	65	22	1470	61	64	21	3	12	8	19	80	0	6	10
pot pie, macaroni Italian, frzn, Swanson	170		180	45	5	8	3	15	15	5	480	20	25	8	2	8	4	9	6	20	15	8
pot pie, turkey, frzn, Banquet	198		370	180	20	31	8	40	45	14	850	35	38	13	3	11	6	10	15	0	4	6
pot pie, turkey, frzn, Morton	198		300	160	18	28	9	45	25	8	1060	44	29	10	2	8	2	8	10	0	4	6
pot pie, turkey, frzn, Swanson	198		440	220	24	37	9	45	20	7	750	31	44	15	2	8	5	11	20	4	4	10
pot pie, turkey, frzn, Swanson Hungry Man	397		650	310	34	52	13	65	45	15	1450	60	65	22	5	20	9	21	100	4	6	10
pot pie, veg & cheese w/broccoli, frzn, Banquet	198		340	160	17	27	7	33	10	3	920	39	39	13	2	9	11	6	25	0	8	4
taco, monster, Jack in the Box	113		290	160	18	27	6	30	40	13	550	23	21	7	3	12	2	11	8	8	20	8
taco, soft, Taco Bell	99		210	90	10	15	4.5	23	30	10	530	22	20	7	2	8	1	12	4	4	8	6
taco supreme, Taco Bell	113		220	120	13	20	6	30	45	15	290	12	13	4	2	8	2	11	6	6	8	6
tostada, Taco Bell	177		300	130	14	22	5	25	15	5	700	29	31	10	11	44	1	11	35	4	15	10

BREADS: BREAD-BASED MEALS/DINNERS[2]

Food Name	Serving Size		Calories	Calories from Fat	Total Fat		Saturated Fat		Cholesterol		Sodium		Total Carbohydrates[6]		Fiber[6]		Sugars[6]	Protein	Vitamin A	Vitamin C[7]	Calcium	Iron
	gm	mL			(g)	%DV	(g)	%DV	(mg)	%DV	(mg)	%DV	(g)	%DV	(g)	%DV	(g)	(g)	(%DV)	(%DV)	(%DV)	(%DV)
burritos, bean & beef, frzn, Michelina's[3]	298		450	160	18	28	6	30	30	10	980	41	57	19	9	36	2	15	40	0	20	20
cheese, sandwich grilled, frzn, Swanson Children	184		460	180	20	31	8	40	30	10	70	3	56	19	5	20	17	14	0	10	25	15
enchilada, beef & cheese fiesta, frzn, Patio Family	340		350	100	11	17	5	24	25	9	1760	73	53	18	7	28	5	11	8	0	15	10
enchilada, beef, frzn, Swanson	390		470	153	17	26	5	25	20	7	1790	75	60	20	10	40	6	20	20	20	15	15
enchiladas, bean & cheese, frzn, Michelina's[10]	298		420	140	15	24	5	27	25	8	1150	48	56	19	8	33	4	14	20	0	40	15
frank on a bun, frzn, Swanson Children[11]	215		350	110	12	18	5	25	35	12	800	33	47	16	3	12	18	14	30	8	10	10
Mexican combination, frzn, Swanson	376		470	160	18	28	6	30	20	7	1620	68	57	19	8	32	9	18	20	50	20	10
Mexican, frzn, Swanson Budget	298		400	140	16	25	7	35	20	7	1350	56	52	17	7	28	6	13	30	25	15	15
Mexican, frzn, Swanson Hungry Man	567		780	320	36	55	16	80	60	20	2120	88	86	29	12	48	18	27	45	8	30	25
pizza, cheese, frzn, Swanson Children	224		350	80	9	14	4	20	15	5	490	20	57	19	7	28	27	10	15	4	20	8
sloppy joe, frzn, Swanson Children	215		290	90	10	15	4	20	70	23	530	22	41	14	3	12	18	8	6	6	4	10
tacos w/cheese sauce, frzn, Swanson Children	204		380	140	15	23	5	25	35	12	760	32	50	17	4	16	20	11	4	4	10	10

Consult a similar product for brand names not listed.

CEREALS: CEREALS, READY-TO-EAT

Food Name	Serving Size	gm	mL	Calories	Calories from Fat	Total Fat (g)	%DV	Saturated Fat (g)	%DV	Cholesterol (mg)	%DV	Sodium (mg)	%DV	Total Carbohydrates (g)	%DV	Fiber (g)	%DV	Sugars (g)	Protein (g)	Vitamin A (%DV)	Vitamin C (%DV)	Calcium (%DV)	Iron (%DV)
All-Bran, Kellogg's	1/2 cup	30		80	10	1	2	0	0	0	0	280	12	22	7	10	40	5	4	15	25	10	25
Almond Raisin Nutri-Grain, Kellogg's	1 1/4 cups	55		200	25	3	5	0	0	0	0	330	14	44	15	4	16	16	4	0	0	2	6
Apple Jacks, Kellogg's	1 cup	30		110	0	0	0	0	0	0	0	135	6	27	9	1	4	14	2	15	25	0	25
Apple Raisin Crisp, Kellogg's	1 cup	55		180	0	0	0	0	0	0	0	340	14	46	15	4	16	16	3	15	0	0	10
Blueberry Squares, Kellogg's	3/4 cup	55		180	10	1	2	0	0	0	0	15	1	44	15	5	20	11	4	0	0	0	90
Bran Buds, Kellogg's	1/3 cup	30		70	10	1	2	0	0	0	0	210	9	24	8	11	45	8	3	15	25	2	25
Coco-Roos, Malt-O-Meal	3/4 cup	30		120	10	1	1	0	0	0	0	190	8	27	9	0	0	14	1	25	25	4	25
Cocoa Krispies, Kellogg's	3/4 cup	30		120	5	0.5	1	0	0	0	0	190	8	27	9	0	0	13	2	15	25	0	10
corn flakes, Kellogg's	1 cup	30		110	0	0	0	0	0	0	0	330	14	26	9	1	4	2	2	15	25	0	45
corn flakes, Malt-O-Meal	1 cup	27		100	0	0	0	0	0	0	0	280	12	23	8	1	4	2	2	25	25	0	15
Corn Pops, Kellogg's	1 cup	30		110	0	0	0	0	0	0	0	95	4	27	9	1	4	13	1	15	25	0	10
Cracklin' Oat Bran, Kellogg's	3/4 cup	55		230	70	8	12	3	15	0	0	180	8	40	13	6	24	18	4	15	25	2	10
Crispix, Kellogg's	1 cup	30		110	0	0	0	0	0	0	0	230	10	26	9	1	4	3	2	15	25	0	10
Crispy Rice, Malt-O-Meal	1 cup	30		120	0	0	0	0	0	0	0	250	11	26	9	0	0	3	2	25	25	0	10
Crunchy Nuggets, TownHouse	1/2 cup	48		180	10	1.5	2	0	0	0	0	220	9	38	13	5	20	4	6	40	0	0	70
Froot Loops, Kellogg's	1 cup	30		120	10	1	2	0.5	3	0	0	150	6	26	9	1	4	14	1	15	25	0	25
Frosted Flakes, Kellogg's	3/4 cup	30		120	0	0	0	0	0	0	0	200	8	28	9	0	0	13	1	15	25	0	25
Frosted Flakes, Malt-O-Meal	3/4 cup	28		110	0	0	0	0	0	0	0	190	8	26	9	0	0	11	1	25	25	0	10
Frosted Mini-Wheats, Kellogg's	1 cup	55		190	10	1	2	0	0	0	0	0	0	45	15	6	24	12	5	0	0	0	90
Fruitful Bran, Kellogg's	1 1/4 cups	55		170	10	1	2	0	0	0	0	330	14	44	15	6	24	16	4	15	0	2	25
Golden Sugar Puffs, Malt-O-Meal	3/4 cup	30		120	0	0	0	0	0	0	0	40	2	26	9	1	4	15	2	25	0	0	10
granola, low-fat, w/raisins, Kellogg's	2/3 cup	55		210	30	3	5	1	0	0	0	135	6	43	14	3	12	16	5	15	0	0	10
Just Right, Fruit & Nut, Kellogg's	1 cup	55		210	15	1.5	2	0	0	0	0	260	11	46	15	3	12	14	4	25	0	0	90
Marshmallow Mateys, Malt-O-Meal	1 cup	27		100	10	1	2	0	0	0	0	170	7	23	8	1	5	11	2	25	25	2	25
Mueslix, Crispy Blend, Kellogg's	2/3 cup	55		200	30	3	5	0	0	0	0	190	8	42	14	4	16	16	4	4	0	2	25
Multi-Grain Flakes, Healthy Choice	1 cup	30		100	0	0	0	0	0	0	0	210	9	25	8	3	12	6	3	10	0	0	35
Product 19, Kellogg's	1 cup	30		110	0	0	0	0	0	0	0	280	12	25	8	1	4	3	3	15	100	0	100

Food Name	Serving Size gm	mL	Calories	Calories from Fat	Total Fat (g)	%DV	Saturated Fat (g)	%DV	Cholesterol (mg)	%DV	Sodium (mg)	%DV	Total Carbohydrates[8] (g)	%DV	Fiber[8] (g)	%DV	Sugars[8] (g)	Protein (g)	Vitamin A (%DV)	Vitamin C[7] (%DV)	Calcium (%DV)	Iron (%DV)
puffed rice, Malt-O-Meal	16		60	0	0	0	0	0	0	0	0	0	14	5	0	0	0	1	0	0	0	25
puffed wheat, Malt-O-Meal	14		50	0	0	0	0	0	0	0	0	0	10	3	0	0	0	2	0	0	0	25
raisin bran, Kellogg's	55		170	10	1	2	0	0	0	0	310	13	43	14	7	28	18	5	15	0	4	25
raisin bran, Malt-O-Meal	61		200	10	1	2	0	0	0	0	290	12	47	16	7	28	18	5	25	0	2	100
Rice Krispies, Kellogg's	30		110	0	0	0	0	0	0	0	320	13	26	9	1	4	3	2	15	25	0	10
Special K, Kellogg's	30		110	0	0	0	0	0	0	0	250	10	21	7	1	4	3	6	15	25	0	45
Toasty O's, apple cinn, Malt-O-Meal	27		110	20	2	3	0	0	0	0	170	7	21	7	2	7	10	2	25	25	2	25
Toasty O's, honey & nut, Malt-O-Meal	30		110	10	1	2	0	0	0	0	270	11	24	8	2	7	11	3	25	25	2	25
Toasty O's, Malt-O-Meal	30		110	15	2	3	0	0	0	0	280	12	22	7	3	11	1	3	25	25	4	45
Tootie Fruities, Malt-O-Meal	30		110	10	1	1	0	0	0	0	150	6	26	9	0	0	14	2	25	25	0	25

Consult a similar product for brand names not listed.

CEREALS: CEREALS SERVED WARM

Food Name	Serving Size	gm	mL	Calories	Calories from Fat	Total Fat (g)	%DV	Saturated Fat (g)	%DV	Cholesterol (mg)	%DV	Sodium (mg)	%DV	Total Carbohydrates (g)	%DV	Fiber (g)	%DV	Sugars (g)	Protein (g)	Vitamin A (%DV)	Vitamin C (%DV)	Calcium (%DV)	Iron (%DV)
couscous w/raisins & almonds, dry mix, Knorr	1/4 package	39		150	10	1	2	0	0	0	0	340	14	30	10	1	5	4	5	0	0	2	6
Cream of Rice	1/4 cup	46		170	0	0	0	0	0	0	0	0	0	38	13	<1	2	0	3	0	0	0	10
Cream of Wheat, inst	3 tbsp	33		120	0	0	0	0	0	0	0	0	0	26	9	1	4	0	4	0	0	4	50
Cream of Wheat, inst, apple 'n cinn	1 package	35		130	0	0	0	0	0	0	0	300	12	29	10	1	5	13	2	25	0	4	45
Cream of Wheat, inst, apple granola crunch	1 package	43		150	5	0.5	1	0	0	0	0	220	9	34	11	2	6	16	3	25	0	6	50
Cream of Wheat, inst, brown sugar cinn	1 package	35		130	0	0	0	0	0	0	0	220	9	29	10	1	4	12	2	25	0	4	45
Cream of Wheat, inst, cinn toast	1 package	35		130	0	0	0	0	0	0	0	170	7	29	10	1	4	12	2	25	0	4	45
Cream of Wheat, quick	3 tbsp	33		120	0	0	0	0	0	0	0	85	4	25	8	1	4	0	3	0	0	4	50
Cream of Wheat, reg	3 tbsp	33		120	0	0	0	0	0	0	0	0	0	26	9	1	4	0	4	0	0	4	50
Malt-O-Meal	3 tbsp	35		120	0	0	0	0	0	0	0	0	0	28	9	1	4	0	3	0	0	0	60
Malt-O-Meal, apple & cinn	1/3 cup	61		220	0	0	0	0	0	0	0	10	0	51	17	1	5	19	4	0	0	0	100
Malt-O-Meal, choc	1/3 cup	61		220	5	0.5	1	0	0	0	0	0	0	50	17	2	8	13	5	0	0	0	100
Malt-O-Meal, maple & brown sugar	1/3 cup	61		220	0	0	0	0	0	0	0	10	0	51	17	1	5	19	4	0	0	0	100

CRACKERS

Food Name	Serving Size	gm	mL	Calories	Calories from Fat	Total Fat (g)	%DV	Saturated Fat (g)	%DV	Cholesterol (mg)	%DV	Sodium (mg)	%DV	Total Carbohydrates (g)	%DV	Fiber (g)	%DV	Sugars (g)	Protein (g)	Vitamin A (%DV)	Vitamin C (%DV)	Calcium (%DV)	Iron (%DV)
bacon cheddar, Frito-Lay	1 package	40		190	80	9	14	2.5	11	<5	1	410	17	25	8	1	4	3	3	0	0	10	8
bacon flavored, Nabisco	15 crackers	31		160	70	8	13	1.5	7	0	0	460	19	19	6	<1	3	2	3	0	0	0	0
Better Cheddars, Nabisco	22 crackers	30		150	70	8	12	2	10	<5	0	290	12	17	6	<1	3	<1	4	4	0	4	6
Captain Wafers, Lance	4 crackers	14		70	25	2.5	4	0.5	2	0	0	105	4	9	3	0	0	1	1	0	0	0	2
Cheese Nips, Nabisco	29 crackers	30		150	60	6	10	1.5	8	0	0	310	13	18	6	<1	3	0	3	0	0	2	6
cheese peanut butter, Keebler	1 package	40		190	80	9	14	2	10	<5	1	420	18	22	7	<1	3	4	6	0	0	0	4
cheese peanut butter, Nabisco Nabs	6 sandwiches	40		190	80	10	15	2	10	0	0	390	16	24	8	1	5	3	4	0	0	2	8
cheese peanut butter, Peter Pan	1 package	41		210	90	10	16	2.5	13	0	0	350	15	23	8	1	5	3	5	0	0	8	8
Cheese Tid-Bit, Nabisco	32 crackers	30		150	70	8	13	1.5	8	0	0	420	18	17	6	<1	2	<1	2	0	0	4	6
Chicken in a Biskit, Nabisco	14 crackers	30		160	80	9	15	1.5	8	0	0	270	11	17	6	<1	2	2	2	0	0	0	6
Crown Pilot, Nabisco	1 cracker	17		70	15	1.5	3	0	0	0	0	85	4	13	4	<1	2	0	1	0	0	0	4
Gold-N-Chee, Lance	½ cup	28		130	50	5	8	1.5	7	0	0	290	12	18	6	1	4	0	3	0	0	2	4
Golden Toast & Cheddar, Frito-Lay	1 package	45		240	130	14	22	4	21	5	2	440	18	25	8	1	4	5	4	0	0	10	6
Harvest Crisps, Five Grain, Nabisco	13 crackers	31		130	30	3.5	6	0.5	3	0	0	300	12	23	8	1	5	4	3	8	6	2	15
Harvest Crisps, Ital Herb, Nabisco	13 crackers	31		130	30	3.5	5	0.5	3	0	0	460	19	22	7	<1	3	3	3	4	4	6	6
jalapeno & cheddar, Doritos	1 package	45		230	120	13	20	4	18	<5	1	450	19	26	9	1	3	5	3	0	0	8	6
melba toast, garlic, Lance	6 slices	15		60	10	1	1	0	0	0	0	95	4	11	4	0	0	<1	2	0	0	0	4
melba toast, onion/sesame, Lance	6 slices	15		60	0	0.5	1	0	0	0	0	100	4	12	4	0	0	<1	2	0	0	0	4
melba toast, plain, oblong, Lance	4 slices	18		70	5	0.5	1	0	0	0	0	120	5	14	5	0	0	<1	3	0	0	0	4
melba toast, plain, round, Lance	6 slices	15		60	10	1.5	2	0	0	0	0	105	4	11	4	0	0	<1	2	0	0	0	4
Munch'ems, original, Keebler	30			130	45	5	8	1	5	0	0	350	15	20	7	<1	3	1	3	0	0	0	4
Oat Thins, Nabisco	18 crackers	30		140	50	6	9	1	5	0	0	190	8	20	7	2	8	2	3	0	0	0	6
Original Club Partners, Keebler	4 crackers	14		70	25	3	5	1	5	0	0	160	7	9	3	<1	1	1	1	0	0	0	2
oyster, Lance	1 package	14		60	15	2	3	0.5	2	0	0	135	6	10	3	0	0	0	2	0	0	0	2
oyster, Oysterettes	19 crackers	15		60	20	2.5	4	0.5	3	0	0	150	6	10	3	<1	3	0	1	0	0	0	4
oyster, Premium	23 crackers	15		60	15	1.5	2	0	0	0	0	230	10	11	4	<1	2	0	1	0	0	0	4
oyster, Zesta	42 crackers	15		70	25	2.5	4	1	5	0	0	160	7	10	3	<1	1	0	1	0	0	0	2

Consult a similar product for brand names not listed.

Food Name	Serving Size	gm	mL	Calories	Calories from Fat	Total Fat (g)	%DV	Saturated Fat (g)	%DV	Cholesterol (mg)	%DV	Sodium (mg)	%DV	Total Carbohydrates[8] (g)	%DV	Fiber[6] (g)	%DV	Sugars[5] (g)	Protein (g)	Vitamin A (%DV)	Vitamin C[7] (%DV)	Calcium (%DV)	Iron (%DV)
peanut butter toast, Nabs Nabisco	6 sandwiches	40		190	90	10	15	2	10	0	0	380	16	24	8	1	5	4	4	0	0	0	6
peanut butter toast, Peter Pan	1 package	41		210	100	11	17	2.5	13	0	0	280	12	23	8	<1	1	3	5	0	0	6	8
Ritz, Nabisco	5 crackers	16		80	35	4	6	0.5	4	0	0	135	6	10	3	<1	1	1	1	0	0	2	4
Royal Lunch, Nabisco	1 cracker	11		50	15	2	3	0	0	0	0	65	3	8	3	0	0	<1	<1	0	0	2	2
Rye Twins, Lance	4 crackers	15		70	30	3	5	0.5	2	0	0	130	5	10	3	1	4	0	1	0	0	2	2
saltines, Premium	5 crackers	14		60	15	1.5	3	0	0	0	0	180	7	10	3	<1	2	0	1	0	0	2	4
saltines, Zesta	5 crackers	15		60	20	2	3	0.5	3	0	0	190	8	10	3	<1	2	0	1	0	0	0	2
Sesame Twins, Lance	4 crackers	17		70	15	2	3	0.5	2	0	0	125	5	12	4	1	4	1	2	0	0	2	4
SnackWell's, French onion, Nabisco	32 crackers	30		120	15	2	3	0	0	0	0	290	12	23	8	1	3	2	2	0	0	4	6
SnackWell's, zesty cheese, Nabisco	32 crackers	30		120	20	2	3	0.5	3	<5	1	350	14	23	8	1	3	2	3	0	0	4	6
Sociables, Nabisco	7 crackers	30		80	35	4	6	0.5	3	0	0	150	6	9	3	<1	2	<1	1	0	0	2	4
sourdough, Lance	4 crackers	15		70	30	3	5	0.5	2	0	0	100	4	10	3	0	0	0	1	0	0	0	0
Toasteds Complements, Keebler	9 crackers	29		140	60	6	9	1.5	8	0	0	270	11	19	6	<1	3	3	2	0	0	0	4
Town House, Keebler	5 crackers	16		80	40	4.5	7	1	5	0	0	150	6	9	3	<1	1	1	1	0	0	0	2
Triscuits, Nabisco	7 wafers	31		140	45	5	8	1	4	0	0	170	7	21	7	4	14	0	3	0	0	0	8
Twigs sesame and cheese, Nabisco	15 sticks	30		150	60	7	11	1.5	9	0	0	300	12	17	6	<1	4	0	4	2	0	8	6
Uneeda Biscuit, Nabisco	2 crackers	15		60	15	1.5	3	0	0	0	0	110	5	11	4	<1	2	0	1	0	0	0	4
Veg Thins, Nabisco	14 crackers	31		160	80	9	13	1.5	7	0	0	310	13	19	6	1	4	2	2	15	0	4	6
Waverly, Nabisco	5 crackers	15		70	30	3.5	5	1	4	0	0	135	6	10	3	0	0	0	1	0	0	0	2
wheat cheese, Frito-Lay	1 package	40		200	90	9	14	2	10	<5	0	430	18	24	8	1	4	6	4	NA	NA	NA	NA
wheat snacks, Italian herb, Lance	3/4 cup	39		200	100	11	17	2	10	0	0	430	18	23	8	1	4	3	3	2	0	6	6
wheat snacks, pizza flavored, Lance	3/4 cup	39		200	90	10	15	2	10	0	0	390	16	23	8	1	6	3	3	15	0	6	6
Wheat Thins, Nabisco	16 crackers	29		140	50	6	9	1	6	0	0	170	7	19	6	2	6	2	2	0	0	2	4
Wheat Twins, Lance	4 crackers	15		70	25	3	5	0.5	2	0	0	120	5	10	3	1	4	1	1	0	0	2	4
wheat w/wheat germ, Breton	3 crackers	13		60	25	3	5	1.5	8	0	0	140	6	8	3	0	0	1	2	0	0	0	4
Wheatables, Keebler	26 crackers	30		150	60	7	11	2	10	0	0	320	13	18	6	1	4	2	3	0	0	6	6
Wheatswafers, Lance	4 crackers	14		60	20	2.5	4	0.5	2	0	0	100	4	9	3	1	4	1	2	0	0	2	2

Food Name	Serving Size			Calories	Calories from Fat	Total Fat (g)	%DV	Saturated Fat (g)	%DV	Cholesterol (mg)	%DV	Sodium (mg)	%DV	Total Carbohydrates[c] (g)	%DV	Fiber[d] (g)	%DV	Sugars[e] (g)	Protein (g)	Vitamin A (%DV)	Vitamin C[f] (%DV)	Calcium (%DV)	Iron (%DV)
		gm	mL																				
Wheatswafers, multi-grain, Lance	4 crackers	15		70	25	2.5	4	0.5	3	0	0	100	4	10	3	<1	3	1	2	0	0	2	2
Wheatsworth, Nabisco	5 crackers	16		80	30	3.5	5	0.5	3	0	0	170	7	10	3	1	3	1	2	0	0	0	4
zwieback, Nabisco	1 piece	8		35	10	1	2	0.5	3	0	0	10	0	5	0	<1	0	1	1	0	0	0	4

Consult a similar product for brand names not listed.

GRAIN-BASED DESSERTS: BROWNIES, CAKES, AND SNACK CAKES

Food Name	Serving Size	gm	mL	Calories	Calories from Fat	Total Fat (g)	%DV	Saturated Fat (g)	%DV	Cholesterol (mg)	%DV	Sodium (mg)	%DV	Total Carbohydrates[6] (g)	%DV	Fiber[6] (g)	%DV	Sugars[6] (g)	Protein (g)	Vitamin A (%DV)	Vitamin C[7] (%DV)	Calcium (%DV)	Iron (%DV)
brownie, choc raspberry, Pepperidge	1/2 piece	46		200	80	9	14	4	21	20	6	100	4	27	9	<1	2	20	2	2	0	0	10
brownie, Frosted Fudge, Little Debbie	1 brownie	43		180	90	10	15	2	9	5	2	135	6	25	8	<1	3	19	1	0	0	0	4
brownie, fudge nut, Lance	1 package	78		340	110	13	19	3	15	20	6	180	7	56	19	2	6	26	3	0	0	2	10
brownie, fudge, Little Debbie	1 brownie	61		270	120	13	20	2.5	12	15	4	170	7	40	13	1	4	28	2	0	0	2	8
brownie, peanut butter swirl, Pepperidge	1/2 piece	46		220	120	13	20	6	29	5	2	115	5	19	6	0	0	9	6	0	0	0	8
brownie, ultimate choc, Pepperidge	1/2 piece	46		200	90	10	15	5	25	50	17	150	6	24	8	1	4	18	3	0	0	2	4
brownie, walnut fudge, Pepperidge	1/2 piece	46		210	100	11	18	5	25	10	4	110	5	23	8	0	0	17	3	2	0	0	8
loaf cake, apple raisin, Harry & David	1/4 cake	92		340	130	14	22	5	26	45	15	280	12	48	16	2	7	26	5	2	0	4	4
snack cake, Banana Twins, Little Debbie	1 cake	62		250	90	10	15	1.5	8	10	3	190	8	39	13	0	0	29	2	15	0	0	6
snack cake, Choc Twins, Little Debbie	1 cake	62		250	80	9	13	1.5	8	20	6	290	12	43	14	1	3	31	2	0	0	2	6
snack cake, Devil Cremes, Little Debbie	1 cake	47		190	70	8	13	1.5	7	0	0	170	7	29	10	0	0	20	1	0	0	0	4
snack cake, Devil Squares, Little Debbie	1 cake	62		270	120	13	20	3	14	0	0	190	8	39	13	1	3	31	2	0	0	2	6
snack cake, Golden Cremes, Little Debbie	1 cake	42		170	70	7	11	2	8	0	0	180	7	25	8	0	0	18	2	0	0	2	4
snack cake, spice, Little Debbie	1 cake	70		300	130	15	23	3	16	10	3	240	10	43	14	1	2	35	2	0	0	0	4
snack cake, Star Crunch, Little Debbie	1 cake	31		140	50	6	9	1	5	0	0	85	4	21	7	0	0	15	1	0	0	2	2
snack cake, strawberry shortcake, Little Debbie	1 cake	61		240	80	8	13	1.5	8	15	5	160	7	41	14	0	0	33	2	0	0	0	4
snack cake, Swiss Rolls, Lance	1 cake	35		170	80	9	13	4.5	23	10	3	130	5	23	8	<1	2	13	1	0	0	0	2
snack cake, Swiss Rolls, Little Debbie	1 cake	61		260	110	12	18	2	11	15	5	180	7	39	13	1	2	31	1	0	0	2	4
snack cake, Zebra, Little Debbie	1 cake	74		330	150	16	25	3	15	0	0	180	8	45	15	0	0	36	2	0	0	0	6

GRAIN-BASED DESSERTS: CEREAL/GRANOLA BARS

Food Name	Serving Size	gm	mL	Calories	Calories from Fat	Total Fat (g)	%DV	Saturated Fat (g)	%DV	Cholesterol (mg)	%DV	Sodium (mg)	%DV	Total Carbohydrates (g)	%DV	Fiber (g)	%DV	Sugars (g)	Protein (g)	Vitamin A (%DV)	Vitamin C (%DV)	Calcium (%DV)	Iron (%DV)
all flavors, low fat, Kellogg's	1 bar	21		80	15	1.5	2	0	0	0	0	60	3	16	5	1	4	6	2	10	0	0	10
all flavors, Nutri-Grain	1 bar	37		140	25	3	5	0.5	3	0	0	60	3	27	9	1	4	12	2	15	0	0	10
almond, McKee	1 bar	28		130	60	7	10	2	10	0	0	65	3	17	6	2	6	10	2	0	0	2	2
apple-oatmeal, Lance	1 bar	51		190	60	6	10	1.5	8	10	4	180	8	32	11	1	4	10	2	0	0	2	8
choc chip, fudge-dipped, McKee	1 bar	43		200	90	10	16	4	19	0	0	70	3	27	9	2	7	19	2	0	0	2	4
choc chip, McKee	1 bar	35		160	60	7	11	3	15	0	0	65	3	23	8	2	7	15	2	0	0	2	4
macaroon, fudge-dipped, McKee	1 bar	39		200	110	12	19	7	33	0	0	60	2	21	7	2	10	14	2	0	0	2	4
oats & honey, McKee	1 bar	28		120	45	5	8	2	10	0	0	60	3	19	6	1	5	11	2	0	0	2	2
oats'n honey, Nature Valley	1 bar	22		100	35	4	6	0.5	2	0	0	70	3	16	5	1	5	6	2	0	0	0	2
raisin, McKee	1 bar	35		150	50	6	8	2	11	0	0	65	3	24	8	2	6	16	2	0	0	2	4
w/peanuts, fudge-dipped, McKee	1 bar	44		200	80	9	14	2.5	12	0	0	90	4	28	9	2	8	20	3	0	0	2	4

Consult a similar product for brand names not listed.

GRAIN-BASED DESSERTS: COOKIES

Food Name	Serving Size	gm	mL	Calories	Calories from Fat	Total Fat (g)	%DV	Saturated Fat (g)	%DV	Cholesterol (mg)	%DV	Sodium (mg)	%DV	Total Carbohydrates⁶ (g)	%DV	Fiber⁶ (g)	%DV	Sugars⁶ (g)	Protein (g)	Vitamin A (%DV)	Vitamin C⁷ (%DV)	Calcium (%DV)	Iron (%DV)
animal, Barnum's	12 crackers	31		140	35	4	6	0.5	4	0	0	160	7	23	8	1	3	8	2	0	0	0	6
animal, iced, Keebler	6 cookies	32		140	40	4.5	7	2	10	0	0	130	5	24	8	<1	3	9	2	0	0	0	4
animal, Mrs. Wright's	6 cookies	28		140	60	7	10	4	22	0	0	65	3	20	7	0	0	8	1	0	0	0	2
arrowroot biscuit, National	1 cookie	5		20	5	0.5	0	0	0	0	0	15	0	3	0	<1	0	1	0	0	0	0	0
banana, Big Town	1 cookie	57		250	90	10	15	2.5	13	0	0	160	7	37	12	1	2	21	3	0	0	2	6
Bonnie, Rotary	6 cookies	34		160	60	7	11	2.5	12	10	3	160	7	23	8	0	0	7	3	0	0	0	6
Breakfast Treats, Stella D'oro	1 cookie	23		100	30	3	5	1	5	10	3	80	3	16	5	<1	1	7	1	0	0	0	4
Brown Edge Wafers, Nabisco	5 cookies	29		140	50	6	9	1.5	8	<5	1	90	4	21	7	<1	1	10	1	0	0	0	6
Cameo creme sandwich, Nabisco	2 cookies	28		130	40	5	7	1	5	0	0	105	4	21	7	<1	2	10	1	0	0	0	4
cherry cobbler, Pepperidge	1 cookie	16		70	20	2	3	1	5	5	2	55	2	12	4	<1	1	11	1	0	0	0	0
choc, Big Town	1 cookie	57		250	70	8	12	2.5	13	0	0	160	7	40	13	1	4	21	3	0	0	0	6
choc chip, Chips Ahoy	3 cookies	32		160	70	8	12	2.5	12	0	0	105	4	21	7	1	3	10	2	0	0	0	4
choc chip, Chips Deluxe	1 cookie	15		80	40	4.5	7	1.5	8	0	0	60	3	9	3	0	0	4	1	0	0	0	2
choc chip, chunky, Chips Ahoy	1 cookie	17		80	40	4	7	3	14	10	3	60	2	11	4	<1	2	7	1	0	0	0	2
choc chip, Darlington Cookie Co	1 cookie	23		100	40	4.5	7	1.5	8	5	2	100	4	16	5	0	0	8	1	0	0	0	4
choc chip, Grandma's	1 cookie	39		190	80	9	14	3	15	0	0	135	6	25	8	<1	2	13	2	0	0	0	6
choc chip, Lance	1 cookie	28		130	50	6	9	2.5	13	5	2	75	3	18	6	1	4	10	2	0	0	0	2
choc chip, L-Sters	11 cookies	28		120	40	4	6	1	5	0	0	140	6	20	7	1	4	7	1	0	0	0	0
choc chip'n Toffee, Archway	1 cookie	29		140	60	7	11	1.5	8	5	2	120	5	19	6	1	2	9	1	0	0	0	6
choc chip, reduced fat, Chips Deluxe	1 cookie	15		70	30	3	5	1	5	0	0	70	3	11	4	0	0	5	1	0	0	0	2
choc chip, Soft Batch	1 cookie	16		80	35	3.5	5	1	5	0	0	70	3	10	3	<1	2	6	<1	0	0	0	2
choc chunk, Pepperidge	1 cookie	26		130	60	7	11	3	15	10	3	75	3	16	5	<1	4	8	1	0	0	0	2
Chocomint, Lance	6 cookies	35		190	90	9	15	3.5	18	0	0	100	4	24	8	1	4	17	2	0	0	0	6
choc w/van filling, EL Fudge	3 cookies	35		170	70	8	12	2	10	0	0	125	5	23	8	1	4	14	2	0	0	0	6
cinn honey hearts, fat-free, Archway	3 cookies	28		100	0	0	0	0	0	0	0	120	5	24	8	1	2	13	1	0	0	0	4
cranberry newtons, fat-free, Nabisco	2 cookies	29		100	0	0	0	0	0	0	0	95	4	23	8	1	2	15	1	0	0	0	2
creme wafer, Mrs. Wright's	5 pieces	28		140	60	7	11	1.5	8	0	0	15	1	20	7	<1	1	12	<1	0	0	0	2

Food Name	Serving Size	gm	mL	Calories	Calories from Fat	Total Fat (g)	%DV	Saturated Fat (g)	%DV	Cholesterol (mg)	%DV	Sodium (mg)	%DV	Total Carbohydrates (g)	%DV	Fiber (g)	%DV	Sugars (g)	Protein (g)	Vitamin A (%DV)	Vitamin C (%DV)	Calcium (%DV)	Iron (%DV)
double choc fudge, low fat, Obie's	2 tbsp mix (makes 1 cookie)	23		90	10	1	2	0	0	0	0	130	6	19	6	<1	2	11	1	0	0	0	4
famous choc wafers, Nabisco	5 cookies	32		140	35	4	6	1.5	7	<5	1	230	9	24	8	1	4	11	2	0	0	0	6
fig newtons, Nabisco	2 cookies	31		110	20	2.5	4	1	4	0	0	120	5	20	7	1	6	13	1	0	0	0	4
French van crm sandwich, Keebler	1 cookie	17		80	30	3.5	5	1	5	0	0	85	4	12	4	0	0	6	<1	0	0	0	0
Fudgebutters, Fudge Shoppe	2 cookies	24		130	70	7	11	4	20	<5	1	90	4	14	5	<1	2	9	2	0	0	0	2
fudge'n caramel, Fudge Shoppe	2 cookies	24		120	50	6	9	4	20	<5	1	55	2	16	5	<1	1	12	<1	0	0	0	2
fudge choc chip, Lance	1 cookie	28		130	50	5	8	2	10	<5	1	75	3	19	6	1	4	5	2	0	0	0	8
fudge sticks, Fudge Shoppe	3 cookies	29		150	70	8	12	4.5	23	0	0	55	2	20	7	<1	3	15	1	0	0	0	2
fudge stripes, Fudge Shoppe	3 cookies	32		160	70	8	12	4.5	23	0	0	140	6	21	7	<1	3	10	1	0	0	0	4
fudge w/fudge filling, EL Fudge	3 cookies	34		160	60	7	11	2	10	0	0	100	4	23	8	<1	4	11	2	0	0	0	6
ginger snaps, Nabisco	4 cookies	28		120	25	2.5	4	0.5	2	0	0	170	7	22	7	<1	2	10	1	0	0	2	6
graham crackers, apple cinn, Keebler	8 crackers	30		130	35	4	6	1	5	0	0	200	8	22	7	<1	3	8	2	0	0	0	4
graham crackers, choc-covered, Fudge Shoppe	3 crackers	28		140	60	7	11	4.5	23	0	0	105	4	19	6	<1	3	10	1	0	0	0	4
graham crackers, choc-covered, Nabisco	3 crackers	32		160	70	8	12	5	23	0	0	90	4	21	7	1	5	12	2	0	0	0	4
graham crackers, choc-covered, Rotary	9 crackers	37		190	70	8	13	2	11	0	0	95	4	25	8	1	4	13	3	0	0	0	6
graham crackers, cinn, Honey Maid	10 crackers	32		140	25	3	4	0.5	2	0	0	210	9	26	9	1	3	11	2	0	0	2	8
graham crackers, honey, Honey Maid	8 crackers	28		120	25	3	4	0.5	2	0	0	180	7	22	7	1	3	7	2	0	0	0	6
graham crackers, honey, Keebler	8 crackers	31		150	50	6	9	1.5	8	0	0	140	6	21	7	1	4	6	2	0	0	0	4
graham crackers, Keebler	8 crackers	29		130	30	3	5	1	5	0	0	135	6	23	8	<1	1	7	2	0	0	0	2
graham crackers, Nabisco	8 crackers	28		120	25	3	5	0.5	3	0	0	180	8	22	7	1	4	7	2	0	0	0	6
Grasshopper, Fudge Shoppe	4 cookies	30		150	60	7	11	5	25	0	0	70	3	20	7	<1	3	12	1	0	0	0	4
Krispy Kreem, Keebler	5 pieces	27		140	60	7	11	1.5	8	0	0	50	2	19	6	0	0	13	1	0	0	0	2
Lady Stella assortment, Stella D'oro	3 cookies	28		130	50	5	8	1.5	7	5	2	65	3	19	6	<1	2	8	1	0	0	0	4
lemon, frosted, Archway	1 cookie	28		120	45	5	8	1	5	0	0	110	5	19	6	0	0	15	1	0	0	0	0

Consult a similar product for brand names not listed.

Food Name	Serving Size	gm	mL	Calories	Calories from Fat	Total Fat (g)	%DV	Saturated Fat (g)	%DV	Cholesterol (mg)	%DV	Sodium (mg)	%DV	Total Carbohydrates (g)	%DV	Fiber[6] (g)	%DV	Sugars[6] (g)	Protein (g)	Vitamin A (%DV)	Vitamin C[7] (%DV)	Calcium (%DV)	Iron (%DV)
Mallomars, Nabisco	2 cookies	26		120	45	5	8	3	14	0	0	35	1	17	6	1	2	13	1	0	0	0	2
molasses, Grandma's	1 cookie	39		160	35	4	6	1.5	7	<5	1	230	10	29	10	<1	2	18	2	0	0	2	6
Mystic Mint, Nabisco	1 cookie	17		90	35	4	6	1	5	0	0	65	3	11	4	0	0	8	1	0	0	0	2
Nilla wafers, Nabisco	8 cookies	32		140	40	5	7	1	5	5	2	105	4	24	8	0	0	12	2	0	0	2	4
Nutter Butter, Nabisco	2 cookies	28		130	50	6	9	1	6	<5	1	110	5	19	6	1	3	8	3	0	0	0	4
oatmeal creme, Lance	1 cookie	57		240	90	10	15	2.5	12	0	0	220	9	35	12	1	4	19	3	0	0	2	6
oatmeal raisin, Archway	1 cookie	28		110	35	4	6	1	5	5	1	115	5	19	6	1	3	13	2	0	0	0	6
oatmeal raisin, Soft Batch	1 cookie	16		70	30	3	5	1	5	0	0	65	3	10	3	<1	2	6	<1	0	0	0	0
oatmeal, Darlington Cookie Co	1 cookie	23		100	30	3.5	5	1	5	<5	1	75	3	16	5	<1	2	8	1	0	0	0	4
oatmeal, Lance	1 cookie	28		130	50	6	8	1	6	0	0	90	4	18	6	1	4	4	2	0	0	0	4
oatmeal, Ruth's Golden, Archway	1 cookie	28		120	40	4.5	7	1	5	5	1	135	6	19	6	1	3	11	2	0	0	0	4
Opera Creme, lemon filling, Keebler	1 cookie	17		80	30	3.5	5	1	5	0	0	70	3	12	4	0	0	6	<1	0	0	0	2
Oreos, Nabisco	3 cookies	33		160	60	7	11	1.5	8	0	0	220	9	23	8	1	3	13	2	0	0	0	4
peanut butter creme-filled wafers, Lance	1 cookie	43		230	110	12	19	3	15	0	0	80	3	26	9	2	7	16	4	0	0	6	6
peanut butter, Darlington Cookie Co	1 cookie	23		110	50	6	9	1.5	8	15	5	100	4	13	4	0	0	8	1	0	0	0	4
peanut butter, Grandma's	1 cookie	39		190	80	9	14	2	11	5	2	200	9	22	7	1	2	12	2	0	0	0	6
peanut butter, Lance	1 cookie	28		140	70	8	12	1.5	8	<5	1	65	3	14	5	1	4	10	4	0	0	0	0
Pecan Sandies, Keebler	1 cookie	16		80	45	5	8	1	5	<5	1	75	3	9	3	<1	1	3	<1	0	0	0	2
Pitter Patter, Keebler	1 cookie	18		90	35	4	6	1	5	0	0	115	5	12	4	<1	3	6	2	0	0	0	2
Rainbow Chip, Chips Deluxe	1 cookie	16		80	35	4	6	2	10	<5	1	45	2	10	3	<1	2	5	1	0	0	0	2
raspberry newtons, fat-free, Nabisco	2 cookies	29		100	0	0	0	0	0	0	0	115	5	23	8	<1	2	14	1	0	2	0	2
shortbread, Lorna Doone	4 cookies	29		140	60	7	11	1	6	5	2	130	5	19	6	<1	2	6	2	0	0	0	6
Social Tea Biscuits, Nabisco	6 cookies	28		120	30	4	6	0.5	4	5	2	105	4	20	7	<1	2	7	2	0	0	0	8
sugar, Darlington Cookie Co	1 cookie	23		100	45	5	8	1	5	5	2	100	4	15	5	0	2	7	1	0	0	0	4
sugar wafers, Biscos	8 cookies	28		140	60	6	8	1.5	6	0	0	40	2	21	6	<1	0	13	<1	0	0	0	0
Toffee Sandies, Keebler	1 cookie	16		80	40	4.5	7	1	5	<5	1	55	2	10	3	0	0	5	<1	0	0	0	0
van, Big Town	1 cookie	57		250	100	11	16	2.5	12	0	0	120	5	37	12	1	4	26	3	0	0	0	4

Food Name	Serving Size	gm	mL	Calories	Calories from Fat	Total Fat (g)	%DV	Saturated Fat (g)	%DV	Cholesterol (mg)	%DV	Sodium (mg)	%DV	Total Carbohydrates[§] (g)	%DV	Fiber[§] (g)	%DV	Sugars[§] (g)	Protein (g)	Vitamin A (%DV)	Vitamin C[?] (%DV)	Calcium (%DV)	Iron (%DV)
van sandwich, Grandma's	5 cookies	43		210	90	15	10	2.5	12	5	2	125	5	30	10	<1	2	15	2	0	0	2	6
van sandwich mini, Grandma's	9 cookies	31		150	60	10	7	1.5	9	<5	1	85	4	22	7	<1	1	10	2	0	0	0	6
van sandwich w/fudge filling, EL Fudge	3 cookies	34		170	70	8	12	2	10	<5	1	105	4	24	8	<1	3	11	2	0	0	0	6
van wafers, Keebler	8 cookies	31		150	60	7	11	2	10	0	0	120	5	20	7	<1	2	9	1	0	0	0	2
waffle crm, Biscos	4 cookies	34		180	80	9	14	2	11	0	0	35	1	24	8	<1	1	17	<1	0	0	0	2

Consult a similar product for brand names not listed.

GRAIN-BASED DESSERTS: PASTRY

Food Name	Serving Size	gm	mL	Calories	Calories from Fat	Total Fat (g)	%DV	Saturated Fat (g)	%DV	Cholesterol (mg)	%DV	Sodium (mg)	%DV	Total Carbohydrates[β] (g)	%DV	Fiber[β] (g)	%DV	Sugars[β] (g)	Protein (g)	Vitamin A (%DV)	Vitamin C[γ] (%DV)	Calcium (%DV)	Iron (%DV)
honey bun, frzn, Morton	1 honey bun	64		250	90	10	16	2.5	13	0	0	160	7	35	12	2	7	16	3	0	0	0	8
honey bun, Lance	1 honey bun	85		320	120	13	20	4	19	0	0	200	8	47	16	4	15	13	4	0	0	4	8
Pecan Twirls, Lance	1 package	57		220	80	9	14	4	20	5	2	140	6	32	11	1	4	17	3	0	0	2	10
Pop-Tarts, apple cinn, Kellogg's	1 pastry	52		210	50	5	8	1	5	0	0	170	7	38	13	1	4	17	2	10	0	0	10
Pop-Tarts, blueberry, frosted, Kellogg's	1 pastry	52		200	50	5	8	1	5	0	0	210	9	37	12	1	4	16	2	10	0	0	10
Pop-Tarts, cherry, Kellogg's	1 pastry	52		200	50	5	8	1	5	0	0	220	9	37	12	1	4	16	2	10	0	0	10
Pop-Tarts, choc fudge, frosted, Kellogg's	1 pastry	52		200	40	5	8	1	5	0	0	220	9	37	12	1	4	19	3	10	0	0	10
Toastettes, blueberry, frosted, Nabisco	1 toastette	48		190	45	5	8	1.5	7	0	0	190	8	35	12	1	3	17	2	10	0	0	10
Toastettes, brown sugar cinn, frosted, Nabisco	1 toastette	48		190	45	5	8	1.5	7	0	0	180	7	35	12	1	3	18	2	10	0	0	10
Toastettes, cherry, frosted, Nabisco	1 toastette	48		190	45	5	8	1.5	7	0	0	190	8	35	12	1	3	17	2	10	0	0	10
Toastettes, fudge, frosted, Nabisco	1 toastette	48		190	45	5	8	1.5	7	0	0	280	12	34	11	1	3	18	2	10	0	2	15
Toastettes, strawberry, frosted, Nabisco	1 toastette	48		190	45	5	8	1.5	7	0	0	190	8	35	12	1	3	17	2	10	4	0	10
Toastettes, strawberry, Nabisco	1 toastette	48		190	45	5	8	1.5	7	0	0	200	8	35	12	1	3	17	2	10	4	0	10

GRAIN-BASED DESSERTS: PIES AND SNACK PIES

Food Name	Serving Size	gm	mL	Calories	Calories from Fat	Total Fat (g)	%DV	Saturated Fat (g)	%DV	Cholesterol (mg)	%DV	Sodium (mg)	%DV	Total Carbohydrates (g)	%DV	Fiber (g)	%DV	Sugars (g)	Protein (g)	Vitamin A (%DV)	Vitamin C (%DV)	Calcium (%DV)	Iron (%DV)
apple cranberry, frzn, Mrs. Smith's	1/6 of 8" pie	123		280	100	11	17	2	10	0	0	300	12	43	14	1	4	19	2	0	0	2	0
apple, Dutch, frzn, Mrs. Smith's	1/8 of 9" pie	131		350	130	14	22	3	15	0	0	300	13	53	18	1	4	20	3	0	0	0	2
apple, frzn, Banquet	1/5 pie	113		300	120	13	20	6	30	5	2	370	15	41	14	2	8	22	3	0	0	0	6
apple, frzn, Mrs. Smith's	1/8 of 9" pie	131		310	130	14	22	2.5	13	0	0	380	16	44	15	1	4	18	2	0	0	0	0
banana crm, frzn, Banquet	1/3 pie	132		350	190	21	32	5	25	<5	0	290	12	39	13	1	4	28	3	0	0	4	2
banana crm, frzn, Mrs. Smith's	1/4 of 8" pie	108		290	130	15	23	4	20	0	0	190	8	38	13	1	4	24	2	0	0	2	2
berry, frzn, Mrs. Smith's	1/6 of 8" pie	123		280	100	11	17	2	10	0	0	340	14	44	15	0	0	21	2	0	0	2	2
blackberry, frzn, Banquet	1/5 pie	113		300	110	12	18	5	25	5	2	430	18	45	15	3	12	23	3	0	4	8	6
blackberry, frzn, Mrs. Smith's	1/6 of 8" pie	123		280	100	11	17	2	10	0	0	320	13	43	14	0	0	21	2	0	0	2	4
blueberry, frzn, Banquet	1/5 pie	113		260	110	12	18	5	25	5	2	400	17	36	12	2	8	25	3	0	0	0	2
blueberry, frzn, Mrs. Smith's	1/6 of 8" pie	123		260	100	11	17	2	10	0	0	320	13	39	13	1	4	17	2	0	0	0	2
Boston crm, frzn, Mrs. Smith's	1/8 of 8" pie	69		180	60	7	11	2	10	20	7	170	7	27	9	0	0	19	2	0	0	2	0
cherry, frzn, Banquet	1/5 pie	113		290	120	14	22	6	30	5	2	310	13	39	13	2	8	14	3	4	0	0	2
cherry, frzn, Mrs. Smith's	1/8 of 9" pie	131		310	120	14	22	2.5	13	0	0	400	17	45	15	1	4	19	3	2	0	2	2
choc crm, frzn, Banquet	1/3 pie	132		360	180	20	31	5	25	<5	0	240	10	43	14	3	12	33	3	0	0	4	6
choc crm, frzn, Mrs. Smith's	1/4 of 8" pie	108		330	150	17	26	4	20	0	0	220	9	42	14	1	4	29	2	0	0	2	6
coconut crm, frzn, Banquet	1/3 pie	132		350	180	20	31	6	30	<5	0	250	10	39	13	2	8	30	3	0	0	4	2
coconut crm, frzn, Mrs. Smith's	1/4 of 8" pie	114		340	170	19	29	5	25	0	0	260	11	40	13	0	0	23	2	0	0	2	0
coconut custard, frzn, Mrs. Smith's	1/5 of 8" pie	142		280	110	12	18	5	25	75	25	350	15	35	12	0	0	18	7	0	0	15	4
lemon crm, frzn, Banquet	1/3 pie	132		360	180	20	31	5	25	<5	0	240	10	43	14	2	8	31	3	0	0	4	2
lemon crm, frzn, Mrs. Smith's	1/4 of 8" pie	108		300	140	15	23	4	20	0	0	180	8	41	14	0	0	28	2	0	0	2	0
lemon meringue, frzn, Mrs. Smith's	1/5 of 8" pie	136		300	70	8	12	2	10	65	22	220	9	55	18	0	0	38	2	0	8	0	2
mince, frzn, Mrs. Smith's	1/6 of 8" pie	123		300	100	11	17	2	10	0	0	400	17	48	16	2	8	24	2	0	0	2	4
mincemeat, frzn, Banquet	1/5 pie	113		310	110	13	20	6	30	10	3	430	18	46	15	2	8	26	3	0	0	2	2
peach, frzn, Banquet	1/5 pie	113		260	110	12	18	5	25	5	2	340	14	36	12	2	8	17	3	0	10	0	2
peach, frzn, Mrs. Smith's	1/6 of 8" pie	123		260	100	11	17	2	10	0	0	310	13	38	13	1	4	17	2	2	10	0	2
pecan snack pie, Lance	1 pie	85		350	150	17	26	4	21	25	8	200	8	46	15	3	11	35	4	0	0	0	15

Consult a similar product for brand names not listed.

Food Name	Serving Size	gm	mL	Calories	Calories from Fat	Total Fat (g)	%DV	Saturated Fat (g)	%DV	Cholesterol (mg)	%DV	Sodium (mg)	%DV	Total Carbohydrates[8] (g)	%DV	Fiber[8] (g)	%DV	Sugars[8] (g)	Protein (g)	Vitamin A (%DV)	Vitamin C[7] (%DV)	Calcium (%DV)	Iron (%DV)
pecan, frzn, Mrs. Smith's	1/6 of 8" pie	136		520	210	23	35	4	20	70	23	450	19	73	24	1	4	45	5	2	0	4	4
pumpkin custard, frzn, Mrs. Smith's	1/8 of 9" pie	131		230	70	8	12	2	10	45	15	320	13	36	12	1	4	18	5	8	0	6	2
pumpkin, frzn, Banquet	1/5 pie	140		250	70	8	12	3	15	20	7	340	14	40	13	3	12	21	4	70	0	6	2
raspberry, red, frzn, Mrs. Smith's	1/6 of 8" pie	123		280	100	11	17	2	10	0	0	320	13	43	14	0	0	20	2	0	0	2	2
strawberry crm, frzn, Banquet	1/3 pie	132		340	150	17	26	4	20	<5	0	240	10	44	15	2	8	22	3	0	2	4	2
strawberry rhubarb, frzn, Mrs. Smith's	1/6 of 8" pie	123		280	100	11	17	2	10	0	0	380	16	44	15	0	0	21	2	0	0	4	2

Food Name	Serving Size gm	mL	Calories	Calories from Fat	Total Fat (g)	%DV	Saturated Fat (g)	%DV	Cholesterol (mg)	%DV	Sodium (mg)	%DV	Total Carbohydrates[8] (g)	%DV	Fiber[8] (g)	%DV	Sugars[8] (g)	Protein (g)	Vitamin A (%DV)	Vitamin C[7] (%DV)	Calcium (%DV)	Iron (%DV)
GRAIN-BASED SNACK FOODS																						
Chee-tos, crunchy	1 oz (21 pieces) 28		160	90	16	10	2.5	13	0	0	290	12	15	5	<1	0	1	2	0	0	0	2
Cracker Jack, butter toffee	1 box 35		160	50	6	9	2.5	13	5	2	200	8	26	9	<1	3	19	1	4	0	0	0
Cracker Jack, butter toffee–peanut clusters	½ cup 28		130	40	4.5	7	2	10	5	2	160	7	21	7	<1	2	15	1	4	0	0	0
Cracker Jack (candied popcorn & peanuts)	1 box 35		150	30	3	5	0.5	3	0	0	110	5	28	9	1	4	18	2	0	0	2	2
Fritos	1 oz (32 chips) 28		160	90	10	15	1.5	8	0	0	160	7	15	5	1	4	0	2	0	0	0	0
Funyuns, Frito-Lay 13 pieces	1 oz (about 28		140	60	7	10	1.5	7	0	0	270	11	18	6	<1	1	<1	2	0	0	0	4
Munchos, Frito-Lay	1 oz (about 16 chips) 28		150	90	10	15	2.5	12	0	0	270	11	16	5	1	3	0	2	0	0	0	0
Pizza Chips, cheese, Pizzarias	14 chips 30		150	60	7	11	1.5	8	<5	1	210	9	19	6	1	4	<1	3	0	0	0	2
Pizza Chips, supreme, Pizzarias	14 chips 30		150	70	7	11	1.5	8	0	0	200	8	19	6	1	4	<1	3	0	0	0	2
Pizza Chips, zesty pepperoni, Pizzarias 14 chips	30		150	60	7	11	1.5	8	<5	1	210	9	20	7	<1	3	<1	3	0	0	0	4
popcorn & caramel bar, Lance	1 bar 21		90	0	0	0	0	0	0	0	120	5	20	7	0	0	14	0	0	0	0	2
popcorn, butter, microwave, Chester's	5 cups 40		200	110	12	18	1.5	8	0	0	300	12	22	7	4	15	<1	3	0	0	0	4
popcorn, butter, Smartfood	3 cups 28		150	80	9	14	2	9	5	2	240	10	15	5	1	6	2	2	6	0	0	2
popcorn, cheddar cheese, Smartfood	3 cups 28		160	90	10	15	2	11	5	2	260	11	14	5	2	7	4	3	0	0	4	0
Popscotch, Lance	1 bar 35		160	50	5	8	1	5	0	0	30	1	27	9	2	8	16	2	0	0	0	2
pretzels, Bavarian, Keebler	3 pretzels 32		120	15	2	3	0.5	3	0	0	600	25	23	8	1	4	<1	4	0	0	2	6
pretzels, braids, Keebler	22 pretzels 28		100	10	1	2	0	0	0	0	680	28	21	7	1	5	<1	3	0	0	0	4
pretzels, butter knots, Keebler	7 pretzels 28		100	10	1	2	0	0	0	0	600	25	21	7	1	5	<1	3	0	0	0	6
pretzels, butter knots, mini, Keebler	18 pretzels 30		100	10	1	2	0	0	0	0	770	32	22	7	1	4	<1	3	0	0	0	4
pretzels, knots, Keebler	7 pretzels 28		110	10	1	2	0	0	0	0	530	22	20	7	1	4	<1	3	0	0	0	4

Consult a similar product for brand names not listed.

Food Name	Serving Size (gm)	Serving Size (mL)	Calories	Calories from Fat	Total Fat (g)	Total Fat %DV	Saturated Fat (g)	Saturated Fat %DV	Cholesterol (mg)	Cholesterol %DV	Sodium (mg)	Sodium %DV	Total Carbohydrates (g)	Total Carbohydrates %DV	Fiber (g)	Fiber %DV	Sugars (g)	Protein (g)	Vitamin A (%DV)	Vitamin C (%DV)	Calcium (%DV)	Iron (%DV)
pretzels, Lance	1 package (9 pretzels) 35		140	10	1	2	0	0	0	0	470	20	28	9	<1	3	1	4	0	0	0	6
pretzels, thin twist, Crispy	1 package 32		130	15	2	3	0	0	0	0	730	31	24	8	1	4	3	3	0	0	0	10
tortilla chips, baked orig, Tostitos	1 oz (13 chips) 28		110	5	0.5	1	0	0	0	0	140	6	24	8	2	6	0	3	0	0	4	0
tortilla chips, cheesy quesadilla, Chacho's	14 chips 30		150	70	8	12	1.5	8	<5	1	270	11	18	6	<1	2	1	3	0	0	0	2
tortilla chips, chili & lime, Guiltless Gourmet	18 chips 28		110	15	2	3	0	0	0	0	200	8	22	7	2	8	2	2	0	0	6	2
tortilla chips, cinn crispana, Chacho's	13 chips 30		150	60	7	11	1	5	0	0	75	3	20	7	<1	3	4	2	0	0	0	2
tortilla chips, nacho, Guiltless Gourmet	18 chips 28		110	15	2	3	0	0	0	0	200	8	22	7	2	8	2	2	0	0	6	2
tortilla chips, orig, Guiltless Gourmet	18 chips 28		110	15	2	3	0	0	0	0	160	7	22	7	2	8	0	3	0	0	6	2
tortilla chips, restaurant, Chacho's	15 chips 30		150	70	8	12	1	5	0	0	210	9	18	6	<1	2	<1	2	0	0	0	2
tortilla chips, toasted corn, Doritos	1 oz (18 chips) 28		140	60	6	10	1	5	0	0	65	3	19	6	1	4	0	2	0	0	4	2
tortilla chips, white corn, Guiltless Gourmet	18 chips 28		110	15	2	3	0	0	0	0	140	6	22	7	2	8	0	3	0	0	6	2

PASTA: PASTA

Food Name	Serving Size			Calories	Calories from Fat	Total Fat (g)	%DV	Saturated Fat (g)	%DV	Cholesterol (mg)	%DV	Sodium (mg)	%DV	Total Carbohydrates (g)	%DV	Fiber (g)	%DV	Sugars (g)	Protein (g)	Vitamin A (%DV)	Vitamin C (%DV)	Calcium (%DV)	Iron (%DV)
		gm	mL																				
angel hair, fresh, Contadina	1¼ cups	80		240	30	3	5	1	4	90	30	30	1	43	14	2	9	1	10	0	0	2	15
bow ties, enr, Mueller's	2 oz dry	56		220	25	3	5	0.5	2	65	22	10	0	38	13	1	4	2	8	0	0	0	10
elbows/other pasta,[12] enr, Mueller's	2 oz dry	56		210	10	1	2	0	0	0	0	0	0	42	14	1	4	2	7	0	0	0	10
fettuccine, fresh, Contadina	1¼ cups	83		250	30	3.5	5	1	4	85	31	30	1	45	15	2	9	1	10	0	0	2	15
fettuccine, spinach, fresh, Contadina	1¼ cups	89		270	35	4	6	1	5	105	34	110	4	46	15	4	14	1	12	4	0	6	15
lasagne, enr, Mueller's	2 oz dry	56		210	10	1	2	0	0	0	0	0	0	42	14	1	4	2	7	0	0	0	10
linguine, fresh, Contadina	1 cup	73		220	25	3	5	1	4	85	27	35	1	39	13	2	8	1	9	0	0	2	15
noodles, egg, enr, Kluski	1 cup dry	56		220	30	3	5	1	5	55	18	210	9	40	13	1	4	2	8	0	0	0	10
noodles, enr, No Yolks	2 oz dry	56		210	10	1	2	0	0	0	0	0	0	42	14	2	7	3	7	0	0	0	10
pasta, egg & spinach, enr, Borden	2 oz dry	56		220	30	3	5	1	4	55	18	35	1	40	13	2	8	2	8	2	0	4	10
pasta, egg, enr, Borden	2 oz dry	56		220	30	3	4	1	4	55	18	15	1	40	13	1	4	2	8	0	0	0	10
pasta, enr, Borden	2 oz dry	56		210	10	1	2	0	0	0	0	0	0	42	14	2	7	3	7	0	0	0	10
pasta, spinach, enr, Borden	2 oz dry	56		210	10	1	2	0	0	0	0	25	1	42	14	2	8	2	7	0	0	4	10
pasta, tomato, enr, Borden	2 oz dry	56		210	10	1	2	0	0	0	0	20	1	42	14	1	4	3	7	0	0	0	10
pasta, veg, enr, Borden	2 oz dry	56		210	10	1	2	0	0	0	0	20	1	42	14	1	4	2	7	0	0	2	10
spagh/other pasta,[13] enr, Mueller's	2 oz dry	56		210	10	1	2	0	0	0	0	0	0	42	14	1	4	2	7	0	0	0	10
spagh/other pasta,[14] enr, Napolina	2 oz dry	56		210	10	1	2	0	0	0	0	0	0	42	14	1	4	2	7	0	0	0	10

Consult a similar product for brand names not listed.

PASTA: PASTA-BASED ENTREES[1]

Food Name	Serving Size	gm	mL	Calories	Calories from Fat	Total Fat (g)	%DV	Saturated Fat (g)	%DV	Cholesterol (mg)	%DV	Sodium (mg)	%DV	Total Carbohydrates[8] (g)	%DV	Fiber[8] (g)	%DV	Sugars[8] (g)	Protein (g)	Vitamin A (%DV)	Vitamin C[7] (%DV)	Calcium (%DV)	Iron (%DV)
ABC's/123's & tomato-cheese sauce, cnd, Boyardee	1 cup	255		180	0	0	0	0	0	0	0	910	38	38	13	3	12	10	6	6	2	4	8
ABC's/123's, meatballs, & tomato sauce, cnd, Boyardee	1 cup	245		280	80	9	15	4	20	25	8	930	39	39	13	4	16	10	9	10	0	0	20
Beefaroni,[15] cnd, Boyardee	1 cup	249		260	60	7	11	3	15	25	8	1070	45	37	12	5	20	9	10	10	2	0	10
Beefogetti,[16] cnd, Boyardee	1 cup	245		250	60	7	11	3	15	25	8	990	41	37	12	4	16	9	8	8	0	0	10
Bert, Ernie, meatballs, & tomato sauce, cnd, Boyardee	1 cup	258		250	40	4	6	2	10	25	8	540	23	44	15	3	12	10	9	10	4	0	10
Bert, Ernie, meatballs, & tomato sauce, microwave, Boyardee	1 container	170		150	30	3	5	1	5	20	7	340	14	26	9	3	12	6	10	15	2	0	25
Big Bird & tomato sauce, microwave, Boyardee	1 container	170		150	15	1.5	2	0	0	0	0	350	15	29	10	2	8	8	4	15	0	2	10
Big Bird, Cookie Monster, & tomato sauce, cnd, Boyardee	1 cup	256		220	20	2.5	4	0	0	0	0	240	10	44	15	3	12	12	6	10	0	2	10
Big Bird, Elmo, & meat sauce, cnd, Boyardee	1 cup	254		230	35	4	6	1.5	8	20	7	510	21	41	14	4	16	10	8	10	2	0	10
cannelloni, beef & meat sauce, cnd, Boyardee	1 cup	250		260	80	9	14	3	15	25	8	1210	50	36	12	4	16	4	10	10	0	0	15
cheddar bake & veg, frzn, Lean Cuisine	1 entree	255		220	60	6	10	2	10	20	5	560	23	29	10	3	11	8	12	25	20	25	6
chicken & noodle casserole, frzn, Swanson	1 entree	284		290	80	9	14	3	15	40	13	1000	42	33	11	2	8	3	19	2	2	20	10
chicken & noodles, escalloped, frzn, Stouffer's	1 cup	239		360	190	22	32	9	42	90	29	1010	42	23	7	2	8	5	17	0	0	10	8
chicken & noodles, homestyle, frzn, Stouffer's	1 cup	243		260	120	13	21	3	13	55	17	1020	43	19	6	1	5	10	16	20	2	15	6
chicken & noodles w/veg, frzn, Swanson	1 entree	255		320	140	15	23	8	40	50	17	980	41	32	11	4	16	4	14	10	0	8	8
chicken fettuccine w/veg, frzn, Contadina	1 cup	237		350	200	22	34	11	55	75	24	920	38	21	7	2	10	7	16	20	10	20	2

Food Name	Serving Size	gm	mL	Calories	Calories from Fat	Total Fat (g)	%DV	Saturated Fat (g)	%DV	Cholesterol (mg)	%DV	Sodium (mg)	%DV	Total Carbohydrates (g)	%DV	Fiber (g)	%DV	Sugars (g)	Protein (g)	Vitamin A (%DV)	Vitamin C (%DV)	Calcium (%DV)	Iron (%DV)
Chili Mac,[17] cnd, Boyardee	1 cup	250		260	100	11	17	5	25	30	10	1480	62	30	10	3	12	5	10	10	2	2	15
Cookie Monster, veg, & chicken, microwave, Boyardee	1 container	170		140	30	3	5	1	5	10	3	370	15	21	7	2	8	3	7	45	0	2	10
dinosaurs & tomato-cheese sauce, cnd, Boyardee	1 cup	250		210	0	0	0	0	0	<5	2	1020	43	45	15	4	16	11	6	6	2	2	8
dinosaurs, meatballs, & tomato sauce, cnd, Boyardee	1 cup	247		270	80	9	14	4	20	25	8	930	39	38	13	4	16	10	9	8	0	0	10
Elmo, ABC's, 123's, meatballs, & tomato sauce, cnd, Boyardee	1 cup	257		250	35	4	6	1.5	8	20	7	520	22	44	15	4	16	9	9	10	4	0	8
fettucini & meat sauce, cnd, Boyardee	1 cup	253		230	50	6	9	2.5	13	20	7	940	39	33	11	4	16	8	10	10	4	2	10
fettucini alfredo, 4-cheese, frzn, Budget Gourmet	1 entree	326		480	210	24	37	13	65	55	18	1120	47	48	16	3	12	12	20	10	0	35	4
lasagna al forno,[18] frzn, Contadina	1 cup	234		330	150	17	25	7	32	40	13	1060	44	31	10	4	17	6	14	10	4	20	6
lasagna, cheese, frzn, Budget Gourmet	1 entree	297		370	140	16	25	10	50	60	20	870	36	38	13	5	20	7	20	30	0	40	4
lasagna, cheese, frzn, Celentano	7 oz	196		280	90	10	15	5	25	75	25	660	27	33	11	8	32	2	15	15	15	10	8
lasagna, cheesy veg, frzn, Swanson	1 entree	284		350	120	13	20	7	35	20	7	1360	57	40	13	3	12	5	17	25	10	30	10
lasagna, classic cheese, frzn, Lean Cuisine	1 entree	326		290	60	6	10	3	15	30	9	560	23	38	13	5	20	10	20	25	10	45	10
lasagna, cnd, Libby's Diner	1 container	150		200	60	7	11	3.5	17	15	5	860	36	25	8	3	13	2	9	4	2	10	10
lasagna, 5-cheese, frzn, Lean Cuisine	1 cup	236		230	50	5	8	2.5	11	25	7	580	23	28	9	3	14	5	15	10	10	30	6
lasagna, meat, frzn, Stouffer's	1 cup	215		290	110	12	18	6	27	35	11	710	29	26	9	3	11	6	20	8	4	25	8
lasagna primavera w/veg, frzn, Celentano[19]	10 oz	280		240	60	7	11	4	20	20	7	600	25	33	11	7	28	10	17	20	2	25	15
lasagna primavera w/veg, frzn, Contadina[20]	1 cup	215		210	70	8	12	3	14	20	6	760	32	24	8	3	12	7	10	30	50	25	8
lasagna, sausage, frzn, Contadina	1 cup	228		310	110	13	20	7	31	65	20	960	40	30	10	4	15	8	19	10	10	25	8
lasagna, veg, frzn, Stouffer's	1 cup	225		280	110	12	18	5	22	25	7	590	24	29	10	2	7	6	14	20	0	35	4
lasagna w/beef sauce, cnd, Boyardee	1 cup	249		270	100	11	17	4	20	25	8	920	38	35	12	5	20	12	9	8	0	0	15

Consult a similar product for brand names not listed.

Food Name	Serving Size	gm	mL	Calories	Calories from Fat	Total Fat (g)	%DV	Saturated Fat (g)	%DV	Cholesterol (mg)	%DV	Sodium (mg)	%DV	Total Carbohydrates (g)	%DV	Fiber (g)	%DV	Sugars (g)	Protein (g)	Vitamin A (%DV)	Vitamin C (%DV)	Calcium (%DV)	Iron (%DV)
lasagna w/beef sauce, cnd, Chompsalot	1 cup	255		210	25	3	5	1.5	8	15	5	730	30	39	13	4	16	12	7	8	6	0	10
lasagna w/meat sauce casserole, frzn, Swanson	1 entree	284		330	80	9	14	5	25	25	8	1050	44	41	14	3	12	12	22	10	45	25	15
lasagna w/meat sauce, frzn, Banquet	1 entree	269		260	70	8	12	2	10	10	4	820	34	38	13	5	20	10	10	15	2	8	10
lasagna w/meat sauce, frzn, Swanson	1 entree	284		410	140	15	23	7	35	65	22	1080	45	45	15	5	20	12	24	10	10	40	15
linguini, meatballs, & tomato sauce, frzn, Lean Cuisine	1 cup	231		200	60	6	10	2.5	10	30	9	630	26	24	8	5	20	7	12	10	10	8	10
mac & beef, cnd, Libby's Diner	1 container	189		220	80	9	14	4	20	20	6	760	32	31	10	5	22	2	9	0	0	6	10
mac & beef, frzn, Banquet Family	1 cup	198		230	60	7	11	3	15	25	8	810	34	31	10	3	12	3	6	0	2	10	NA
mac & broccoli, frzn, Swanson Mac & More	1 entree	170		220	70	8	12	3.5	18	20	7	760	32	28	9	2	8	4	9	8	6	15	6
mac & cheese, cnd, Boyardee	1 cup	244		210	25	2.5	4	1.5	8	25	8	1110	46	38	13	2	8	1	8	10	0	8	8
mac & cheese, cnd, Franco-Am	1 cup	252		200	60	7	11	3	15	10	3	1060	44	29	10	4	16	2	8	15	0	10	8
mac & cheese, cnd, Libby's Diner	1 container	205		320	180	20	31	7	34	30	11	1400	58	25	8	2	9	4	12	10	0	25	6
mac & cheese, frzn, Banquet	1 entree	184		200	30	3	5	1.5	8	10	3	750	31	36	12	1	4	10	7	0	0	10	6
mac & cheese, frzn, Banquet Value Meal	1 meal	269		320	100	11	17	3.5	16	20	6	970	40	44	15	4	16	6	11	25	2	15	8
mac & cheese, frzn, Healthy Choice	1 entree	269		320	60	7	11	2.5	13	25	8	580	24	50	17	4	16	13	15	0	0	25	8
mac & cheese, frzn, Lean Cuisine	1 cup	224		260	80	8	13	4	20	25	8	660	28	33	11	3	14	6	14	0	0	25	4
mac & cheese, frzn, Morton Casseroles	1 container	182		200	30	3	4	1.5	6	10	3	600	25	35	11	2	9	2	7	0	0	10	6
mac & cheese, frzn, Stouffer's	1 cup	250		340	120	14	21	6	32	30	10	930	39	38	13	1	6	5	16	0	0	30	4
mac & cheese, frzn, Swanson	1 entree	255		280	90	10	15	5	25	20	7	1050	44	36	12	2	8	2	11	0	0	20	10
mac & cheese, frzn, Swanson Mac & More	1 entree	170		240	80	9	14	4	20	20	7	800	33	30	10	2	8	4	10	8	2	15	8
mac & cheese mix, not prepared, TownHouse	2.5 oz mix	70		260	20	2	3	1.0	5	<5	2	550	23	49	16	2	7	7	9	0	0	10	15

Food Name	Serving Size	gm	mL	Calories	Calories from Fat	Total Fat (g)	%DV	Saturated Fat (g)	%DV	Cholesterol (mg)	%DV	Sodium (mg)	%DV	Total Carbohydrates (g)	%DV	Fiber[g] (g)	%DV	Sugars[6] (g)	Protein (g)	Vitamin A (%DV)	Vitamin C[7] (%DV)	Calcium (%DV)	Iron (%DV)
mac & cheese w/salsa, frzn, Swanson	1 entree	170		210	70	8	12	3	15	15	5	870	36	27	9	2	8	5	8	8	4	15	8
mac & white cheddar, frzn, Swanson Mac & More	1 entree	170		200	60	7	11	3	15	10	3	790	33	27	9	2	8	3	7	0	0	15	6
mac bake casserole, 3-cheese, frzn, Swanson	1 entree	284		400	130	14	22	6	30	20	7	1580	66	53	18	3	12	5	15	10	2	35	10
mac beef casserole w/tomato sauce, frzn, Swanson	1 entree	284		270	45	5	8	5	25	35	12	1060	44	39	13	2	8	11	18	6	20	6	15
mac Ital, frzn, Swanson Mac & More	1 entree	170		180	45	5	8	3	15	15	5	480	20	25	8	2	8	4	9	6	20	15	8
mac, beef, & tomato sauce, frzn, Lean Cuisine	1 cup	220		210	60	7	10	1.5	7	35	10	550	23	25	8	2	9	5	12	8	10	4	10
mac, beef, & tomato, frzn, Stouffer's	1 cup	240		250	80	9	14	3	12	30	10	1270	53	28	9	3	14	10	13	8	10	2	8
manicotti, cheese, frzn, Celentano[21]	2 manicotti	280		450	190	21	33	8	40	85	29	910	38	41	14	9	36	3	24	35	20	40	20
manicotti, cheese, frzn, Contadina	1 manicotti	144		160	70	7	11	3	15	15	5	480	20	15	5	2	7	4	8	4	0	20	4
manicotti Florentine,[22] frzn, Celentano	2 manicotti	280		210	50	6	9	2	10	35	12	600	25	29	10	5	20	7	15	80	0	25	20
Mexi-Mac,[23] frzn, Stouffer's	1 cup	240		220	70	8	11	3	13	20	6	1160	48	29	10	4	16	7	9	8	10	6	8
mostaccioli & meat sauce, frzn, Contadina	1 cup	265		330	100	12	18	5	22	25	8	1150	48	43	14	5	20	12	12	10	10	10	15
ninja turtles & tomato-cheese sauce, cnd, Boyardee	1 cup	252		170	0	0	0	0	0	<5	2	1010	42	38	13	3	12	11	5	6	0	0	8
ninja turtles, meatballs, & tomato sauce, cnd, Boyardee	1 cup	245		260	90	9	14	4	20	30	10	960	40	35	12	4	16	9	8	8	0	0	10
noodles & beef, frzn, Banquet Family	1 cup	198		150	35	4	6	2	10	40	13	1200	50	17	6	2	8	1	12	0	4	2	8
noodles & chicken, frzn, Banquet Family	1 cup	277		210	80	9	14	3	15	40	13	810	34	24	8	2	8	2	10	1	0	6	8
noodles & turkey, frzn, Budget Gourmet	1 entree	304		440	180	20	31	10	50	115	38	840	35	44	15	2	8	4	19	6	0	15	10
noodles romanoff, frzn, Stouffer's	1 cup	250		360	170	19	29	3	16	45	15	1500	63	33	11	2	9	4	14	8	0	15	10
noodles stroganoff w/grnd beef, frzn, Michelina's	1 container	227		310	150	17	26	5	25	55	18	920	38	25	8	2	8	1	14	6	0	4	4

Consult a similar product for brand names not listed.

Food Name	Serving Size	gm mL	Calories	Calories from Fat	Total Fat (g)	%DV	Saturated Fat (g)	%DV	Cholesterol (mg)	%DV	Sodium (mg)	%DV	Total Carbohydrates (g)	%DV	Fiber (g)	%DV	Sugars (g)	Protein (g)	Vitamin A (%DV)	Vitamin C (%DV)	Calcium (%DV)	Iron (%DV)
O-rings, meatballs, & tomato sauce, cnd, Chompsalot	1 cup	250	260	90	10	15	4	20	25	8	780	33	33	11	4	16	12	8	10	0	0	8
pasta, chicken marinara, & veg, frzn, Lean Cuisine	1 entree	269	270	50	6	9	1.5	7	20	7	540	23	38	13	4	19	4	15	25	20	10	10
pasta marinara, chicken, & cheese, frzn, Celentano	10 oz	280	390	170	19	29	4	20	50	17	1040	43	36	12	8	32	9	19	20	0	25	25
pasta w/ricotta & tomato sauce, frzn, Budget Gourmet	1 entree	290	430	200	23	35	8	40	75	25	600	25	41	14	3	12	1	16	10	2	25	10
penne in meat sauce, cnd, Franco-Am	1 cup	252	240	45	5	8	2	10	10	3	1100	46	40	13	3	12	21	9	15	4	8	10
ravioli, beef & meat sauce, cnd, Boyardee	1 cup	244	230	45	5	8	2.5	13	20	7	1150	48	36	12	4	16	5	9	15	4	0	15
ravioli, beef & meat sauce, cnd, Franco-Am	1 cup	252	300	90	10	15	4	20	25	8	1160	48	42	14	3	12	11	11	10	4	4	10
ravioli, beef & tomato sauce, cnd, Franco-Am	1 cup	259	250	50	6	9	2	10	15	5	1160	48	40	13	3	12	14	9	10	0	8	15
ravioli, beef, cnd, Libby's Diner	1 container	205	230	80	9	13	3.5	18	15	4	1040	43	29	10	7	30	1	11	0	0	10	10
ravioli, beef, mini & meat sauce, cnd, Boyardee	1 cup	252	230	45	5	8	2	10	20	7	1120	47	37	12	4	16	6	9	10	2	0	20
ravioli, beef, mini & meat sauce, cnd, Chompsalot	1 cup	249	210	30	4	6	1.5	8	15	5	800	33	37	12	4	16	8	8	10	4	0	15
ravioli, beef, mini & meat sauce, cnd, Franco-Am	1 cup	259	270	70	8	12	2.5	13	15	5	1160	48	36	12	3	12	14	13	6	0	6	10
ravioli, cheese & alfredo-broccoli sauce, frzn, Michelina's	1 container	227	390	220	24	36	12	62	70	22	840	35	28	9	2	8	2	17	25	0	45	10
ravioli, cheese & tomato-beef sauce, cnd, Boyardee	1 cup	246	220	30	3	5	1.5	8	15	5	1280	53	38	13	4	16	6	9	6	2	2	15
ravioli, cheese & tomato sauce, cnd, Boyardee	1 cup	251	210	0	0	0	0	0	<5	2	1070	45	44	15	4	16	9	7	10	2	4	20
ravioli, cheese, frzn, Celentano	6 ravioli	182	360	35	4	6	2	10	35	12	700	29	69	23	1	4	4	12	2	0	25	15
ravioli, cheese, frzn, Contadina	1 cup	87	280	100	12	18	6	31	85	27	350	15	31	10	2	9	3	13	0	0	20	10

Food Name	Serving Size	gm	mL	Calories	Calories from Fat	Total Fat (g)	%DV	Saturated Fat (g)	%DV	Cholesterol (mg)	%DV	Sodium (mg)	%DV	Total Carbohydrates (g)	%DV	Fiber[δ] (g)	%DV	Sugars[δ] (g)	Protein (g)	Vitamin A (%DV)	Vitamin C[γ] (%DV)	Calcium (%DV)	Iron (%DV)
ravioli, cheese, mini & tomato-cheese sauce, cnd, Chompsalot	1 cup	253		210	0	0	0	0	0	<5	2	870	36	45	15	5	20	11	7	6	4	4	15
ravioli, cheese-spinach & green beans, frzn, Smart Ones	1 entree	240		190	15	2	3	0	0	5	2	420	18	37	12	5	20	7	8	30	25	15	10
ravioli, cheese w/meatballs & tomato sauce, cnd, Boyardee	1 cup	248		270	100	11	17	5	25	25	8	1170	49	34	11	3	12	6	10	10	0	2	15
Rigatoni,[24] cnd, Boyardee	1 cup	246		250	60	7	11	2.5	13	25	8	1200	50	38	13	4	16	11	10	10	6	2	20
roller coasters, meatballs, & tomato sauce, cnd, Boyardee	1 cup	245		250	60	7	11	3	15	25	8	990	41	37	12	4	16	9	8	8	0	0	10
sharks & tomato-cheese sauce, cnd, Boyardee	1 cup	252		180	0	0	0	0	0	<5	1	970	40	40	13	3	12	10	6	8	2	2	15
sharks, meatballs, & tomato sauce, cnd, Boyardee	1 cup	245		260	80	9	14	4	20	25	8	940	39	35	12	4	16	10	9	10	2	0	10
shells, cheese stuffed, frzn, Lean Cuisine	1 cup	263		230	70	7	11	3.5	16	25	7	600	25	29	10	3	13	7	13	10	10	25	6
shells w/ricotta, broccoli, & marinara sauce, frzn, Celentano	4 shells	280		190	35	4	6	1	5	15	5	520	22	31	11	4	16	9	12	25	15	15	15
shells w/ricotta, mozzarella, & marinara sauce, frzn, Celentano	3 shells	196		300	130	14	22	7	35	50	17	720	30	30	10	8	32	2	14	25	15	30	10
shells w/ricotta, spinach, & marinara sauce, frzn, Celentano	10 oz	280		240	50	6	9	1.5	8	15	5	630	26	32	11	5	20	0	14	80	15	25	25
spagh & meatballs, cnd, Campbell's Superiore	1 cup	252		270	90	10	15	5	25	30	10	1060	44	35	12	4	16	13	11	10	8	2	15
spagh & meatballs, cnd, Libby's Diner	1 container	184		190	45	5	8	2	10	20	6	940	39	27	9	2	10	2	10	4	0	6	10
spagh & tomato-cheese sauce, cnd, Franco-Am	1 cup	252		210	20	2	3	1	5	5	2	1020	43	41	14	3	12	14	7	10	0	4	10
spagh, meatballs & tomato sauce, cnd, Boyardee	1 cup	240		250	90	10	15	4	20	25	8	950	40	32	11	3	12	7	9	6	4	0	15
spagh, meatballs, & tomato sauce, cnd, Franco-Am	1 cup	252		270	90	10	15	5	25	30	10	1060	44	35	12	4	16	13	11	10	8	2	15
Spaghettios & tomato-cheese sauce, cnd, Franco-Am	1 cup	252		190	20	2	3	0.5	3	5	2	990	41	36	12	2	8	12	5	15	0	4	10

Consult a similar product for brand names not listed.

Food Name	Serving Size	gm	mL	Calories	Calories from Fat	Total Fat (g)	%DV	Saturated Fat (g)	%DV	Cholesterol (mg)	%DV	Sodium (mg)	%DV	Total Carbohydrates[δ] (g)	%DV	Fiber[δ] (g)	%DV	Sugars[δ] (g)	Protein (g)	Vitamin A (%DV)	Vitamin C[7] (%DV)	Calcium (%DV)	Iron (%DV)
Spaghettios Garfield Pizzos & beef, cnd, Franco-Am	1 cup	252		260	100	11	17	5	25	20	7	1150	48	31	10	5	20	10	11	10	2	4	15
Spaghettios Garfield Pizzos, cnd, Franco-Am	1 cup	252		190	20	2	3	0.5	3	5	2	990	41	36	12	2	8	12	5	15	0	4	10
Spaghettios, franks, & tomato sauce, cnd, Franco-Am	1 cup	252		250	100	11	17	5	25	25	8	1210	50	32	11	4	16	11	10	10	6	4	10
Spaghettios, meatballs, & tomato sauce, cnd, Franco-Am	1 cup	252		260	100	11	17	5	25	20	7	1150	48	31	10	5	20	10	11	10	2	4	15
spirals & chicken, cnd, Libby's Diner	1 container	93		130	40	4	7	1	4	15	4	980	41	16	5	4	19	2	8	8	0	0	0
Swedish meatballs & pasta, frzn, Lean Cuisine	1 entree	258		290	80	8	13	3	10	55	18	590	24	32	11	3	13	2	22	2	0	4	10
tortellini, beef & pork, frzn, Contadina	³⁄₄ cup	85		270	70	8	12	3	13	55	17	400	16	38	13	2	9	2	12	2	0	6	10
tortellini, cheese & tomato sauce, cnd, Boyardee	1 cup	258		230	10	1	2	0	0	15	5	770	32	46	15	5	20	12	9	15	6	8	15
tortellini, cheese & tomato sauce, cnd, Franco-Am	1 cup	255		240	40	4	6	2	10	25	8	1140	48	44	15	2	8	18	8	15	0	20	8
tortellini, cheese, frzn, Contadina	³⁄₄ cup	85		260	50	6	9	2.5	12	35	11	290	11	41	13	1	6	2	11	0	0	10	8
tortellini, meat & meat sauce, cnd, Franco-Am	1 cup	255		260	80	9	14	4	20	30	10	1140	48	36	12	2	8	15	9	15	0	8	10
tortellini, spinach & cheese, frzn, Contadina	³⁄₄ cup	87		260	60	6	9	3	14	55	18	390	16	39	13	3	12	2	13	4	0	15	10
tortelloni, chicken & prosciutto, frzn, Contadina	1 cup	109		360	120	13	20	4	19	75	23	440	18	46	15	3	11	3	15	2	0	8	15
tuna noodle casserole, frzn, Stouffer's	1 cup	250		310	150	17	26	2.5	12	30	10	1110	46	24	8	1	4	7	14	0	0	15	8
tuna noodle casserole, frzn, Swanson	1 entree	284		320	100	11	17	6	30	25	8	800	33	38	13	1	4	4	16	2	0	15	10
turkey tetrazzini, frzn, Stouffer's	1 cup	244		310	150	17	26	6	27	60	18	850	36	24	8	3	13	5	15	0	0	8	6
twists & meat sauce, cnd, Franco-Am	1 cup	252		250	45	5	8	2	10	10	3	1160	48	41	14	2	8	21	9	15	0	8	10
X&Os & meatballs, cnd, Boyardee	1 cup	241		260	90	10	15	4	20	20	7	1060	44	35	12	4	16	10	9	8	0	0	10
X&Os & tomato-cheese sauce, cnd, Boyardee	1 cup	256		190	0	0	0	0	0	0	0	990	41	41	14	3	12	10	6	6	2	2	10

Food Name	Serving Size		gm	mL	Calories	Calories from Fat	Total Fat (g)	%DV	Saturated Fat (g)	%DV	Cholesterol (mg)	%DV	Sodium (mg)	%DV	Total Carbohydrates[6] (g)	%DV	Fiber[6] (g)	%DV	Sugars[6] (g)	Protein (g)	Vitamin A (%DV)	Vitamin C[7] (%DV)	Calcium (%DV)	Iron (%DV)
X-men & tomato-cheese sauce, cnd, Boyardee	1 cup		258		210	0	0	0	0	0	0	0	820	34	46	15	6	24	14	6	6	0	2	8
X-men, meatballs, & tomato sauce, cnd, Boyardee	1 cup		256		270	70	8	12	3	15	25	8	960	40	41	14	4	16	11	9	10	0	0	10

Consult a similar product for brand names not listed.

PASTA: PASTA-BASED MEALS/DINNERS[2]

Food Name	Serving Size	gm	mL	Calories	Calories from Fat	Total Fat (g)	%DV	Saturated Fat (g)	%DV	Cholesterol (mg)	%DV	Sodium (mg)	%DV	Total Carbohydrates[d] (g)	%DV	Fiber[d] (g)	%DV	Sugars[d] (g)	Protein (g)	Vitamin A (%DV)	Vitamin C[7] (%DV)	Calcium (%DV)	Iron (%DV)
beef stroganoff w/noodles, frzn, Michelina's[25]	1 meal	171		410	160	18	28	7	35	70	23	750	31	42	14	5	20	1	20	15	0	15	6
mac & cheese, frzn, Swanson Budget	1 meal	291		320	100	11	17	7	35	20	7	960	40	43	14	6	24	16	10	90	4	20	6
pasta & chicken, frzn, Swanson Budget	1 meal	255		250	100	11	17	6	30	40	13	660	28	30	10	5	20	9	9	140	4	6	8
ravioli, frzn, Swanson Children	1 meal	312		440	90	10	15	4	20	25	8	540	23	73	24	8	32	42	12	2	50	10	10
rings, frzn, Swanson Children	1 meal	340		380	110	12	18	6	30	25	8	780	33	57	19	4	16	36	12	10	40	6	10
sirloin beef tips, noodles, & gravy, frzn, Swanson	1 meal	283		280	90	10	15	5	25	50	17	510	21	32	11	5	20	14	16	100	4	4	15
spagh & meatballs, frzn, Swanson Budget	1 meal	284		300	110	12	18	6	30	20	7	1050	44	36	12	5	20	13	11	140	30	6	10
wheels & cheese, frzn, Swanson Children	1 meal	312		390	100	11	17	4	20	15	5	1110	46	60	20	8	32	29	12	70	8	20	8

PASTA: PASTA-BASED SOUPS

Food Name	Serving Size	gm	mL	Calories	Calories from Fat	Total Fat (g)	%DV	Saturated Fat (g)	%DV	Cholesterol (mg)	%DV	Sodium (mg)	%DV	Total Carbohydrates (g)	%DV	Fiber (g)	%DV	Sugars (g)	Protein (g)	Vitamin A (%DV)	Vitamin C (%DV)	Calcium (%DV)	Iron (%DV)
beef flavor noodle, dry mix, Campbell's	1 package	48		120	15	1.5	2	0.5	3	20	7	1260	53	22	7	1	4	4	5	10	0	2	6
beef noodle, cnd cond, Campbell's	1/2 cup	126		70	25	2.5	4	1	5	15	5	920	38	8	3	1	4	6	5	2	0	2	6
beef pasta, chunky, cnd rts, Campbell's	1 can	305		190	35	4	6	1	5	20	7	1200	50	23	8	3	12	6	16	70	2	6	15
chicken alphabet, cnd cond, Campbell's	1/2 cup	126		80	20	2	3	1	5	10	3	880	37	11	4	1	4	1	4	15	0	2	4
chicken & stars, cnd cond, Campbell's	1/2 cup	126		70	20	2	3	0.5	3	0	1	1010	42	9	3	1	4	1	3	15	2	2	4
chicken chicken noodle noodle, frzn conc, Stouffer's	1/2 cup	122		130	60	6	11	2	10	25	8	740	31	13	4	1	6	1	5	30	6	2	4
chicken chicken noodle noodle, frzn rts, Stouffer's	1 cup	244		130	80	9	14	2.5	10	25	8	840	35	9	3	1	5	1	4	8	2	2	2
chicken flavor noodle, dry mix, Knorr	1/3 package	25		90	10	1	2	0.5	2	15	5	800	33	17	6	0	0	3	3	0	0	0	2
chicken noodle, chunky, cnd rts, Campbell's	1 can	305		160	30	3.5	5	1	5	25	8	1310	55	20	7	3	12	4	12	60	4	4	8
chicken noodle, chunky, rts microwave, Campbell's	1 container	298		160	45	5	7	2	10	35	12	1060	44	17	6	3	12	4	12	50	0	4	8
chicken noodle, cnd cond, Campbell's	1/2 cup	126		60	20	2	3	1	5	15	5	980	41	8	3	1	4	1	3	6	0	2	4
chicken noodle, cnd rts, Campbell's Home Cookin'	1 cup	245		100	30	3.5	5	1	5	15	5	980	41	11	4	1	4	4	7	60	0	4	4
chicken noodle, creamy, cnd cond, Campbell's	1/2 cup	124		130	60	7	11	2	10	15	5	880	37	12	4	2	8	2	5	25	0	2	4
chicken noodle, dry mix, Campbell's	1 package	46		130	20	2	3	0.5	3	20	7	1320	55	23	8	1	4	3	5	8	0	2	6
chicken noodle, homestyle, cnd cond, Campbell's	1/2 cup	126		70	25	2.5	4	1.5	8	20	7	970	40	9	3	1	4	1	4	15	2	2	4
chicken noodle O's, cnd cond, Campbell's	1/2 cup	126		80	25	3	5	1	5	15	5	980	41	10	3	1	4	1	4	20	2	2	6

Consult a similar product for brand names not listed.

Food Name	Serving Size (gm)	(mL)	Serving Size	Calories	Calories from Fat	Total Fat (g)	%DV	Saturated Fat (g)	%DV	Cholesterol (mg)	%DV	Sodium (mg)	%DV	Total Carbohydrates (g)	%DV	Fiber (g)	%DV	Sugars (g)	Protein (g)	Vitamin A (%DV)	Vitamin C (%DV)	Calcium (%DV)	Iron (%DV)
chicken noodle, rts microwave, Campbell's	220		1 container	90	35	4	6	1.5	8	20	7	850	35	10	3	1	4	2	5	35	2	6	2
chicken noodle w/mushrooms, chunky, cnd rts, Campbell's	305		1 can	150	40	4.5	7	1.5	8	30	10	1150	48	13	4	1	4	2	14	15	2	4	4
curly noodle & chicken broth, cnd cond, Campbell's	126		½ cup	80	25	2.5	4	1	5	15	5	840	35	12	4	1	4	1	3	15	0	2	6
double noodle & chicken broth, cnd cond, Campbell's	126		½ cup	100	25	2.5	4	1	5	15	5	810	34	15	5	2	8	1	4	30	0	2	6
egg noodles, veg & chicken broth, dry mix, Campbell's	52		1 package	150	20	2	3	1	5	20	7	980	41	27	9	2	8	6	6	50	0	4	8
hearty noodle w/veg, dry mix, Campbell's	42		1 package	150	20	2	3	0.5	3	20	7	1050	44	28	9	1	4	3	6	15	0	2	6
noodles & chicken broth, dry mix, Campbell's	27		3 tbsp	100	15	2	2	0.5	3	10	3	790	33	18	6	1	4	3	4	0	0	0	4
noodles & chicken broth, dry mix, Mrs. Grass	18		¼ carton	60	15	2	2	0.5	2	20	7	880	37	10	3	0	0	1	2	0	0	0	2
noodles & grnd beef, cnd cond, Campbell's	126		½ cup	100	35	4	6	2	10	25	8	900	38	11	4	2	8	1	5	20	0	2	6
oriental noodle, dry mix, Knorr	55		1 package	210	25	3	4	0.5	2	20	6	830	35	39	13	2	9	2	7	15	2	2	15
oriental noodle, pork, dry mix, Sanwa	40		½ block	180	60	7	11	4	20	0	0	760	32	26	9	1	4	2	4	0	0	0	8
ramen noodle, beef, dry mix, Sanwa	40		½ block	180	60	7	11	4	20	0	0	870	36	26	9	1	4	2	4	0	0	0	8
ramen noodle, chicken, dry mix, Campbell's	62		½ package	280	100	11	17	5	25	0	0	1360	57	40	13	3	12	3	5	15	2	2	10
ramen noodle, chicken, dry mix, Sanwa	65		1 package	310	120	13	20	5	25	0	0	1080	45	41	14	2	8	3	6	10	2	2	10
ramen noodle, oriental, low fat, dry mix, Campbell's	62		1 package	220	15	1.5	2	0.5	3	0	0	1360	57	45	15	2	8	3	6	50	0	4	15
ramen noodle, shrimp, dry mix, Campbell's	62		1 package	310	130	14	22	4	20	0	0	1020	43	40	13	2	8	3	6	15	0	2	10
ramen noodle, tomato veg, dry mix, Sanwa	65		1 package	310	130	14	22	5	25	0	0	860	36	40	13	2	8	4	6	15	60	4	10

Food Name	Serving Size	gm	mL	Calories	Calories from Fat	Total Fat (g)	%DV	Saturated Fat (g)	%DV	Cholesterol (mg)	%DV	Sodium (mg)	%DV	Total Carbohydrates (g)	%DV	Fiber (g)	%DV	Sugars (g)	Protein (g)	Vitamin A (%DV)	Vitamin C (%DV)	Calcium (%DV)	Iron (%DV)
ramen noodle, veg beef, dry mix, Sanwa	1 package	65		300	120	13	20	4	20	0	0	1410	59	40	13	2	8	3	6	10	0	2	10
stroganoff beef, chunky, cnd rts, Campbell's	1 can	305		310	140	16	25	6	30	45	15	1180	49	28	9	4	16	4	16	50	0	8	15
turkey noodle, cnd cond, Campbell's	½ cup	126		80	25	2.5	4	1	5	15	5	970	40	10	3	1	4	1	4	10	0	2	4
veg beef flavored noodle, dry mix, Mrs. Grass	¼ carton	20		70	10	1	2	0	0	0	0	1030	43	11	4	0	0	1	3	6	0	4	2
veg, hearty w/pasta, cnd cond, Campbell's	½ cup	126		90	10	1	2	0	0	0	0	830	35	18	6	2	8	8	2	45	0	2	4

Consult a similar product for brand names not listed.

Food Name	Serving Size	gm	mL	Calories	Calories from Fat	Total Fat (g)	%DV	Saturated Fat (g)	%DV	Cholesterol (mg)	%DV	Sodium (mg)	%DV	Total Carbohydrates[8] (g)	%DV	Fiber[8] (g)	%DV	Sugars[8] (g)	Protein (g)	Vitamin A (%DV)	Vitamin C[7] (%DV)	Calcium (%DV)	Iron (%DV)
RICE: RICE AND RICE-BASED ENTREES[1]																							
chicken & rice stir fry casserole, frzn, Swanson	1 entree	284		240	30	3	5	1	5	20	7	1200	50	40	13	2	8	9	12	70	25	4	6
chicken fried rice, frzn, Yu Sing	1 container	227		260	50	6	9	2	10	60	20	730	31	38	13	2	10	2	13	2	0	6	4
confetti rice, frzn, Stouffer's	1 cup	248		220	35	4	6	1.5	8	10	2	930	39	42	14	1	5	3	4	0	0	0	2
rice, brown, long grain, uncooked, S&W	1/4 cup	42		150	10	1	2	0	0	0	0	0	0	32	11	1	4	0	3	0	0	0	4
rice, brown, quick (parboiled), uncooked, S&W	1/2 cup	43		150	10	1	2	0	0	0	0	5	0	33	11	2	8	0	4	0	0	2	4
rice in cheese sauce, Budget Gourmet[26]	1 entree	297		330	120	13	20	8	40	65	22	840	35	36	12	2	8	6	17	20	2	20	15
rice pilaf, basmati, dry mix, Knorr	1/4 package	42		150	5	0.5	1	0	0	0	0	390	16	33	11	1	4	0	3	15	0	2	0
rice pilaf, harvest, dry mix, Knorr	1/4 package	26		90	5	0.5	1	0	0	0	0	360	15	20	7	<1	2	0	2	20	0	0	2
rice pilaf, jasmine, dry mix, Knorr	1/4 package	37		130	10	1	1	0	0	0	0	130	5	28	9	<1	1	0	3	2	2	2	6
rice, white, enr, long/med grain, uncooked, TownHouse	1/4 cup	45		150	0	0	0	0	0	0	0	0	0	33	11	1	6	0	4	0	0	0	8
rice, white, long grain, uncooked, S&W	1/4 cup	45		150	0	0	0	0	0	0	0	0	0	35	12	0	0	0	3	0	0	0	8
rice, wild, uncooked, S&W	1/2 cup	75		110	5	1	2	0	0	0	0	0	0	58	19	3	12	0	10	0	0	0	4

Food Name	Serving Size	gm	mL	Calories	Calories from Fat	Total Fat (g)	%DV	Saturated Fat (g)	%DV	Cholesterol (mg)	%DV	Sodium (mg)	%DV	Total Carbohydrates[5] (g)	%DV	Fiber[6] (g)	%DV	Sugars[5] (g)	Protein (g)	Vitamin A (%DV)	Vitamin C[7] (%DV)	Calcium (%DV)	Iron (%DV)
RICE: RICE-BASED SOUPS																							
chicken flavored w/rice, dry mix, Mrs. Grass	¼ carton	23		80	10	1	2	0	0	0	0	1000	42	15	5	0	0	1	2	0	0	0	4
chicken rice, chunky, cnd rts, Campbell's	1 cup	245		140	30	3	5	1	5	25	8	840	35	18	6	2	8	2	9	80	2	4	4
chicken rice, cnd rts, Campbell's Home Cookin'	1 can	305		140	20	2	3	0.5	3	20	7	1130	47	21	7	2	8	5	8	60	6	4	6
chicken rice, rts microwave, Campbell's	1 container	298		120	25	2.5	4	1	5	10	3	1130	47	20	7	2	8	4	5	50	0	4	2
chicken w/rice, cnd cond, Campbell's	½ cup	126		70	25	2	4	1	5	<5	1	830	35	9	3	0	0	0	3	8	0	0	2
chicken w/wild rice, cnd cond, Campbell's	½ cup	126		70	20	2.5	3	0.5	3	10	3	900	38	9	3	1	4	1	3	8	25	2	2
mushroom & rice, cnd rts, Campbell's Home Cookin'	1 cup	245		80	5	0.5	1	0	0	0	0	820	34	16	5	2	8	2	3	50	4	4	2
tomato rice, cnd cond, Campbell's	½ cup	126		120	20	2	3	0.5	3	5	1	790	33	23	8	1	4	11	2	8	10	2	2

Consult a similar product for brand names not listed.

Vegetables

VEGETABLES AND VEGETABLE JUICES

Food Name	Serving Size	gm	mL	Calories	Calories from Fat	Total Fat (g)	%DV	Saturated Fat (g)	%DV	Cholesterol (mg)	%DV	Sodium (mg)	%DV	Total Carbohydrates (g)	%DV	Fiber (g)	%DV	Sugars (g)	Protein (g)	Vitamin A (%DV)	Vitamin C (%DV)	Calcium (%DV)	Iron (%DV)
artichoke hearts, bottled, S&W	3 pieces	80		30	0	0	0	0	0	0	0	200	8	5	2	0	0	0	2	2	6	0	6
artichoke hearts, marinated, bottled, S&W	2 pieces	28		20	15	2	3	0	0	0	0	80	3	2	1	1	4	0	0	0	10	0	0
asparagus pieces, cnd, S&W	6 pieces	128		15	0	0	0	0	0	0	0	260	11	4	1	1	4	1	2	10	35	0	4
asparagus, raw	5 spears	93		25	0	0	0	0	0	0	0	0	0	4	1	2	8	2	2	10	15	2	2
asparagus spears, cnd, S&W	3 pieces	89		10	0	0	0	0	0	0	0	170	7	3	1	1	4	1	1	8	25	0	2
asparagus spears, cnd, Tender Green	1/2 cup	124		20	0	0	0	0	0	0	0	420	17	3	1	1	4	0	2	8	30	0	2
asparagus tips, cnd, Tender Green	1/2 cup	124		20	0	0	0	0	0	0	0	420	17	3	1	1	4	0	2	8	30	0	2
bean salad, deli style, cnd, S&W	1/2 cup	127		80	0	0	0	0	0	0	0	670	28	20	7	4	16	0	4	10	2	4	4
bean salad, marinated, cnd, S&W	1/2 cup	130		70	0	0	0	0	0	0	0	1410	59	16	5	3	12	6	3	6	2	4	4
beets, julienne, cnd, S&W	1/2 cup	123		30	0	0	0	0	0	0	0	230	10	7	2	1	4	6	1	0	2	0	4
beets, pickled, sliced, cnd, Del Monte	1/2 cup	127		80	0	0	0	0	0	0	0	380	16	19	6	2	8	16	1	0	6	0	2
beets, pickled, sliced/whole, cnd, S&W	1 oz	28		15	0	0	0	0	0	0	0	50	2	4	1	1	4	4	0	0	0	0	0
beets, sliced, cnd, Del Monte	1/2 cup	123		35	0	0	0	0	0	0	0	290	12	8	3	2	8	5	1	0	4	0	2
beets, sliced, cnd, S&W	1/2 cup	123		30	0	0	0	0	0	0	0	230	10	7	2	1	4	6	1	0	0	0	4
beets, small, whole, cnd, S&W	1/2 cup	123		30	0	0	0	0	0	0	0	230	10	7	2	1	4	6	1	0	0	0	4
broccoli au gratin, frzn, Stouffer's	1/2 cup	121		120	50	6	9	2	9	15	5	450	18	11	3	2	8	4	6	4	6	15	2
broccoli, chopped, frzn, Bel-Air	3/4 cup	85		25	0	0	0	0	0	0	0	20	1	4	1	2	9	1	2	10	60	2	2
broccoli, raw	1 medium stalk	148		45	0	0.5	1	0	0	0	0	55	2	8	3	5	20	3	5	15	220	6	6
cabbage, green, raw	1/12 medium head	84		25	0	0	0	0	0	0	0	20	1	5	2	2	8	3	1	0	70	4	2
cabbage, red, sweet & sour, cnd, S&W	2 tbsp	30		15	0	0	0	0	0	0	0	160	7	3	1	0	0	2	0	0	2	0	0
carrots, crinkle cut, frzn, Bel-Air	2/3 cup	85		40	0	0	0	0	0	0	0	50	2	8	3	2	8	4	0	90	0	2	2
carrots, julienne/sliced/tiny whole, cnd, S&W	1/2 cup	123		25	5	0.5	1	0	0	0	0	250	10	6	2	2	8	4	1	220	4	2	4

Food Name	Serving Size	gm	mL	Calories	Calories from Fat	Total Fat (g)	%DV	Saturated Fat (g)	%DV	Cholesterol (mg)	%DV	Sodium (mg)	%DV	Total Carbohydrates[6] (g)	%DV	Fiber[6] (g)	%DV	Sugars[6] (g)	Protein (g)	Vitamin A (%DV)	Vitamin C[7] (%DV)	Calcium (%DV)	Iron (%DV)
carrots, raw	1 medium	78		35	0	0	0	0	0	0	0	40	2	8	3	2	8	5	1	270	10	2	0
carrots, sliced, cnd, Del Monte	1/2 cup	123		35	0	0	0	0	0	0	0	300	13	8	3	3	12	5	0	300	6	2	2
cauliflower, raw	1/6 medium head	99		25	0	0	0	0	0	0	0	30	1	5	2	2	8	2	2	0	100	2	2
celery, raw	2 medium stalks	110		20	0	0	0	0	0	0	0	100	4	5	2	2	8	0	1	2	15	4	2
coleslaw, Safeway Deli Shop	1/3 cup	82		130	60	7	11	0.5	3	5	2	330	14	17	6	1	6	15	1	10	60	4	4
corn, cream style, white, cnd, Del Monte	1/2 cup	125		100	0	0	0	0	0	0	0	360	15	21	7	2	8	6	2	0	6	0	2
corn, cream style, yellow, cnd, Del Monte	1/2 cup	125		90	5	0.5	1	0	0	0	0	360	15	20	7	2	8	5	2	0	10	0	2
corn, cream style, yellow, cnd, S&W	1/2 cup	128		100	10	1	2	0	0	0	0	340	14	24	8	1	4	6	2	0	2	0	2
corn-on-the-cob, yellow, raw	1 medium ear	90		80	10	1	2	0	0	0	0	0	0	18	6	3	12	5	3	2	10	0	2
corn, white, cnd, Del Monte	1/2 cup	125		80	0	0	0	0	0	0	0	360	15	17	6	2	8	7	2	0	15	0	2
corn, yellow, cnd, Del Monte	1/2 cup	125		90	10	1	2	0	0	0	0	360	15	18	6	3	10	6	2	0	10	0	2
corn, yellow, cnd, S&W	1/2 cup	125		90	10	1	2	0	0	0	0	340	14	14	5	2	8	5	2	0	4	0	2
corn, yellow, cnd, Safeway Select	1/2 cup	125		80	10	1	2	0	0	0	0	360	15	16	5	2	8	6	2	0	4	0	0
corn, yellow, sweet'n crisp, cnd, S&W	1/4 cup	85		70	15	1.5	2	0	0	0	0	170	7	12	4	2	8	6	2	4	4	0	0
cucumber, raw	1/3 medium	99		15	0	0	0	0	0	0	0	0	0	3	1	1	4	2	1	4	10	2	2
French fries, crinkle, frzn, Lynden Farms	3 oz	85		120	40	4	7	1.5	9	<5	1	45	2	20	6	3	11	0	2	0	6	0	2
French fries, frzn, Lynden Farms	3 oz	85		120	35	4	6	1.5	7	<5	1	50	2	20	7	2	9	0	2	0	6	0	2
French fries, Hardee's	1 medium serving	142		350	130	15	23	4	19	0	0	150	6	49	16	NA	NA	NA	5	NA	NA	NA	NA
French fries, Jack in the Box	1 jumbo serving	142		430	180	20	29	5	25	0	0	220	9	58	17	4	16	0	6	0	45	0	8
French fries, McDonald's	1 large serving	147		450	200	22	33	4	19	0	0	290	12	57	19	5	21	0	6	0	30	2	6

Consult a similar product for brand names not listed.

Food Name	Serving Size	gm	mL	Calories	Calories from Fat	Total Fat (g)	%DV	Saturated Fat (g)	%DV	Cholesterol (mg)	%DV	Sodium (mg)	%DV	Total Carbohydrates (g)	%DV	Fiber (g)	%DV	Sugars (g)	Protein (g)	Vitamin A (%DV)	Vitamin C (%DV)	Calcium (%DV)	Iron (%DV)
French fries, shoestring, frzn, Lynden Farms	3 oz	85		140	50	6	9	1.5	7	<5	1	60	3	23	7	2	10	0	2	0	4	0	0
French fries, steak, frzn, Lynden Farms	3 oz	85		130	45	5	7	2.5	12	5	2	70	3	21	7	2	8	0	2	0	2	0	2
French fries, steakhouse w/skins, frzn, Lynden Farms	3 oz	85		110	30	3	5	1.5	7	<5	1	55	2	20	7	2	11	0	2	0	6	0	2
French fries, Wendy's	1 medium serving	130		390	170	19	29	3	15	0	0	120	5	50	17	5	20	0	5	0	10	2	6
garden salad, dill, cnd, S&W	1/2 cup	127		50	0	0	0	0	0	0	0	560	23	14	4	3	12	6	2	140	0	4	2
garden salad, marinated, cnd, S&W	1/2 cup	127		50	0	0	0	0	0	0	0	880	37	13	4	3	12	10	2	190	0	4	0
green & wax beans, cut, cnd, S&W	1/2 cup	120		20	0	0	0	0	0	0	0	135	6	3	1	2	8	2	1	4	8	0	4
green bean mushroom casserole, frzn, Stouffer's	1/2 cup	119		130	80	8	13	2	10	15	4	490	20	12	4	2	7	4	3	4	0	8	2
green beans, cut, cnd, S&W	1/2 cup	120		20	0	0	0	0	0	0	0	340	14	4	1	2	8	2	1	6	6	2	4
green beans, dilled, cnd, S&W	1 oz	28		20	0	0	0	0	0	0	0	125	5	5	2	1	4	3	0	0	0	0	0
green beans, French style, cnd, Blue Lake	1/2 cup	121		20	0	0	0	0	0	0	0	360	15	4	1	2	6	2	1	6	8	2	4
green beans, French style, cnd, S&W	1/2 cup	120		20	0	0	0	0	0	0	0	340	14	4	1	2	8	2	1	6	6	2	4
green beans, French style, frzn, Bel-Air	1 cup	83		25	0	0	0	0	0	0	0	10	0	4	1	2	8	2	1	4	2	2	2
green beans, raw	3/4 cup	83		25	0	0	0	0	0	0	0	0	0	5	2	3	12	2	1	4	10	4	2
green beans, vertical pack, cnd, S&W	1/2 cup	120		20	0	0	0	0	0	0	0	340	14	4	1	2	8	2	1	6	6	2	4
green beans, whole, cnd, Blue Lake	1/2 cup	121		20	0	0	0	0	0	0	0	360	15	4	1	2	6	2	1	6	8	2	4
green beans, whole, cnd, S&W	1/2 cup	120		20	0	0	0	0	0	0	0	340	14	4	1	2	8	2	1	6	6	2	4
green beans, whole, frzn, Bel-Air	3/4 cup	83		25	5	0	1	0	0	0	0	10	0	4	1	2	7	2	1	2	2	2	0
hominy, white, cnd, Sun Vista	1/2 cup	122		65	5	0	0	0	0	0	0	530	22	18	6	3	13	0	2	0	4	0	2
hominy, yellow, cnd, Sun Vista	1/2 cup	123		70	0	0	0	0	0	0	0	540	22	19	6	3	13	0	2	0	4	0	2
Italian beans, cut, cnd, Del Monte	1/2 cup	121		30	0	0	0	0	0	0	0	360	15	6	2	3	12	2	1	4	15	2	4

Food Name	Serving Size	gm	mL	Calories	Calories from Fat	Total Fat (g)	%DV	Saturated Fat (g)	%DV	Cholesterol (mg)	%DV	Sodium (mg)	%DV	Total Carbohydrates (g)	%DV	Fiber (g)	%DV	Sugars (g)	Protein (g)	Vitamin A (%DV)	Vitamin C (%DV)	Calcium (%DV)	Iron (%DV)
lettuce, iceberg, raw	1/6 medium head	89		15	0	0	0	0	0	0	0	10	0	3	1	1	4	2	1	4	6	2	2
lettuce, leaf, raw	1 1/2 cups shredded	85		15	0	0	0	0	0	0	0	30	1	4	1	2	8	2	1	40	6	4	0
lima beans, green, cnd, Del Monte	1/2 cup	126		80	0	0	0	0	0	0	0	360	15	15	5	4	16	0	4	2	15	2	8
mixed veg, cnd, Del Monte	1/2 cup	124		40	0	0	0	0	0	0	0	360	15	8	3	2	8	3	2	45	10	2	4
mixed veg, cnd, S&W	1/2 cup	125		35	0	0	0	0	0	0	0	370	15	7	2	2	8	3	1	90	6	2	4
mixed veg, frzn, Bel-Air	2/3 cup	85		60	5	0	1	0	0	0	0	30	1	13	4	3	12	2	2	50	10	2	4
mushrooms, raw	5 medium	84		20	0	0	0	0	0	0	0	0	0	3	1	1	4	0	3	0	2	0	2
onion, green, raw	1/4 cup chopped	25		10	0	0	0	0	0	0	0	5	0	2	1	1	4	1	0	2	8	0	0
onion, mature, raw	1 medium	148		60	0	0	0	0	0	0	0	5	0	14	5	3	12	9	2	0	20	4	2
onion rings, frzn, Mrs. Paul's	7 rings	85		230	110	12	18	2.5	13	0	0	450	19	29	10	1	4	4	3	0	2	2	4
onions, cocktail, bottled, S&W	12 pieces	30		5	0	0	0	0	0	0	0	300	13	1	0	0	0	1	0	0	0	0	0
onions, small/tiny whole, cnd, S&W	1/2 cup	113		40	0	0	0	0	0	0	0	410	17	8	3	1	4	5	0	0	0	0	2
peas & carrots, cnd, Del Monte	1/2 cup	128		60	0	0	0	0	0	0	0	360	15	11	4	2	8	4	2	100	20	2	4
peas & carrots, cnd, S&W	1/2 cup	123		50	0	0	0	0	0	0	0	330	14	10	3	3	12	4	3	100	15	2	6
peas & onions, cnd, S&W	1/2 cup	123		40	0	0	0	0	0	0	0	530	22	11	4	3	12	1	3	10	15	0	6
peas, early June, cnd, Sun Vista	1/2 cup	122		80	0	0	0	0	0	0	0	510	21	18	6	5	20	2	6	4	4	2	6
peas, petit pois/sweet, cnd, S&W	1/2 cup	125		70	0	0	0	0	0	0	0	330	14	12	4	4	16	4	4	10	15	2	6
peas, sweet, cnd, Del Monte	1/2 cup	125		60	0	0	0	0	0	0	0	360	15	11	4	4	16	6	3	8	30	2	8
pepper, green, raw	1 medium	148		30	0	0	0	0	0	0	0	0	0	7	2	2	8	4	1	8	190	2	2
peppers, banana, hot, Vlasic	1 oz	28		5	0	0	0	0	0	0	0	480	20	1	0	0	0	1	0	0	15	0	0
peppers, banana, mild, Vlasic	1 oz	28		5	0	0	0	0	0	0	0	480	20	1	0	0	0	1	0	0	15	0	0
peppers, bell pepper salsa, Vlasic Zesters	2 tbsp	32		15	0	0	0	0	0	0	0	210	9	4	1	0	0	4	0	2	2	0	0
peppers, cherry, mild/hot, Vlasic	1 oz	28		10	0	0	0	0	0	0	0	480	20	2	1	0	0	2	0	0	10	0	0
peppers, chile, green, diced, mild, Ortega	2 tbsp	25		10	0	0	0	0	0	0	0	20	1	2	1	0	0	<1	<1	4	50	0	2

Consult a similar product for brand names not listed.

Food Name	Serving Size	gm	mL	Calories	Calories from Fat	Total Fat (g)	%DV	Saturated Fat (g)	%DV	Cholesterol (mg)	%DV	Sodium (mg)	%DV	Total Carbohydrates (g)	%DV	Fiber (g)	%DV	Sugars (g)	Protein (g)	Vitamin A (%DV)	Vitamin C (%DV)	Calcium (%DV)	Iron (%DV)
peppers, chile, green, whole, mild, Ortega	1 pepper	36		15	0	0	0	0	0	0	0	30	1	3	1	<1	2	<1	<1	6	70	0	2
peppers, chili, hot, Del Monte	4 peppers	28		10	0	0	0	0	0	0	0	610	25	3	1	<1	2	2	0	0	45	0	2
peppers, garden onion, Vlasic Zesters	2 tbsp	32		15	0	0	0	0	0	0	0	250	10	4	1	0	0	4	0	2	2	0	0
peppers, Ital tomato, Vlasic Zesters	2 tbsp	32		10	0	0	0	0	0	0	0	240	10	3	1	0	0	2	0	4	2	0	0
peppers, jalapeño, diced, hot, Ortega	2 tbsp	29		10	0	0	0	0	0	0	0	25	1	3	1	0	0	1	<1	4	60	0	2
peppers, jalapeño, hot, Vlasic	1/4 cup	30		10	0	0	0	0	0	0	0	490	20	2	1	0	0	2	0	10	6	0	0
peppers, jalapeño salsa, Vlasic Zesters	2 tbsp	32		15	0	0	0	0	0	0	0	230	10	4	1	0	0	3	0	2	0	0	0
peppers, jalapeño, whole, cnd, Del Monte	1 pepper	20		3	0	0	0	0	0	0	0	230	9	<1	0	<1	2	<1	0	0	6	0	0
peppers, Mexican, hot, tiny, Vlasic	1 oz	28		10	0	0	0	0	0	0	0	480	20	2	1	0	0	2	0	0	0	0	0
peppers, mushroom & onion, Vlasic Zesters	2 tbsp	32		10	0	0	0	0	0	0	0	170	7	3	1	0	0	3	0	2	0	2	0
peppers, pepperoncini salad, Vlasic	1 oz	28		5	0	0	0	0	0	0	0	440	18	1	0	0	0	1	0	0	0	0	0
peppers, rings, sweet, Vlasic	1 oz	28		25	0	0	0	0	0	0	0	170	7	6	2	0	0	6	0	0	15	0	0
peppers, rings/chunks, mild/hot, Vlasic	1 oz	28		5	0	0	0	0	0	0	0	480	20	1	0	0	0	1	0	0	15	0	0
pimentos, whole, cnd, S&W	2 1/4 oz	63		20	0	0	0	0	0	0	0	180	8	3	1	0	0	0	1	8	50	2	4
potato au gratin, box mix, not prepared, Idahoan	1/3 cup mix	30		110	10	1.5	2	0.5	3	0	0	600	25	23	8	2	7	1	2	0	6	4	0
potato au gratin, frzn, Stouffer's	1/2 cup	145		170	60	7	10	2	9	15	4	660	27	20	7	2	8	4	6	0	2	15	2
potato, hash brown, frzn, Lynden Farms	2/3 cup	69		150	60	6	10	3	15	5	2	60	2	22	7	2	9	0	2	0	4	0	2
potato, mashed, complete mix, not prepared, Idahoan[27]	1/3 cup mix	26		100	15	2	3	0.5	3	0	0	310	13	19	7	2	8	0	2	4	4	0	2
potato, mashed, mix, not prepared, Idahoan[28]	1/3 cup mix	23		80	0	0	0	0	0	0	0	15	1	18	6	2	6	0	2	0	6	0	0
potato, new, whole, cnd, S&W	1/2 cup	124		60	0	0	0	0	0	0	0	260	11	14	5	1	4	0	1	0	0	6	2

Food Name	Serving Size	gm	mL	Calories	Calories from Fat	Total Fat (g)	%DV	Saturated Fat (g)	%DV	Cholesterol (mg)	%DV	Sodium (mg)	%DV	Total Carbohydrates[8] (g)	%DV	Fiber[8] (g)	%DV	Sugars[8] (g)	Protein (g)	Vitamin A (%DV)	Vitamin C[7] (%DV)	Calcium (%DV)	Iron (%DV)
potato, raw	1 medium	148		100	0	0	0	0	0	0	0	0	0	26	9	3	12	3	4	0	45	2	6
potato salad, southern, Safeway Deli Shop	1/2 cup	172		220	100	11	17	2	9	5	2	640	27	27	9	3	12	11	12	2	2	0	4
potato, scalloped, mix, not prepared, Idahoan	1/3 cup mix	30		110	15	1.5	2	0.5	3	0	0	430	18	23	8	3	11	1	2	0	2	6	0
potato, scalloped, frzn, Stouffer's	1/2 cup	131		140	50	6	9	0.5	3	5	1	500	21	18	6	2	7	3	4	0	0	10	2
potato, sliced/whole, cnd, Del Monte	2/3 cup	155		60	0	0	0	0	0	0	0	360	15	13	4	2	8	0	1	0	20	2	2
potato, Taters, frzn, Lynden Farms	9 taters	85		150	60	7	11	2.5	13	5	2	300	12	20	7	2	10	0	2	0	15	0	2
pumpkin butter, Smucker's	1 tbsp	19		45	0	0	0	0	0	0	0	25	1	11	4	0	0	11	0	0	0	0	0
pumpkin, cnd, solid pack, Libby's	1/2 cup	122		60	5	1	0.5	0	0	0	0	5	0	15	5	4	17	4	2	350	8	2	10
pumpkin pie mix, cnd, Libby's	1/2 cup	131		100	0	0	0	0	0	0	0	150	6	25	8	2	7	22	<1	160	2	2	4
radishes, raw	7 radishes	85		15	0	0	0	0	0	0	0	25	1	3	1	0	0	0	1	0	30	2	0
sauerkraut, Claussen	1/4 cup	30		5	0	0	0	0	0	0	0	210	9	1	0	1	4	0	1	0	6	0	0
sauerkraut, cnd, Del Monte	1/2 cup	120		15	0	0	0	0	0	0	0	700	30	4	2	2	8	0	1	0	30	0	2
sauerkraut, cnd, S&W	2 tbsp	30		5	0	0	0	0	0	0	0	180	8	2	1	0	0	0	0	0	4	0	0
sauerkraut ice, cnd, S&W	1 can	30		35	0	0	0	0	0	0	0	1950	81	7	2	0	0	2	0	20	10	8	
spinach, cnd, Del Monte	1/2 cup	115		30	0	0	0	0	0	0	0	360	15	4	1	2	8	0	2	50	40	10	6
spinach, cnd, S&W	1/2 cup	127		30	0	0	0	0	0	0	0	440	18	4	1	2	8	1	3	70	20	8	15
spinach, chopped, frzn, Bel-Air	1 cup	81		20	0	0	0	0	0	0	0	110	5	2	1	2	7	1	2	110	10	6	2
spinach, creamed, frzn, Stouffer's	1/2 cup	129		210	150	17	26	2.5	13	30	8	460	19	9	3	2	8	3	4	50	10	10	6
squash casserole, frzn Stouffer's	1/2 cup	119		150	70	9	13	3.5	15	30	9	370	16	9	3	2	8	3	7	0	2	20	4
squash, summer, raw	1/2 medium	98		20	0	0	0	0	0	0	0	0	0	4	1	2	8	2	1	6	30	2	2
succotash, cnd, S&W	1/2 cup	125		100	10	1	2	0	0	0	0	340	14	19	6	2	8	4	3	0	6	0	2
sweet potato, candied, frzn, Mrs. Paul's	5 oz	140		300	10	1	2	0.5	3	0	0	130	5	73	24	3	12	47	1	100	8	15	6
sweet potato, raw	1 medium (5" long, 2" diameter)	130		130	0	0	0	0	0	0	0	45	2	33	11	4	16	7	2	440	30	2	2
sweet potato, whipped, frzn Stouffer's	1/2 cup	127		180	50	6	9	1	5	0	0	410	17	29	10	3	14	20	2	140	4	2	2

Consult a similar product for brand names not listed.

Food Name	Serving Size	gm	mL	Calories	Calories from Fat	Total Fat (g)	%DV	Saturated Fat (g)	%DV	Cholesterol (mg)	%DV	Sodium (mg)	%DV	Total Carbohydrates (g)	%DV	Fiber (g)	%DV	Sugars (g)	Protein (g)	Vitamin A (%DV)	Vitamin C (%DV)	Calcium (%DV)	Iron (%DV)
tomato aspic, cnd, S&W	1/2 cup	126		50	0	0	0	0	0	0	0	570	24	14	5	2	7	8	1	10	6	10	4
tomatoes, crushed, cnd, Contadina	1/4 cup	61		20	0	0	0	0	0	0	0	150	6	4	1	1	4	3	<1	8	10	2	2
tomatoes, crushed, cnd, S&W	1/4 cup	61		20	0	0	0	0	0	0	0	95	4	4	1	1	5	2	1	6	12	2	4
tomatoes in jce, cnd, S&W	1/2 cup	121		25	0	0	0	0	0	0	0	190	8	4	1	1	4	4	1	20	15	4	15
tomatoes, Ital w/basil, cnd, S&W	1/2 cup	121		25	0	0	0	0	0	0	0	220	9	4	1	1	5	3	1	10	20	2	4
tomatoes in jce, no-salt, cnd, S&W	1/2 cup	121		25	0	0	0	0	0	0	0	30	1	4	1	1	4	3	1	20	15	0	10
tomatoes in puree, cnd, S&W	1/2 cup	120		30	0	0	0	0	0	0	0	410	17	6	2	2	6	3	2	10	10	0	6
tomatoes, Ital, in jce, cnd, S&W	1/2 cup	121		25	0	0	0	0	0	0	0	190	8	4	1	1	4	4	1	20	15	4	15
tomatoes, stewed, cnd, Contadina	1/2 cup	123		40	0	0	0	0	0	0	0	250	10	9	3	1	4	5	1	8	15	4	4
tomatoes, stewed, cnd, Del Monte	1/2 cup	126		35	0	0	0	0	0	0	0	360	15	9	3	2	8	7	1	10	25	2	2
tomatoes, stewed, cnd, S&W	1/2 cup	123		35	0	0	0	0	0	0	0	270	11	7	2	2	8	5	1	10	20	4	8
tomatoes, stewed, Ital recipe, cnd, S&W	1/2 cup	123		35	0	0	0	0	0	0	0	270	11	7	2	2	7	5	1	10	20	4	8
tomatoes, stewed, Ital style, cnd, Contadina	1/2 cup	123		40	0	0	0	0	0	0	0	260	11	8	3	1	5	5	1	6	4	4	2
tomatoes, stewed, Mexican style, cnd, Contadina	1/2 cup	123		40	0	0	0	0	0	0	0	220	9	9	3	1	4	4	1	6	4	4	2
tomatoes, stewed, no-salt, cnd, S&W	1/2 cup	123		35	0	0	0	0	0	0	0	15	1	7	2	2	8	5	1	10	20	4	8
tomatoes, whole, peeled, cnd, Contadina	1/2 cup	126		25	0	0	0	0	0	0	0	220	9	4	1	1	5	3	1	10	20	2	4
tomatoes, whole, peeled, cnd, Del Monte	1/2 cup	126		25	0	0	0	0	0	0	0	160	7	6	2	2	8	4	1	10	25	2	2
tomatoes, whole, peeled, cnd, S&W	1/2 cup	121		25	0	0	0	0	0	0	0	220	9	4	1	1	5	3	1	10	20	2	4
tomatoes, whole, peeled, no-salt, cnd, S&W	1/2 cup	119		20	0	0	0	0	0	0	0	90	4	4	1	1	6	3	2	6	10	0	15
tomato jce, cnd, Campbell's	8 fl oz (1 cup)	243		50	0	0	0	0	0	0	0	860	36	9	3	1	4	7	2	20	40	2	8
tomato jce, cnd, Del Monte	8 fl oz (1 cup)	240		40	0	0	0	0	0	0	0	550	23	7	2	0	0	7	3	15	25	0	15

Food Name	Serving Size	gm	mL	Calories	Calories from Fat	Total Fat (g)	Total Fat %DV	Saturated Fat (g)	Saturated Fat %DV	Cholesterol (mg)	Cholesterol %DV	Sodium (mg)	Sodium %DV	Total Carbohydrates[5] (g)	%DV	Fiber[6] (g)	%DV	Sugars[8] (g)	Protein (g)	Vitamin A (%DV)	Vitamin C[7] (%DV)	Calcium (%DV)	Iron (%DV)
tomato jce, cnd, S&W	1 can (5.5 fl oz)		163	30	0	0	0	0	0	0	0	380	16	5	2	0	0	5	2	10	100	0	10
tomato jce, cnd, S&W	8 fl oz (1 cup)		163	40	0	0	0	0	0	0	0	550	23	7	2	0	0	7	2	15	100	0	15
tomato, raw	1 medium	148		35	0	0.5	1	0	0	0	0	5	0	7	2	1	4	4	1	20	40	2	2
V8 bloody Mary mix, cnd, Campbell's	11 ½ fl oz	349		70	0	0	0	0	0	0	0	1800	75	13	4	2	8	13	3	15	80	4	6
V8 veg jce, cnd, Campbell's	8 fl oz (1 cup)	243		50	0	0	0	0	0	0	0	620	26	10	3	1	4	8	1	40	100	4	6
V8 veg jce, lightly tangy, cnd, Campbell's	8 fl oz (1 cup)	243		60	0	0	0	0	0	0	0	340	14	11	4	1	4	9	2	60	100	4	6
V8 veg jce, picante, cnd, Campbell's	8 fl oz (1 cup)	243		50	0	0	0	0	0	0	0	680	28	10	3	1	4	7	2	40	100	4	6
V8 veg jce, spicy hot, cnd, Campbell's	8 fl oz (1 cup)	243		50	0	0	0	0	0	0	0	780	33	10	3	1	4	7	2	40	60	2	4
wax beans, cut, cnd, Del Monte	½ cup	121		20	0	0	0	0	0	0	0	360	15	4	1	2	8	2	0	0	10	2	2
wax beans, cut, cnd, S&W	½ cup	120		20	0	0	0	0	0	0	0	400	17	4	1	1	4	2	1	0	6	2	2
yams & apples, frzn, Stouffer's	½ cup	130		170	25	3	4	1	2	0	0	110	5	35	12	2	7	27	1	80	30	2	2
yams, candied, cnd S&W	½ cup	141		170	0	0	0	0	0	0	0	360	15	46	15	4	16	21	2	40	8	2	6
zucchini w/Ital tom sauce, cnd, Del Monte	½ cup	121		30	0	0	0	0	0	0	0	490	20	7	2	1	4	1	1	6	15	0	4

Consult a similar product for brand names not listed.

VEGETABLE-BASED ENTREES[1]

Food Name	Serving Size	gm	mL	Calories	Calories from Fat	Total Fat (g)	%DV	Saturated Fat (g)	%DV	Cholesterol (mg)	%DV	Sodium (mg)	%DV	Total Carbohydrates[8] (g)	%DV	Fiber[8] (g)	%DV	Sugars[8] (g)	Protein (g)	Vitamin A (%DV)	Vitamin C[7] (%DV)	Calcium (%DV)	Iron (%DV)
cabbage w/beef & tom sauce, frzn, Stouffer's	1 cabbage roll	217		210	80	14	10	2	11	25	8	970	40	21	7	4	18	6	9	4	6	4	8
cajun stew (veg, chicken, & sausage), frzn, Stouffer's	1 cup	255		210	110	12	19	3	15	55	17	900	37	13	4	5	22	6	12	10	40	6	8
corn fritters, frzn, Mrs. Paul's	1 fritter	63		130	60	7	11	2	10	5	2	310	13	16	5	1	4	4	3	0	0	2	4
eggplant parmigiana, frzn, Celentano	1 cup (8 oz)	224		360	230	25	38	5	25	25	9	640	27	25	9	15	60	6	9	40	15	15	10
eggplant parmigiana, frzn, Mrs. Paul's	½ cup	118		220	130	14	22	4	20	10	3	530	22	19	6	3	12	9	5	10	8	10	6
eggplant rollettes, frzn, Celentano	10 oz	280		330	130	15	23	4	20	55	18	660	28	39	13	7	28	10	11	25	0	25	15
heartland medley, frzn, Lean Cuisine[29]	1 cup	243		170	45	5	7	1	5	30	10	730	30	18	6	3	14	4	12	25	4	2	6
ital veg & chicken, frzn, Budget Gourmet	1 entree	255		240	50	6	9	2	10	25	8	560	23	37	12	3	12	4	10	50	15	6	8
pepper, green w/beef & tom sauce, frzn, Stouffer's	1 pepper w/sauce	196		170	60	7	11	2	7	25	6	830	35	18	6	2	9	6	8	6	10	2	6
potato, baked w/broccoli & cheese, Wendy's	1 potato	411		470	120	14	22	3	15	5	2	470	20	80	27	9	36	6	9	35	120	20	25
potato, baked w/chili & cheese, Wendy's	1 potato	439		620	220	24	37	9	45	40	13	780	33	83	28	9	36	7	20	20	60	35	30
potatoes, scalloped & ham, frzn, Swanson Entree	1 entree	255		290	110	12	18	8	40	45	15	1020	43	29	10	4	16	4	16	0	10	20	4
Szechuan veg, chicken, noodles, & sauce, frzn, Budget Gourmet	1 entree	283		330	90	10	15	2	10	15	5	1020	43	46	15	4	16	3	15	15	4	4	10
taco salad w/shell and salsa, Taco Bell	1 salad	535		840	470	52	80	15	75	75	25	1670	70	62	21	13	52	8	32	150	40	25	35
veg chow mein, frzn, Stouffer's	½ cup	130		60	30	3	5	1	2	0	0	710	30	8	3	1	3	2	0	4	10	0	0
veg lo mein, beef strips, & sauce, frzn, Healthy Choice	1 entree	340		330	30	5	5	1	4	20	6	500	21	55	18	5	18	2	20	20	30	4	25

VEGETABLE-BASED SOUPS

Food Name	Serving Size	gm	mL	Calories	Calories from Fat	Total Fat (g)	%DV	Saturated Fat (g)	%DV	Cholesterol (mg)	%DV	Sodium (mg)	%DV	Total Carbohydrates (g)	%DV	Fiber (g)	%DV	Sugars (g)	Protein (g)	Vitamin A (%DV)	Vitamin C (%DV)	Calcium (%DV)	Iron (%DV)
asparagus, crm of, cnd cond, Campbell's	½ cup	124		110	60	7	11	2	10	<5	1	910	38	9	3	1	4	2	3	6	6	2	2
broccoli, crm of, cnd cond, Campbell's	½ cup	124		100	50	6	9	2.5	13	5	1	770	32	9	3	1	4	2	2	6	4	2	2
broccoli, crm of, frzn rts, Stouffer's	1 cup	238		300	190	22	33	8	36	45	14	950	40	14	4	4	14	11	11	4	8	35	2
celery, crm of, cnd cond, Campbell's	½ cup	124		110	60	7	11	2.5	13	<5	1	900	38	9	3	1	4	1	2	6	0	2	2
chicken flavor veg, dry mix, Knorr	1 package	30		100	0	0	0	0	1	0	0	840	35	21	7	0	0	0	3	10	20	4	6
corn chowder, frzn rts, Stouffer's	1 cup	235		280	160	19	28	3	11	5	1	810	34	20	6	2	8	11	6	10	4	15	0
corn, golden, cnd cond, Campbell's	½ cup	124		120	30	3.5	5	1	5	<5	1	730	30	20	7	2	8	7	2	10	0	2	2
country veg, cnd rts, Campbell's Home Cookin'	1 can	305		130	20	2	3	0	0	5	2	940	39	26	9	2	8	8	4	120	2	8	6
French onion, cnd cond, Campbell's	½ cup	126		70	25	2.5	4	0	0	<5	1	980	41	10	3	1	4	5	2	0	4	2	2
French onion, dry mix, Knorr	⅓ package	13		45	10	1	1	0.5	2	<5	0	980	41	8	3	0	0	1	1	0	6	0	0
French onion, frzn conc, Stouffer's	½ cup	122		70	30	3	5	1	5	5	1	1670	69	10	3	2	7	6	1	0	0	2	2
gumbo, dry mix, Campbell's	1 package	53		170	20	2	3	0.5	3	5	1	950	40	34	11	2	8	6	4	4	10	4	2
hearty veg w/pasta, chunky, cnd rts, Campbell's	1 cup	245		130	25	3	5	0.5	3	0	0	1080	45	21	7	3	12	6	4	0	2	8	10
Ital veg, cnd rts, Campbell's Home Cookin'	1 can	305		130	45	5	8	2	10	5	2	1070	45	17	6	3	12	7	3	140	6	8	6
leek, dry mix, Knorr	⅓ package	17		70	25	3	5	1	4	<5	0	780	33	9	3	0	0	1	2	0	2	0	2
Mediterranean veg, chunky, cnd rts, Campbell's	1 cup	245		140	45	5	8	1.5	8	5	2	850	35	21	7	1	4	6	4	100	2	6	10
Mexican pepper, crm of, cnd cond, Campbell's	½ cup	124		110	60	7	11	2	10	<5	1	860	36	10	3	2	8	1	2	0	2	2	2
minestrone, chunky, cnd rts, Campbell's	1 cup	245		140	45	5	8	1.5	8	5	2	800	33	22	7	2	8	4	5	90	8	8	10
minestrone, cnd cond, Campbell's	½ cup	126		100	20	2	3	0.5	3	0	1	960	40	16	5	4	16	3	5	20	2	4	6
minestrone, cnd rts, Campbell's Home Cookin'	1 cup	245		120	20	2	3	1	5	5	2	990	41	19	6	3	12	5	4	70	2	6	6
minestrone, cnd rts, Progresso	8 oz	227		120	20	2	3	0	0	0	0	960	40	21	7	5	20	4	5	20	0	4	8

Consult a similar product for brand names not listed.

Food Name	Serving Size	gm	mL	Calories	Calories from Fat	Total Fat (g)	Total Fat %DV	Saturated Fat (g)	Saturated Fat %DV	Cholesterol (mg)	Cholesterol %DV	Sodium (mg)	Sodium %DV	Total Carbohydrates (g)	Total Carbohydrates %DV	Fiber (g)	Fiber %DV	Sugars (g)	Protein (g)	Vitamin A (%DV)	Vitamin C (%DV)	Calcium (%DV)	Iron (%DV)
minestrone, frzn conc, Stouffer's	1/2 cup	119		110	25	3	5	1	5	5	5	1010	42	16	5	3	13	3	4	15	2	4	6
minestrone, frzn rts, Stouffer's	1 cup	243		80	25	3	5	1	5	5	5	930	39	11	4	3	11	3	3	15	2	6	6
mushroom, crm of, cnd cond, Campbell's	1/2 cup	124		110	60	7	11	2.5	13	<5	1	870	36	9	3	1	4	1	2	0	0	2	2
mushroom, crm of, cnd rts, Campbell's Home Cookin'	1 can	305		210	150	17	26	5	25	20	7	1210	50	12	4	3	12	1	4	0	0	0	2
mushroom, golden, cnd cond, Campbell's	1/2 cup	124		80	25	3	5	1	5	5	1	930	39	10	3	1	4	1	2	15	0	2	0
onion, creamy, cnd cond, Campbell's	1/2 cup	124		110	50	6	9	1.5	8	20	7	910	38	13	4	1	4	4	2	6	0	2	4
onion, dry mix, Campbell's	2 tbsp	15		50	10	1	2	0	0	0	0	760	32	10	3	0	3	7	1	0	0	2	0
onion-mushroom recipe, dry mix, Mrs. Grass	1/3 package	16		60	10	1	2	0	0	0	0	1080	45	10	3	0	0	2	2	0	0	0	4
pepper pot, cnd cond, Campbell's	1/2 cup	126		100	45	5	8	2	10	15	5	1020	43	9	3	1	4	1	4	20	2	2	4
potato, crm of, cnd cond, Campbell's	1/2 cup	124		100	25	3	5	1.5	8	10	3	890	37	14	5	1	4	2	2	0	0	2	4
potato, crm of, frzn rts, Stouffer's	1 cup	261		270	100	11	17	4	18	25	8	1180	49	32	11	2	10	16	11	0	0	35	2
potato ham chowder, chunky, cnd rts, Campbell's	1 can	305		270	160	18	28	9	45	25	8	1050	44	20	7	3	12	1	7	0	0	2	6
potato leek, dry mix, Knorr	1 package	34		120	0	0	0	0	1	0	0	970	40	24	8	1	4	4	4	15	4	15	10
southwest veg, cnd rts, Campbell's Home Cookin'	1 cup	245		130	25	2	4	0.5	3	0	0	750	31	24	8	4	16	4	3	90	4	6	6
spring veg, dry mix, Knorr	1/3 package	9		25	0	0	0	0	0	0	0	570	24	5	2	0	0	0	1	40	25	0	2
tom bisque, cnd cond, Campbell's	1/2 cup	126		130	25	3	5	1.5	8	5	1	900	38	24	8	2	8	15	2	10	25	4	4
tom, cnd cond, Campbell's	1/2 cup	124		100	20	2	3	0	0	0	0	730	30	18	6	2	8	10	2	10	30	2	4
tom, crm of, cnd cond, Campbell's	1/2 cup	124		110	25	2	4	1	5	5	2	860	36	21	7	1	4	14	1	10	20	2	4
tom, fiesta, cnd cond, Campbell's	1/2 cup	126		70	0	0	0	0	0	0	0	860	36	16	5	1	4	8	1	8	10	10	4
tom, frzn conc, Stouffer's	1/2 cup	121		100	30	4	5	1.5	7	5	2	1100	46	14	5	3	11	5	3	20	8	4	6
tom garden, cnd rts, Campbell's Home Cookin'	1 can	305		150	35	4	6	2	10	5	2	900	38	27	9	4	16	13	5	50	2	10	8
tom, ital, cnd cond, Campbell's	1/2 cup	126		100	5	0.5	1	0	0	0	0	820	34	23	8	2	8	16	2	15	30	4	6

Food Name	Serving Size	gm	mL	Calories	Calories from Fat	Total Fat (g)	%DV	Saturated Fat (g)	%DV	Cholesterol (mg)	%DV	Sodium (mg)	%DV	Total Carbohydrates[6] (g)	%DV	Fiber[6] (g)	%DV	Sugars[6] (g)	Protein (g)	Vitamin A (%DV)	Vitamin C[7] (%DV)	Calcium (%DV)	Iron (%DV)
tom veg, dry mix, Campbell's	1 package	48		130	15	2	3	1	5	15	5	900	38	25	8	2	8	9	5	50	0	6	8
Tuscany minestrone, cnd rts, Campbell's Home Cookin'	1 can	305		200	70	8	12	2	10	5	2	1100	46	26	9	6	24	5	6	80	6	10	15
veg beef, cnd cond, Campbell's	½ cup	126		80	20	2	3	1	5	10	3	810	34	10	3	2	8	2	5	40	0	2	4
veg beef, cnd rts, Campbell's Home Cookin'	1 can	305		150	25	2.5	4	1.5	8	10	3	1260	53	22	7	4	16	7	8	100	0	6	8
veg beef, old fashioned, chunky, cnd rts, Campbell's	1 can	305		180	50	6	9	2	10	20	7	1090	45	20	7	4	16	4	13	120	6	6	10
veg beef, rts microwave, Campbell's	1 container	220		90	20	2	3	1	5	10	3	780	33	13	4	2	8	2	5	50	6	6	2
veg beef w/barley, frzn conc, Stouffer's	½ cup	130		170	90	10	16	3.5	17	15	4	1270	53	14	5	3	11	4	5	25	6	2	4
veg beef w/barley, frzn rts, Stouffer's	1 cup	242		150	80	9	13	1	3	10	3	990	41	12	4	2	10	3	6	20	2	2	6
veg, Calif, cnd cond, Campbell's	½ cup	126		60	10	1	2	0	0	0	0	850	35	10	3	2	8	2	3	20	50	2	2
veg, cnd cond, Campbell's	½ cup	126		80	15	1.5	2	0.5	3	<5	1	920	38	14	5	2	8	7	3	30	2	2	4
veg, cnd rts, Progresso Healthy Classics	1 cup	238		80	10	1.5	2	0	0	5	2	470	19	13	4	1	6	2	4	60	2	4	8
veg, dry mix, Campbell's	2 tbsp	11		35	0	0	0	0	0	0	0	650	27	7	2	0	0	5	<1	10	0	0	0
veg, dry mix, Knorr	¼ package	10		30	0	0	0	0	0	0	0	730	30	6	2	1	4	1	1	20	4	2	2
veg, homestyle, cnd cond, Campbell's	½ cup	126		70	20	2	3	0.5	3	0	0	970	40	10	3	2	8	4	2	40	2	4	4
veg, old fashioned, cnd cond, Campbell's	½ cup	126		70	25	2.5	4	0.5	3	<5	1	950	40	10	3	2	8	2	2	50	0	2	4
veg recipe, dry mix, Mrs. Grass	¼ packet	12		35	0	0	0	0	0	0	0	900	38	7	2	1	4	2	1	4	0	2	2
veg, rts microwave, Campbell's	1 container	220		100	20	2	3	0.5	3	0	0	850	35	17	6	2	8	4	3	60	4	6	4
veg soup & recipe mix, Knorr	2 tbsp	10		30	5	0.5	1	0	0	0	0	730	30	6	2	1	4	2	1	20	4	2	2
vegetarian veg, frzn conc, Stouffer's	½ cup	126		100	25	3	4	1	3	0	0	860	36	16	5	4	15	4	3	30	8	4	6

Consult a similar product for brand names not listed.

VEGETABLE PRODUCTS: PICKLES AND PICKLE RELISHES

Food Name	Serving Size	gm	mL	Calories	Calories from Fat	Total Fat (g)	%DV	Saturated Fat (g)	%DV	Cholesterol (mg)	%DV	Sodium (mg)	%DV	Total Carbohydrates (g)	%DV	Fiber (g)	%DV	Sugars (g)	Protein (g)	Vitamin A (%DV)	Vitamin C[7] (%DV)	Calcium (%DV)	Iron (%DV)
bread & butter midgets, Vlasic Milwaukee's[1]	1 oz	28		40	0	0	0	0	0	0	0	230	10	10	3	0	0	10	0	0	0	0	0
bread & butter sandwich stackers, Vlasic	1 oz	28		30	0	0	0	0	0	0	0	170	7	7	2	0	0	7	0	0	0	0	0
bread'n butter chips, Claussen	4 slices	28		20	0	0	0	0	0	0	0	170	7	4	1	0	0	3	0	0	0	0	0
dill chips, Del Monte	5 chips	28		5	0	0	0	0	0	0	0	310	13	1	0	0	0	0	0	0	0	6	0
dill spears, Claussen	1 spear	34		5	0	0	0	0	0	0	0	320	13	1	0	0	0	0	0	0	0	0	0
dill spears, Vlasic Deli Kosher/Polish	1 oz	28		5	0	0	0	0	0	0	0	310	13	1	0	0	0	1	0	0	0	0	0
hamburger relish, Del Monte	1 tbsp	17		20	0	0	0	0	0	0	0	220	9	6	2	<1	2	5	0	4	0	0	0
hot dog relish, Del Monte	1 tbsp	16		15	0	0	0	0	0	0	0	140	6	4	1	<1	2	3	0	0	0	0	0
sour, New York deli style, Claussen	½ pickle	28		5	0	0	0	0	0	0	0	260	11	1	0	0	0	<1	0	0	0	0	0
sweet chips, Del Monte	5 chips	28		40	0	0	0	0	0	0	0	210	9	10	3	<1	3	10	0	0	0	0	0
sweet India relish w/curry, Vlasic	1 tbsp	15		15	0	0	0	0	0	0	0	140	6	4	1	0	0	4	0	0	0	0	0
sweet relish, Claussen	1 tbsp	15		15	0	0	0	0	0	0	0	85	4	3	1	0	0	2	0	0	0	0	0
sweet relish, Del Monte	1 tbsp	16		20	0	0	0	0	0	0	0	125	5	5	2	0	0	5	0	0	0	0	0
sweet, Vlasic	1 oz	28		40	0	0	0	0	0	0	0	170	7	10	3	0	0	10	0	0	0	0	0

Food Name	Serving Size	gm	mL	Calories	Calories from Fat	Total Fat (g)	%DV	Saturated Fat (g)	%DV	Cholesterol (mg)	%DV	Sodium (mg)	%DV	Total Carbohydrates (g)	%DV	Fiber (g)	%DV	Sugars (g)	Protein (g)	Vitamin A (%DV)	Vitamin C (%DV)	Calcium (%DV)	Iron (%DV)
VEGETABLE PRODUCTS: POTATO-BASED CHIPS AND SNACKS																							
baked potato flavor, Tato Skins	18 chips	28		144	72	8	12	2	8	0	0	160	6	17	6	<1	2	<1	1	0	0	0	0
bbq, Lay's	1 oz (15 chips)	28		160	90	10	16	3	15	0	0	200	8	15	5	1	4	2	2	0	10	0	2
cheddar, O'Boisies	16 chips	28		150	90	10	15	2	10	0	0	135	6	15	5	1	6	<1	2	0	0	0	0
cheese'n bacon, Tato Skins	18 chips	28		150	80	9	14	1.5	8	0	0	170	7	17	6	1	4	<1	<1	0	0	0	0
Fabulous Fries, Pik-Nik	2/3 cup	29		150	80	9	14	2	10	0	0	120	5	16	5	1	4	<1	2	0	4	0	2
Ketchup 'n Fries, Pik-Nik	2/3 cup	31		160	90	10	16	2	11	0	0	160	7	17	6	1	4	2	2	0	6	0	4
orig, Lay's	1 oz (20 chips)	28		150	90	10	15	3	15	0	0	180	8	15	5	1	2	2	2	0	10	0	0
orig, O'Boisies	16 chips	28		150	80	9	14	2	10	0	0	180	8	15	5	1	5	<1	1	0	2	0	2
orig, Pringles	14 chips	28		160	90	11	17	3	14	0	0	170	7	15	5	1	4	0	1	0	6	0	0
orig, Ruffles	1 oz (12 chips)	28		160	90	10	16	2.5	13	0	0	180	8	14	5	1	4	0	2	0	10	0	2
ridges orig, Pringles	12 chips	28		150	90	10	17	2.5	14	0	0	150	6	15	5	1	4	0	1	0	6	0	0
shoestrings, 50% less salt, Pik-Nik	3/4 cup	31		165	105	12	18	3	13	0	0	60	2	16	5	1	5	0	2	0	0	0	2
shoestrings, Pik-Nik	2/3 cup	29		160	95	10	16	3	13	0	0	105	4	15	5	1	4	1	1	0	6	0	2
shoestrings, Santa Fe bbq, Pik-Nik	2/3 cup	34		180	110	12	19	3	14	0	0	240	10	18	6	2	6	0	2	0	2	0	4
shoestrings, sour crm & cheddar, Pik-Nik	2/3 cup	33		180	120	13	20	3	14	0	0	130	5	17	6	2	6	0	2	0	0	0	2
sour crm & onion, O'Boisies	15 chips	28		150	80	9	14	2	10	0	0	190	8	15	5	1	5	1	2	0	0	0	0
sour crm & onion, Ruffles	1 oz (11 chips)	28		150	90	10	15	3	14	0	0	180	8	15	5	1	4	1	2	0	10	0	2
sour crm'n onion, Tato Skins	18 chips	28		150	90	10	15	1.5	8	0	0	160	7	16	5	1	4	<1	<1	0	0	0	0

Consult a similar product for brand names not listed.

VEGETABLE PRODUCTS: TOMATO-BASED DIPS, PASTES, SALSAS, AND SAUCES

Food Name	Serving Size	gm	mL	Calories	Calories from Fat	Total Fat (g)	%DV	Saturated Fat (g)	%DV	Cholesterol (mg)	%DV	Sodium (mg)	%DV	Total Carbohydrates (g)	%DV	Fiber (g)	%DV	Sugars (g)	Protein (g)	Vitamin A (%DV)	Vitamin C (%DV)	Calcium (%DV)	Iron (%DV)
bbq sauce, hickory flavor, Open Pit	2 tbsp	34		50	0	0	0	0	0	0	0	380	16	11	4	0	0	9	0	0	0	0	0
chili hot dog sauce, Armour Star	1/4 cup	62		120	80	9	14	4	20	20	7	310	13	6	2	0	0	1	4	4	0	0	6
chili sauce, Del Monte	1 tbsp	18		20	0	0	0	0	0	0	0	480	20	5	2	0	0	4	0	10	2	0	0
chili sauce, S&W Steakhouse	1 tbsp	17		15	0	0	0	0	0	0	0	180	8	4	1	0	0	2	0	0	0	0	0
cooking sauce, ital tom, herb & garlic, S&W	1 tbsp	17		15	10	1	1	0	0	0	0	150	6	0	0	0	0	1	0	2	0	0	0
ketchup, Del Monte	1 tbsp	17		15	0	0	0	0	0	0	0	190	8	4	1	0	0	4	0	2	2	0	0
ketchup, Heinz	1 tbsp	17		15	0	0	0	0	0	0	0	190	8	4	1	0	0	4	0	6	0	0	0
ketchup, Smucker's	1 tbsp	17		25	0	0	0	0	0	0	0	110	5	7	2	0	0	6	0	0	0	0	0
marinara sauce, Barilla	1/2 cup	126		80	35	4	6	1	5	0	0	450	19	10	3	3	12	6	2	10	2	8	4
marinara sauce, Campbell's	1/2 cup	125		90	10	1	2	0	0	0	0	510	21	18	6	2	8	11	2	20	25	4	4
marinara sauce, Contadina	1/2 cup	125		80	35	4	6	0	0	0	0	390	16	9	3	2	8	6	1	10	10	2	4
marinara sauce, Prego	1/2 cup	125		110	50	6	9	1.5	8	0	0	670	28	12	4	3	12	8	2	20	30	4	4
pasta sauce, green & black olive, Barilla	1/2 cup	126		100	50	6	9	1.5	8	0	0	710	30	9	3	3	12	6	2	10	2	6	4
pasta sauce, mushroom & garlic, Barilla	1/2 cup	126		80	30	3.5	5	0.5	3	0	0	500	21	9	3	3	12	5	2	15	2	6	4
pasta sauce, spicy pepper, Barilla	1/2 cup	126		80	30	3.5	5	0.5	3	0	0	570	24	9	3	3	12	7	2	15	2	8	4
pasta sauce, sweet pepper & garlic, Barilla	1/2 cup	126		70	30	3.5	5	0.5	3	0	0	580	24	8	3	3	12	6	1	10	15	6	4
pasta sauce, tomato & basil, Barilla	1/2 cup	126		70	20	2.5	4	0.5	3	0	0	570	24	10	3	3	12	7	2	10	2	8	4
picante sauce, hot, Sun Vista	2 tbsp	32		10	0	0	0	0	0	0	0	260	11	2	1	0	0	<1	0	4	2	0	4
picante sauce, mild, Sun Vista	2 tbsp	31		5	0	0	0	0	0	0	0	200	8	2	1	0	0	<1	0	6	0	0	4
pizza sauce, chunky, Contadina	1/4 cup	63		30	0	0	0	0	0	0	0	280	12	6	2	1	4	2	<1	4	15	2	2
pizza sauce, Contadina	1/4 cup	63		35	10	1.5	2	0	0	0	0	350	15	6	2	1	3	1	1	8	8	2	4
salsa, garden style, mild/med, Ortega	2 tbsp	41		10	0	0	0	0	0	0	0	140	6	3	1	0	0	<1	1	0	6	0	0
salsa, hot, Sun Vista	2 tbsp	32		5	0	0	0	0	0	0	0	170	7	2	1	<1		1	0	4	4	0	0
salsa, Marie's	2 tbsp	31		10	0	0	0	0	0	0	0	250	10	2	1	0	0	2	0	2	8	0	0

Food Name	Serving Size gm	mL	Calories	Calories from Fat	Total Fat (g)	%DV	Saturated Fat (g)	%DV	Cholesterol (mg)	%DV	Sodium (mg)	%DV	Total Carbohydrates[6] (g)	%DV	Fiber[8] (g)	%DV	Sugars[6] (g)	Protein (g)	Vitamin A (%DV)	Vitamin C[7] (%DV)	Calcium (%DV)	Iron (%DV)
salsa, med, Guiltless Gourmet	30		10	0	0	0	0	0	0	0	140	4	2	1	0	0	1	0	2	6	2	2
salsa, med/mild, S&W	61		20	0	0	0	0	0	0	0	190	8	4	1	1	3	3	1	4	4	0	4
salsa, Mexicana, Del Monte	32		5	0	0	0	0	0	0	0	200	8	2	1	1	4	0	0	6	2	0	0
salsa, mild, Frito-Lay	33		15	0	0	0	0	0	0	0	230	9	3	1	1	3	1	<1	8	0	0	0
salsa, mild, Safeway Select	28		10	0	0	0	0	0	0	0	150	6	2	1	0	0	0	0	0	0	0	0
salsa, mild, Sun Vista	32		5	0	0	0	0	0	0	0	210	9	0	0	0	0	<1	0	4	4	0	0
salsa, roasted garlic, Marie's	31		10	0	0	0	0	0	0	0	230	10	2	1	0	0	2	0	2	8	0	0
salsa, thick & chunky, hot, Ortega	31		10	0	0	0	0	0	0	0	210	9	2	0	0	0	1	0	2	6	0	0
salsa, thick & chunky, med/mild, Ortega	31		10	0	0	0	0	0	0	0	320	14	2	0	0	0	1	0	2	4	0	0
salsa, verde, Del Monte	32		10	0	0	0	0	0	0	0	280	12	2	1	<1	2	1	0	0	4	0	4
salsa w/chipotle, S&W	61		20	0	0	0	0	0	0	0	190	8	4	1	<1	0	3	<1	4	4	0	4
salsa w/cilantro, S&W	61		20	0	0	0	0	0	0	0	190	8	4	1	1	3	3	1	4	4	0	4
seafood cocktail sauce, Del Monte	78		100	0	0	0	0	0	0	0	910	38	24	8	0	0	22	1	20	0	0	0
seafood cocktail sauce, S&W	20		20	0	0	0	0	0	0	0	220	9	5	2	0	0	4	0	0	0	0	0
sloppy joe sauce, Del Monte	67		70	0	0	0	0	0	0	0	680	28	16	5	0	0	13	1	50	20	0	6
sloppy joe sauce, Libby's	78		45	0	0	0	0	0	0	0	430	18	10	3	1	3	4	1	6	10	2	2
spagh sauce, Del Monte	125		80	10	0	0	0	0	0	0	470	19	15	5	<1	3	10	2	10	35	4	8
spagh sauce, Campbell's	125		120	15	1.5	2	0	0	0	0	550	23	25	8	2	8	17	2	15	15	2	6
spagh sauce, extra garlic & onion, Campbell's	125		60	10	1	2	0	0	<5	0	370	15	12	4	2	8	8	3	25	25	6	2
spagh sauce, garden combo, Prego	130		90	10	1	2	0.5	3	0	0	480	20	16	5	3	12	12	2	25	50	2	4
spagh sauce, garlic & cheese, Prego	125		130	30	3.5	5	1	5	0	0	610	25	22	7	3	12	14	3	30	30	6	6
spagh sauce, garlic supreme, Prego	126		130	25	3	5	0.5	3	0	0	570	24	23	8	3	12	15	3	20	8	6	8
spagh sauce, green peppers & mushrooms, Del Monte	125		70	10	1	1	0	0	0	0	320	13	13	4	<1	2	6	2	15	40	4	8
spagh sauce, grnd beef, Campbell's	126		100	15	1.5	2	0	0	<1	0	600	25	19	6	2	8	12	2	15	15	2	6
spagh sauce, Ital, Campbell's	125		120	15	1.5	2	0	0	<5	0	550	23	25	8	2	8	12	2	15	15	2	6

Consult a similar product for brand names not listed.

Food Name	Serving Size	gm	mL	Calories	Calories from Fat	Total Fat (g)	%DV	Saturated Fat (g)	%DV	Cholesterol (mg)	%DV	Sodium (mg)	%DV	Total Carbohydrates (g)	%DV	Fiber (g)	%DV	Sugars (g)	Protein (g)	Vitamin A (%DV)	Vitamin C (%DV)	Calcium (%DV)	Iron (%DV)
spagh sauce, meat, Del Monte	1/2 cup	125		70	15	1.5	3	0	0	<5	0	390	16	13	4	<1	3	10	3	15	35	4	6
spagh sauce, meat, Prego	1/2 cup	125		140	50	6	9	1.5	8	5	2	500	21	21	7	3	12	13	3	25	20	4	10
spagh sauce, mushroom & extra spice, Prego	1/2 cup	130		120	35	4	6	0	0	0	0	510	21	19	6	3	12	12	2	30	15	4	4
spagh sauce, mushroom & garlic, Campbell's	1/2 cup	125		90	10	1	2	0	0	0	0	540	23	19	6	2	8	10	2	15	15	2	6
spagh sauce, mushroom & green pepper, Prego	1/2 cup	130		120	40	4.5	6	0.5	3	5	2	430	18	18	6	6	24	11	2	20	6	6	6
spagh sauce, mushroom & onion, Prego	1/2 cup	125		110	25	3	5	1	5	5	2	500	21	18	6	3	12	11	2	15	15	4	4
spagh sauce, mushroom & tomato, Prego	1/2 cup	130		110	35	3	5	1	5	0	0	510	21	19	6	3	12	8	2	25	15	2	6
spagh sauce, mushroom, Campbell's	1/2 cup	125		100	10	1	2	0	0	0	0	530	22	22	7	2	8	15	2	15	20	2	6
spagh sauce, mushroom parmesan, Prego	1/2 cup	126		120	30	3.5	5	1	5	10	3	570	24	19	6	3	12	12	3	20	15	8	6
spagh sauce, mushroom, Prego	1/2 cup	125		150	45	5	8	1.5	8	0	0	670	28	23	8	3	12	14	2	25	25	4	6
spagh sauce, mushroom supreme, Prego	1/2 cup	130		130	40	4.5	7	0.5	3	5	2	490	20	21	7	3	12	13	3	20	10	4	8
spagh sauce, onion & garlic, Prego	1/2 cup	125		110	45	3	5	0.5	3	0	0	420	18	19	6	3	12	12	2	25	35	4	6
spagh sauce, Prego	1/2 cup	125		140	40	4.5	7	1.5	8	5	2	610	25	23	8	2	8	15	2	20	15	4	8
spagh sauce, S&W	1/4 cup	61		20	0	0	0	0	0	0	0	210	9	4	1	1	4	3	1	10	2	0	6
spagh sauce, sausage & pepper, Prego	1/2 cup	125		180	80	9	14	2.5	13	10	3	570	24	22	7	3	12	12	4	20	35	6	8
spagh sauce, 3-cheese, Prego	1/2 cup	125		100	20	2	3	0.5	3	0	0	480	20	20	7	3	12	14	3	15	40	6	8
spagh sauce, tomato & basil, Prego	1/2 cup	125		110	30	3	5	0.5	3	5	2	420	18	19	6	3	12	12	2	25	35	4	6
spagh sauce, tomato, onion, & garlic, Prego	1/2 cup	130		110	30	4	5	1	5	0	0	480	20	19	6	3	12	13	2	15	25	4	4
spagh sauce, tomato parmesan, Prego	1/2 cup	126		120	30	3	5	1	5	5	2	570	24	19	6	3	12	13	3	20	15	8	6
spagh sauce, tomato supreme, Prego	1/2 cup	126		120	25	3	5	0.5	3	0	0	580	24	20	7	3	12	14	2	20	15	6	6

Food Name	Serving Size gm	mL	Calories	Calories from Fat	Total Fat (g)	%DV	Saturated Fat (g)	%DV	Cholesterol (mg)	%DV	Sodium (mg)	%DV	Total Carbohydrates[8] (g)	%DV	Fiber[6] (g)	%DV	Sugars[8] (g)	Protein (g)	Vitamin A (%DV)	Vitamin C[7] (%DV)	Calcium (%DV)	Iron (%DV)
spagh sauce, veg supreme, Prego	130	½ cup	90	30	3	5	0.5	3	5	2	490	20	15	5	3	12	10	2	25	4	4	4
spagh sauce, zesty basil, Prego	130	½ cup	110	15	2	2	0.5	3	0	0	510	21	22	7	3	12	15	2	30	15	6	2
spagh sauce, zesty oregano, Prego	125	½ cup	140	30	3	5	1	5	0	0	580	24	25	8	3	12	15	2	25	25	4	6
taco sauce, hot, Ortega	16	1 tbsp	10	0	0	0	0	0	0	0	120	5	2	1	0	0	1	0	2	0	0	0
taco sauce, med/mild, Ortega	16	1 tbsp	10	0	0	0	0	0	0	0	125	5	2	1	0	0	1	0	2	0	0	0
tomato paste, Contadina	33	2 tbsp	30	0	0	0	0	0	0	0	20	1	6	2	1	6	3	2	10	10	0	4
tomato paste, Del Monte	33	2 tbsp	30	0	0	0	0	0	0	0	25	1	7	2	2	8	5	1	15	15	0	2
tomato paste, S&W	33	2 tbsp	30	0	0	0	0	0	0	0	20	1	6	2	1	4	3	2	10	10	0	4
tomato sauce, Contadina	61	¼ cup	20	0	0	0	0	0	0	0	280	12	4	1	<1	2	1	<1	6	0	0	2
tomato sauce, Del Monte	61	¼ cup	20	0	0	0	0	0	0	0	340	14	4	1	<1	3	4	<1	4	8	0	2
tomato sauce, garden Ital herb, S&W	122	½ cup	35	0	0	0	0	0	0	0	470	20	9	3	2	8	7	2	20	4	2	10
tomato sauce, garden mild Mexican, S&W	61	¼ cup	20	0	0	0	0	0	0	0	190	8	4	1	1	3	3	1	4	4	0	4
tomato sauce, garden orig, S&W	61	¼ cup	20	0	0	0	0	0	0	0	200	8	4	1	1	0	2	0	6	8	2	8
tomato sauce, Ital, Contadina	61	¼ cup	15	0	0	0	0	0	0	0	320	13	4	1	1	3	1	<1	6	10	0	2
tomato sauce, S&W	61	¼ cup	20	0	0	0	0	0	0	0	300	11	4	1	1	4	2	1	6	4	0	4
tomato sauce, thick & zesty, Contadina	62	¼ cup	20	0	0	0	0	0	0	0	340	14	3	1	1	4	2	1	8	8	0	4
tomato, sun-dried dip, Marie's	28	2 tbsp	140	130	14	22	2	10	15	5	135	6	2	1	<1	1	<1	<1	0	0	0	0

Consult a similar product for brand names not listed.

Fruit

FRUIT

Food Name	Serving Size gm	mL	Calories	Calories from Fat	Total Fat (g)	%DV	Saturated Fat (g)	%DV	Cholesterol (mg)	%DV	Sodium (mg)	%DV	Total Carbohydrates (g)	%DV	Fiber (g)	%DV	Sugars (g)	Protein (g)	Vitamin A (%DV)	Vitamin C (%DV)	Calcium (%DV)	Iron (%DV)
apple fritters, frzn, Mrs. Paul's	2 fritters	125	260	100	11	17	3.5	18	5	2	570	24	36	12	2	8	15	3	0	10	4	6
apple, raw	1 medium	154	80	0	0	0	0	0	0	0	0	0	22	7	5	20	16	0	2	8	0	2
applesauce, Gravenstein, cnd/bottled, S&W	1/2 cup	122	90	0	0	0	0	0	0	0	5	0	21	7	1	4	13	0	2	0	0	4
applesauce, Gravenstein, unsweetened, cnd, S&W	1/2 cup	122	50	0	0	0	0	0	0	0	5	0	13	4	2	8	10	0	2	2	0	2
apples, escalloped, frzn, Stouffer's	2/3 cup	158	170	20	2	4	0	2	0	0	5	0	37	12	3	10	32	1	0	40	0	0
apple rings, spiced, S&W	2 pieces	32	25	0	0	0	0	0	0	0	20	1	7	2	1	4	6	0	0	0	0	0
apple slices, dried, Del Monte	1/3 cup	40	80	0	0	0	0	0	0	0	310	13	23	8	5	19	18	0	0	2	0	2
apricot, dried, Del Monte	1/3 cup	40	80	0	0	0	0	0	0	0	5	0	25	8	6	24	19	2	90	8	2	10
apricot, heavy syrup, cnd, Del Monte	1/2 cup	127	100	0	0	0	0	0	0	0	10	0	26	9	1	4	25	0	40	8	0	2
apricot, heavy syrup, whole, peeled, cnd, S&W	1/2 cup	129	110	0	0	0	0	0	0	0	15	1	26	9	1	4	27	1	8	2	0	0
apricot, lite syrup, cnd, Del Monte	1/2 cup	122	60	0	0	0	0	0	0	0	10	0	16	5	1	4	15	0	40	8	0	2
avocado, raw	1/3 medium	30	55	45	5	8	1	5	0	0	0	0	3	1	3	12	0	1	0	4	0	0
banana, raw	1 medium	126	110	0	0	0	0	0	0	0	0	0	22	7	5	20	16	0	2	8	0	2
blueberries, wild Maine, heavy syrup, cnd, S&W	1/3 cup	100	70	0	0	0	0	0	0	0	0	0	16	5	6	24	12	0	0	4	2	6
cantaloupe, raw	1/4 medium	134	50	0	0	0	0	0	0	0	25	1	12	4	1	4	11	1	100	80	2	2
cherries, dark, sweet, heavy syrup, cnd, S&W	1/2 cup	133	140	0	0	0	0	0	0	0	10	0	34	11	1	4	26	1	0	2	0	2
cherries, glacé, green/red, S&W	5 pieces	32	80	0	0	0	0	0	0	0	20	1	20	7	0	0	16	0	0	0	0	4
cherries, maraschino, green/red, S&W	1 cherry	8	10	0	0	0	0	0	0	0	0	0	3	1	0	0	3	0	0	0	0	0
cherries, red, heavy syrup, cnd, Del Monte	1/2 cup	120	100	0	0	0	0	0	0	0	10	0	24	8	<1	2	24	<1	0	20	2	2
cherries, red, tart, cnd, TownHouse	1/2 cup	122	35	0	0	0	0	0	0	0	15	1	7	2	1	4	7	1	15	0	0	0
cherries, Royal Anne, sweet, light syrup, cnd, S&W	1/2 cup	133	140	0	0	0	0	0	0	0	15	1	33	11	1	4	26	1	0	4	0	2

Food Name	Serving Size	gm	mL	Calories	Calories from Fat	Total Fat (g)	%DV	Saturated Fat (g)	%DV	Cholesterol (mg)	%DV	Sodium (mg)	%DV	Total Carbohydrates (g)	%DV	Fiber (g)	%DV	Sugars (g)	Protein (g)	Vitamin A (%DV)	Vitamin C (%DV)	Calcium (%DV)	Iron (%DV)
cherries, sweet, raw	21 cherries	140		90	0	0	1	0	0	0	0	0	0	22	7	3	12	19	2	2	15	2	2
cherry pie filling, cnd, Lucky Leaf	½ cup	85		60	0	0	0	0	0	0	0	10	1	14	5	0	0	8	0	10	0	0	0
crab apple, spiced, S&W	1 piece	25		35	0	0	0	0	0	0	0	15	1	8	3	1	4	5	0	0	0	0	0
cranberry sauce, jellied/whole, cnd, S&W	¼ cup	70		100	0	0	0	0	0	0	0	15	1	26	9	1	4	17	0	0	0	0	0
cranberry sauce, whole berry, cnd, Ocean Spray	¼ cup	70		110	0	0	0	0	0	0	0	35	1	28	9	1	4	27	0	0	0	0	0
currents, zante, S&W	¼ cup	40		130	0	0	0	0	0	0	0	10	0	31	10	2	8	29	1	0	0	2	6
date, Del Monte	5-6 dates	40		120	0	0	0	0	0	0	0	0	0	31	10	3	14	29	1	0	0	2	2
date, Sun World	5-6 dates	40		120	0	0	0	0	0	0	0	0	0	31	10	3	14	29	1	0	0	2	2
fig, kadota, S&W	5 pieces	140		140	10	1	2	0	0	0	0	5	0	32	11	3	12	18	0	0	0	6	4
fruit cocktail, heavy syrup, cnd, Del Monte	½ cup	127		100	0	0	0	0	0	0	0	10	0	24	8	1	4	23	0	4	4	0	2
fruit cocktail, heavy syrup, cnd, S&W	½ cup	128		90	0	0	0	0	0	0	0	15	1	23	8	1	4	22	0	4	2	0	0
fruit cocktail, jce pak, cnd, Del Monte	½ cup	124		60	0	0	0	0	0	0	0	10	0	15	5	1	4	14	0	4	4	0	2
fruit cocktail, jce pak, cnd, S&W	½ cup	126		80	0	0	1	0	0	0	0	20	1	20	7	2	8	13	1	6	2	0	2
grapefruit, jce pak, cnd, S&W	⅔ cup	150		50	0	0	0	0	0	0	0	25	1	14	5	0	0	9	0	0	40	2	4
grapefruit, jce pak, cnd, TownHouse/Safeway	⅔ cup	150		50	0	0	0	0	0	0	0	25	1	14	5	0	0	9	0	0	40	2	4
grapefruit, raw	½ medium	154		60	0	0	0	0	0	0	0	0	0	16	5	6	24	10	1	15	110	2	0
grapes, light syrup, cnd, S&W	½ cup	133		130	0	0	0	0	0	0	0	35	1	33	11	<1	<1	31	<1	4	6	0	8
grapes, raw	1½ cups	138		90	10	1	2	0	0	0	0	0	0	24	8	1	4	23	1	2	25	2	2
grapes, Thompson, heavy syrup, cnd, S&W	½ cup	123		100	0	0	0	0	0	0	0	20	1	23	8	<1	<1	19	<1	0	0	0	8
honeydew melon, raw	1/10 melon	134		50	0	0	0	0	0	0	0	35	1	13	4	1	4	12	1	2	45	0	2
kiwifruit, raw	2 medium	148		100	10	1	2	0	0	0	0	0	0	24	8	4	16	16	2	2	240	6	4
lemon, raw	1 medium	58		15	0	0	0	0	0	0	0	5	0	5	2	1	4	1	0	0	40	2	0
lime, raw	1 medium	67		20	0	0	0	0	0	0	0	0	0	7	2	2	8	0	0	0	35	0	0

Consult a similar product for brand names not listed.

Food Name	Serving Size	gm	mL	Calories	Calories from Fat	Total Fat (g)	%DV	Saturated Fat (g)	%DV	Cholesterol (mg)	%DV	Sodium (mg)	%DV	Total Carbohydrates[B] (g)	%DV	Fiber[B] (g)	%DV	Sugars[B] (g)	Protein (g)	Vitamin A (%DV)	Vitamin C[7] (%DV)	Calcium (%DV)	Iron (%DV)
mandarin oranges, ice pak, cnd, S&W	2/3 cup	156		70	0	0	0	0	0	0	0	0	0	16	5	0	0	16	1	25	70	2	2
mandarin oranges, light syrup, cnd, Del Monte	1/2 cup	126		80	0	0	0	0	0	0	0	10	0	19	6	<1	2	19	0	0	20	0	4
mandarin oranges, light syrup, cnd, S&W	2/3 cup	154		100	0	0	0	0	0	0	0	15	1	23	8	1	4	21	1	11	30	0	4
mandarin oranges, light syrup, cnd, Safeway	1/2 cup	140		80	0	0	0	0	0	0	0	20	7	20	1	1	4	19	1	6	35	2	4
mincemeat, S&W	1/4 cup	95		180	20	2	4	1.5	8	0	0	210	9	43	14	4	16	37	<1	0	10	4	25
mixed fruit, chunky, heavy syrup, cnd, Del Monte	1/2 cup	127		100	0	0	0	0	0	0	0	10	0	24	8	1	4	23	0	4	4	0	2
mixed fruit, chunky, ice pak, cnd, S&W	1/2 cup	123		70	0	0	0	0	0	0	0	20	1	19	6	3	12	14	1	4	2	0	0
mixed fruit, chunky, ice pak, cnd, Safeway	1/2 cup	124		60	0	0	0	0	0	0	0	10	0	15	5	1	4	14	0	4	4	0	2
mixed fruit, dried, Del Monte	1/3 cup	40		110	0	0	0	0	0	0	0	50	2	30	10	5	18	17	<1	25	2	0	6
nectarine, raw	1 medium	140		70	0	0.5	1	0	0	0	0	0	0	16	5	2	8	12	1	4	15	0	2
olives, black,[30] colossal, Vlasic	2 olives	15		20	15	2	3	0	0	0	0	110	5	1	0	0	0	0	0	0	0	0	0
olives, black,[30] extra large, pitted, S&W	3 olives	14		25	20	2.5	4	0	0	0	0	110	5	1	0	0	0	0	0	0	0	0	0
olives, black,[30] extra large, Vlasic	3 olives	14		25	20	2.5	4	0	0	0	0	115	5	1	0	0	0	0	0	25	0	0	0
olives, black,[30] jalapeno, chopped/sliced, Vlasic	1 tbsp	15		25	20	2.5	4	0	0	0	0	115	5	1	0	0	0	0	0	4	0	0	0
olives, black,[30] jumbo, pitted, S&W	3 olives	18		25	20	2	3	0	0	0	0	135	6	1	0	0	0	0	0	0	0	0	0
olives, black,[30] jumbo, Vlasic	3 olives	18		25	20	2	3	0	0	0	0	135	6	1	0	0	0	0	0	0	0	0	0
olives, black,[30] large, pitted, Vlasic	4 olives	15		25	20	2.5	4	0	0	0	0	55	2	1	0	0	0	0	0	0	0	0	0
olives, black,[30] small, pitted, Vlasic	6 olives	15		25	20	2.5	4	0	0	0	0	115	5	1	0	0	0	0	0	0	0	0	0
olives, black,[30] small/med/large, Vlasic	4-6 olives	15		25	20	2.5	4	0	0	0	0	115	5	1	0	0	0	0	0	0	0	0	0
olives, black,[30] super colossal, Vlasic	1 olive	10		15	10	1	2	0	0	0	0	75	3	1	0	0	0	0	0	0	0	0	0

Food Name	Serving Size	gm	mL	Calories	Calories from Fat	Total Fat (g)	%DV	Saturated Fat (g)	%DV	Cholesterol (mg)	%DV	Sodium (mg)	%DV	Total Carbohydrates[6] (g)	%DV	Fiber[6] (g)	%DV	Sugars[6] (g)	Protein (g)	Vitamin A (%DV)	Vitamin C[7] (%DV)	Calcium (%DV)	Iron (%DV)
olives, black,[30] super colossal, with pits, S&W	1 olive	11		15	10	1.5	2	0	0	0	0	80	3	1	0	0	0	0	0	0	0	0	0
olives, green,[31] alcaparrado, Vlasic	1 tbsp	15		20	15	1.5	2	0	0	0	0	250	10	1	0	0	0	0	0	0	0	0	0
olives, green,[31] Manzanilla, stuffed, S&W	3 olives	14		25	20	2	3	0	0	0	0	240	10	1	0	0	0	0	0	0	0	0	0
olives, green,[31] pitted, Vlasic	8 olives	15		20	20	2	3	0	0	0	0	280	12	1	0	0	0	0	0	0	0	0	0
olives, green,[31] queen, S&W	2 olives	13		20	15	2	3	0	0	0	0	220	9	1	0	0	0	0	0	0	0	0	0
olives, green,[31] queen, stuffed, large, S&W	1 olive	10		10	10	1	2	0	0	0	0	180	8	1	0	0	0	0	0	0	0	0	0
olives, green,[31] queen, stuffed, med, S&W	2 olives	16		20	15	1.5	2	0	0	0	0	290	12	1	0	0	0	0	0	0	0	0	0
olives, green,[31] queen, stuffed, small, S&W	2 olives	14		15	15	1.5	2	0	0	0	0	250	10	1	0	0	0	0	0	0	0	0	0
olives, green,[31] queen, stuffed, Vlasic	2 olives	16		20	15	1.5	2	0	0	0	0	340	14	1	0	0	0	0	0	0	0	0	0
olives, green,[31] queen, whole, Vlasic	2 olives	14		20	15	1.5	2	0	0	0	0	320	13	1	0	0	0	0	0	0	0	0	0
olives, green,[31] sliced, Vlasic	1 tbsp	15		20	15	1.5	2	0	0	0	0	320	13	1	0	0	0	0	0	0	0	0	0
olives, green,[31] stuffed, Vlasic	6 olives	16		20	20	2	3	0	0	0	0	350	15	1	0	0	0	0	0	0	0	0	0
orange, raw	1 medium	154		70	0	0	0	0	0	0	0	0	0	21	7	7	28	14	1	2	130	6	2
peach, cling, heavy syrup, cnd, S&W	1/2 cup	128		100	0	0	0	0	0	0	0	10	0	24	8	3	1	23	1	6	2	0	0
peach, cling, ice pak, cnd, S&W Natural Style	1/2 cup	126		80	0	0	0	0	0	0	0	20	1	19	6	4	1	13	1	8	2	0	0
peach, cling, spiced, heavy syrup, cnd, S&W	1 peach	123		100	0	0	0	0	0	0	0	20	1	23	8	<1		18	<1	10	0	0	0
peach, dried, Del Monte	1/3 cup	40		90	0	0	0	0	0	0	0	0	0	26	9	5	21	21	1	10	10	0	6
peach, freestone, heavy syrup, cnd, S&W	1/2 cup	140		100	0	0	0	0	0	0	0	50	2	23	8	0	0	22	<1	10	2	0	0
peach, heavy syrup, cnd, Del Monte	1/2 cup	127		100	0	0	0	0	0	0	0	10	0	24	8	4	1	23	0	6	8	0	2
peach, ice pak, cnd, Del Monte	1/2 cup	124		60	0	0	0	0	0	0	0	10	0	15	5	4	1	14	0	6	8	0	2
peach, raw	1 medium	98		40	0	0	0	0	0	0	0	0	0	10	3	2	8	9	1	2	10	0	0

Consult a similar product for brand names not listed.

Food Name	Serving Size	gm	mL	Calories	Calories from Fat	Total Fat (g)	%DV	Saturated Fat (g)	%DV	Cholesterol (mg)	%DV	Sodium (mg)	%DV	Total Carbohydrates (g)	%DV	Fiber (g)	%DV	Sugars (g)	Protein (g)	Vitamin A (%DV)	Vitamin C (%DV)	Calcium (%DV)
peach, syrup pak w/cinn, cnd, S&W Sweet Memory Sun	1/2 cup	130		70	0	0	0	0	0	0	0	15	1	19	6	<1	0	17	<1	8	8	2
peach, syrup pak, cnd, S&W Calif Sun	1/2 cup	130		80	0	0	0	0	0	0	0	20	1	20	7	1	4	14	<1	4	100	0	2
peach, syrup pak, cnd, S&W Tropical Sun	1/2 cup	130		80	0	0	0	0	0	0	0	15	1	19	6	0	0	16	<1	8	100	0	0
pear halves, Bartlett, heavy syrup, cnd, S&W	1/2 cup	130		90	0	0	0	0	0	0	0	10	0	22	8	2	8	18	0	0	2	0	2
pear halves, Bartlett, jce pak, cnd, S&W	1/2 cup	125		80	0	0	0	0	0	0	0	10	0	21	7	2	8	17	0	0	2	0	2
pear halves, heavy syrup, cnd, Del Monte	1/2 cup	127		100	0	0	0	0	0	0	0	10	0	24	8	1	4	23	0	0	4	0	0
pear halves in pear jce, Townhouse/Safeway	1/2 cup	125		60	0	0	0	0	0	0	0	10	1	14	5	1	5	14	0	0	0	0	0
pear, jce pak, cnd, Del Monte	1/2 cup	124		60	0	0	0	0	0	0	0	10	0	15	5	1	4	14	0	0	4	0	0
pear, raw	1 medium	166		100	10	1	2	0	0	0	0	0	0	25	8	4	16	17	1	0	10	2	0
pear, syrup pak, cnd, S&W Calif Sun	1/2 cup	135		80	0	0	0	0	0	0	0	10	0	19	6	<1	0	14	<1	0	100	0	2
pineapple chunks, heavy syrup, cnd, Del Monte	1/2 cup	123		90	0	0	0	0	0	0	0	10	0	24	8	1	4	22	0	0	20	0	2
pineapple chunks, jce pak, cnd, Del Monte	1/2 cup	122		70	0	0	0	0	0	0	0	10	0	17	6	1	4	15	0	0	20	0	2
pineapple glacé, slices, natural/green/red, S&W	1 piece	63		180	0	0	0	0	0	0	0	40	2	46	15	0	0	43	0	0	0	0	0
pineapple glacé, wedges, natural/tricolor, S&W	5 pieces	29		80	0	0	0	0	0	0	0	20	1	21	7	0	0	20	0	0	0	0	0
pineapple, raw	2 slices	112		60	0	0	0	0	0	0	0	10	0	16	5	1	4	13	1	0	25	2	2
pineapple, slices, cnd, S&W	2 pieces	117		90	0	0	0	0	0	0	0	10	0	23	8	1	4	21	0	0	20	0	2
plum, purple, cnd, S&W	1/2 cup	133		130	0	0	0	0	0	0	0	15	1	33	11	2	8	26	0	20	2	0	0
plum, raw	2 medium	132		80	10	1	2	0	0	0	0	0	0	19	6	2	8	10	1	6	20	0	0
prune, Del Monte	1/4 cup	40		120	0	0	0	0	0	0	0	5	0	29	10	3	11	14	1	10	4	0	4

Food Name	Serving Size gm	mL	Calories	Calories from Fat	Total Fat (g)	%DV	Saturated Fat (g)	%DV	Cholesterol (mg)	%DV	Sodium (mg)	%DV	Total Carbohydrates[8] (g)	%DV	Fiber[8] (g)	%DV	Sugars[8] (g)	Protein (g)	Vitamin A (%DV)	Vitamin C[7] (%DV)	Calcium (%DV)	Iron (%DV)
prune, stewed, heavy syrup, cnd, S&W	140		210	0	0	0	0	0	0	0	15	1	52	17	4	16	25	2	15	6	0	4
raisins, Del Monte	40		120	0	0	0	0	0	0	0	20	1	33	11	5	18	28	1	0	8	2	4
raisins, golden, Del Monte	40		120	0	0	0	0	0	0	0	20	1	33	11	5	18	28	1	0	8	2	4
raisins, golden/dark, S&W	40		130	0	0	0	0	0	0	0	10	0	31	10	2	8	29	1	0	0	2	6
raisins w/strawberry yogurt coating, Del Monte	26		110	25	3	4	2.5	14	0	0	25	1	20	7	<1	3	17	2	0	0	4	0
raisins w/van yogurt coating, Del Monte	26		110	25	3	4	2.5	14	0	0	25	1	20	7	<1	3	17	2	0	0	4	0
strawberries, raw	147		45	0	0	0	0	0	0	0	0	0	12	4	4	16	8	1	0	160	2	4
sweet potato'n apples, candied, frzn, Mrs. Paul's	175		270	0	0	0	0	0	5	2	90	4	66	22	3	12	47	0	50	20	15	6
tangerine, raw	109		50	0	0.5	1	0	0	0	0	0	0	15	5	3	12	12	1	0	50	4	0
tropical fruit salad, light syrup, cnd, Del Monte	126		80	0	0	0	0	0	0	0	10	0	21	7	1	4	20	0	4	80	0	2
watermelon, raw	280		80	0	0	0	0	0	0	0	10	0	27	9	2	8	25	1	20	25	2	4

1/16 melon (2 cups diced)

Consult a similar product for brand names not listed.

FRUIT JUICES AND JUICE DRINKS

Food Name	Serving Size	gm	mL	Calories	Calories from Fat	Total Fat (g)	%DV	Saturated Fat (g)	%DV	Cholesterol (mg)	%DV	Sodium (mg)	%DV	Total Carbohydrates[6] (g)	%DV	Fiber[6] (g)	%DV	Sugars[6] (g)	Protein (g)	Vitamin A (%DV)	Vitamin C[7] (%DV)	Calcium (%DV)	Iron (%DV)
apple ice, cnd, Bombay	8 fl oz (1 cup)	240		100	0	0	0	0	0	0	0	25	1	25	8	0	0	22	0	0	190	2	2
apple ice, cnd, S&W	8 fl oz (1 cup)	237		120	0	0	0	0	0	0	0	0	0	30	10	0	0	25	0	0	0	0	0
apple ice, Ocean Spray	8 fl oz (1 cup)	240		110	0	0	0	0	0	0	0	35	1	28	9	0	0	28	0	0	0	0	2
apple ice, Tropicana	8 fl oz (1 cup)	240		120	0	0	0	0	0	0	0	25	1	29	10	0	0	26	<1	0	50	2	0
apple raspberry blackberry ice, Tropicana	8 fl oz (1 cup)	240		130	0	0	0	0	0	0	0	20	1	32	11	0	0	31	0	0	0	0	0
apricot nectar, cnd, S&W	5 ½ oz	173		100	0	0	0	0	0	0	0	10	1	24	8	1	4	19	1	50	50	0	2
berry punch, Tropicana	8 fl oz (1 cup)	240		130	0	0	0	0	0	0	0	15	1	32	11	0	0	30	0	0	0	0	0
blueberry cranberry drink, Ocean Spray	8 fl oz (1 cup)	240		160	0	0	0	0	0	0	0	35	1	41	14	0	0	41	0	0	100	0	0
cherry cranberry drink, Ocean Spray	8 fl oz (1 cup)	240		160	0	0	0	0	0	0	0	35	1	39	13	0	0	39	0	0	100	0	4
citrus cranberry ice drink, Ocean Spray	8 fl oz (1 cup)	240		140	0	0	0	0	0	0	0	35	1	35	12	0	0	35	0	0	100	0	0
citrus medley, Tropicana	8 fl oz (1 cup)	240		120	0	0	0	0	0	0	0	25	1	31	10	0	0	27	<1	0	35	2	0
citrus peach ice drink, Ocean Spray	8 fl oz (1 cup)	240		120	0	0	0	0	0	0	0	35	1	30	10	0	0	30	0	6	100	0	0
citrus punch, Tropicana	8 fl oz (1 cup)	240		140	0	0	0	0	0	0	0	15	1	36	12	0	0	32	0	0	0	0	0
cranberry apple drink, Ocean Spray	8 fl oz (1 cup)	240		160	0	0	0	0	0	0	0	35	1	41	14	0	0	40	0	0	100	0	0
cranberry apricot drink, Ocean Spray	8 fl oz (1 cup)	240		160	0	0	0	0	0	0	0	35	1	40	13	0	0	40	0	30	0	0	0
cranberry juice cocktail, Ocean Spray	8 fl oz (1 cup)	240		140	0	0	0	0	0	0	0	35	1	34	11	0	0	34	0	0	100	0	2
cranberry medley, Tropicana	8 fl oz (1 cup)	240		120	0	0	0	0	0	0	0	20	1	29	10	0	0	26	<1	0	0	0	2
cranberry raspberry strawberry drink, Tropicana	8 fl oz (1 cup)	240		120	0	0	0	0	0	0	0	5	0	31	10	0	0	30	0	0	0	0	0
cranberry strawberry drink, Ocean Spray	8 fl oz (1 cup)	240		140	0	0	0	0	0	0	0	35	1	36	12	0	0	35	0	0	100	0	0
fruit medley, Tropicana	8 fl oz (1 cup)	240		130	0	0	0	0	0	0	0	25	1	32	11	0	0	27	<1	0	6	2	0
fruit punch, Ocean Spray	8 fl oz (1 cup)	240		130	0	0	0	0	0	0	0	35	1	32	11	0	0	32	0	0	100	0	0
fruit punch, Tropicana	8 fl oz (1 cup)	240		130	0	0	0	0	0	0	0	15	1	32	11	0	0	30	0	0	0	0	0
grape cranberry drink, Ocean Spray	8 fl oz (1 cup)	240		170	0	0	0	0	0	0	0	35	1	41	14	0	0	41	0	0	100	0	0

Food Name	Serving Size	gm	mL	Calories	Calories from Fat	Total Fat (g)	%DV	Saturated Fat (g)	%DV	Cholesterol (mg)	%DV	Sodium (mg)	%DV	Total Carbohydrates[6] (g)	%DV	Fiber[6] (g)	%DV	Sugars[6] (g)	Protein (g)	Vitamin A (%DV)	Vitamin C[7] (%DV)	Calcium (%DV)	Iron (%DV)
grape jce, Tropicana	8 fl oz (1 cup)		240	160	0	0	0	0	0	0	0	25	1	39	13	0	0	36	<1	0	0	0	4
grapefruit jce, cnd, Bombay	8 fl oz (1 cup)		240	90	0	0	0	0	0	0	0	20	1	21	7	0	0	15	<1	0	150	0	0
grapefruit jce, cnd, S&W	6 fl oz (¾ cup)		177	80	0	0	0	0	0	0	0	0	0	18	6	0	0	18	1	0	80	0	0
grapefruit jce, Ocean Spray	8 fl oz (1 cup)		240	100	0	0	0	0	0	0	0	35	1	24	8	0	0	23	1	0	100	2	0
grapefruit jce, Tropicana	8 fl oz (1 cup)		240	90	0	0	0	0	0	0	0	0	0	22	7	0	0	17	<1	0	100	2	0
grapefruit, pink, drink, Tropicana	8 fl oz (1 cup)		240	120	0	0	0	0	0	0	0	20	1	29	10	0	0	28	0	0	8	0	0
grapefruit, pink, jce cocktail, Ocean Spray	8 fl oz (1 cup)		240	110	0	0	0	0	0	0	0	35	1	28	9	0	0	28	<1	0	100	0	0
grapefruit, red & tangerine, jce drink, Ocean Spray	8 fl oz (1 cup)		240	130	0	0	0	0	0	0	0	35	1	32	11	0	0	32	0	0	100	0	0
grapefruit, red, jce drink, Ocean Spray	8 fl oz (1 cup)		240	130	0	0	0	0	0	0	0	35	1	33	11	0	0	33	0	0	100	0	0
grapefruit, red, jce, Tropicana	8 fl oz (1 cup)		240	90	0	0	0	0	0	0	0	0	0	22	7	0	0	17	<1	0	50	2	0
guava & passion fruit jce drink, Mauna La'i	8 fl oz (1 cup)		240	130	0	0	0	0	0	0	0	35	1	32	11	0	0	32	0	10	100	0	0
guava fruit jce drink, Mauna La'i	8 fl oz (1 cup)		240	130	0	0	0	0	0	0	0	35	1	32	11	0	0	32	0	0	100	0	0
Hawaiian Punch	8 fl. oz (1 cup)		240	120	0	0	0	0	0	0	0	100	4	30	10	0	0	29	0	0	100	0	0
lemonade, Ocean Spray	8 fl oz (1 cup)		240	110	0	0	0	0	0	0	0	35	1	29	10	0	0	29	0	0	100	0	0
lemonade, Tropicana	10 fl oz (1 ¼ cups)		300	140	0	0	0	0	0	0	0	20	1	35	12	0	0	32	0	0	0	0	0
lemonade w/cranberry jce, Ocean Spray	8 fl oz (1 cup)		240	110	0	0	0	0	0	0	0	35	1	26	9	0	0	26	0	0	100	0	0
lemonade w/raspberry jce, Ocean Spray	8 fl oz (1 cup)		240	110	0	0	0	0	0	0	0	35	1	27	9	0	0	27	0	0	100	0	0
mango & guava fruit jce drink, Mauna La'i	8 fl oz (1 cup)		240	130	0	0	0	0	0	0	0	35	1	33	11	0	0	33	0	0	100	0	0
orange cranberry drink, Tropicana	8 fl oz (1 cup)		240	130	0	0	0	0	0	0	0	15	1	32	11	0	0	31	0	0	6	0	0
orange cranberry jce drink, Ocean Spray	8 fl oz (1 cup)		240	130	0	0	0	0	0	0	0	15	1	32	11	0	0	31	0	0	6	0	0
orange jce, cnd, Bombay	8 fl oz (1 cup)		240	110	0	0	0	0	0	0	0	20	1	25	8	0	0	23	1	2	200	0	0

Consult a similar product for brand names not listed.

Food Name	Serving Size	gm	mL	Calories	Calories from Fat	Total Fat (g)	%DV	Saturated Fat (g)	%DV	Cholesterol (mg)	%DV	Sodium (mg)	%DV	Total Carbohydrates[6] (g)	%DV	Fiber[6] (g)	%DV	Sugars[6] (g)	Protein (g)	Vitamin A (%DV)	Vitamin C[7] (%DV)	Calcium (%DV)	Iron (%DV)
orange jce, cnd, S&W	6 fl oz (¾ cup)		177	90	0	0	0	0	0	0	0	0	0	22	7	0	0	22	1	0	100	0	0
orange jce, Ocean Spray	8 fl oz (1 cup)		240	120	0	0	0	0	0	0	0	35	1	31	10	0	0	31	1	0	130	2	2
orange jce, Tropicana	8 fl oz (1 cup)		240	110	0	0	0	0	0	0	0	0	0	26	9	0	0	22	<1	0	50	2	0
orange jce, valencia, FloridaGold	8 fl oz (1 cup)		240	110	0	0	0	0	0	0	0	0	0	27	9	0	0	24	<1	0	130	0	0
orange peach drink, Tropicana	8 fl oz (1 cup)		240	120	0	0	0	0	0	0	0	20	1	31	10	0	0	30	0	0	15	0	0
orange raspberry drink, Tropicana	8 fl oz (1 cup)		240	120	0	0	0	0	0	0	0	20	1	31	10	0	0	30	0	0	6	0	0
orange strawberry banana drink, Tropicana	8 fl oz (1 cup)		240	120	0	0	0	0	0	0	0	20	1	29	10	0	0	28	0	0	10	0	0
orange strawberry guava drink, Tropicana	8 fl oz (1 cup)		240	120	0	0	0	0	0	0	0	20	1	29	10	0	0	28	0	0	6	0	0
pineapple jce, cnd, Bombay	8 fl oz (1 cup)		240	110	0	0	0	0	0	0	0	25	1	27	9	0	0	24	1	0	200	2	2
pineapple jce, cnd, S&W	12 fl oz (1½ cups)		355	180	0	0	0	0	0	0	0	20	1	45	15	3	12	42	1	0	100	6	6
pineapple jce, cnd, S&W	8 fl oz (1 cup)		240	110	0	0	0	0	0	0	0	15	1	29	10	2	8	27	0	0	100	4	4
pineapple jce, cnd, Del Monte	6 fl oz (¾ cup)		177	90	0	0	0	0	0	0	0	10	0	23	8	2	8	22	0	0	100	2	4
pineapple jce, Del Monte	8 fl oz (1 cup)		240	110	0	0	0	0	0	0	0	15	1	29	10	2	8	27	0	0	100	4	4
pineapple punch, Tropicana	10 fl oz (1¼ cups)		300	130	0	0	0	0	0	0	0	25	1	33	11	0	0	30	0	0	0	0	0
prune jce, cnd, S&W	8 fl oz (1 cup)		240	180	0	0	0	0	0	0	0	10	0	41	14	1	4	23	2	4	15	0	15
prune jce, Del Monte	8 fl oz (1 cup)		240	170	0	0	0	0	0	0	0	20	1	43	14	1	4	27	1	0	0	2	6
raspberry cranberry drink, Ocean Spray	8 fl oz (1 cup)		240	140	0	0	0	0	0	0	0	35	1	36	12	0	0	36	0	0	100	0	0

FRUIT SPREADS

Food Name	Serving Size	gm	mL	Calories	Calories from Fat	Total Fat (g)	%DV	Saturated Fat (g)	%DV	Cholesterol (mg)	%DV	Sodium (mg)	%DV	Total Carbohydrates[5] (g)	%DV	Fiber[6] (g)	%DV	Sugars[8] (g)	Protein (g)	Vitamin A (%DV)	Vitamin C[7] (%DV)	Calcium (%DV)	Iron (%DV)
All Fruit, apricot, Polaner	1 tbsp	18		40	0	0	0	0	0	0	0	0	0	10	3	0	0	10	0	0	6	0	0
All Fruit, black cherry, Polaner	1 tbsp	18		40	0	0	0	0	0	0	0	0	0	10	3	0	0	8	0	0	0	0	0
All Fruit, blueberry, Polaner	1 tbsp	17		40	0	0	0	0	0	0	0	5	0	9	3	0	0	10	0	0	0	0	0
All Fruit, grape, Polaner	1 tbsp	19		40	0	0	0	0	0	0	0	0	0	10	3	0	0	10	0	0	0	0	0
All Fruit, orange/other flavors,[32] Polaner	1 tbsp	18		40	0	0	0	0	0	0	0	0	0	10	3	0	0	9	0	0	0	0	0
All Fruit, peach, Polaner	1 tbsp	18		40	0	0	0	0	0	0	0	0	0	10	3	0	0	8	0	0	6	0	0
apple butter, Dutch Girl/Mary Ellen	1 tbsp	18		35	0	0	0	0	0	0	0	0	0	9	3	0	0	10	0	0	0	0	0
apple butter, Smucker's	1 tbsp	19		45	0	0	0	0	0	0	0	10	0	11	4	0	0	10	0	0	0	0	0
Fruit Spread, Smucker's	1 tbsp	19		45	0	0	0	0	0	0	0	0	0	11	4	0	0	10	0	0	0	0	0
peach butter, Smucker's	1 tbsp	19		45	0	0	0	0	0	0	0	10	0	11	4	0	0	10	0	0	0	0	0
preserves/jam/jelly/marmalade, Smucker's	1 tbsp	20		50	0	0	0	0	0	0	0	0	0	13	4	0	0	12	0	0	0	0	0
preserves, light, Smucker's	1 tbsp	17		20	0	0	0	0	0	0	0	5	0	5	2	0	0	4	0	0	0	0	0
preserves, low sugar, Smucker's	1 tbsp	17		25	0	0	0	0	0	0	0	0	0	6	2	0	0	5	0	0	0	0	0
Simply Fruit-Spreadable Fruit, Smucker's	1 tbsp	20		50	0	0	0	0	0	0	0	0	0	13	4	0	0	12	0	0	0	0	0
Super Spreaders & Peanuts Fruit Spread, Smucker's	1 tbsp	19		40	0	0	0	0	0	0	0	10	1	10	3	0	0	9	0	0	50	0	0

Consult a similar product for brand names not listed.

Milk, Cheese, Yogurt, and other Dairy Products

CHEESE AND CHEESE PRODUCTS

Food Name	Serving Size	gm	mL	Calories	Calories from Fat	Total Fat (g)	%DV	Saturated Fat (g)	%DV	Cholesterol (mg)	%DV	Sodium (mg)	%DV	Total Carbohydrates[a] (g)	%DV	Fiber[b] (g)	%DV	Sugars[b] (g)	Protein (g)	Vitamin A (%DV)	Vitamin C[7] (%DV)	Calcium (%DV)	Iron (%DV)
Am cheese spread, Easy Cheese	2 tbsp	34		100	60	7	11	4	22	25	8	400	17	2	1	0	0	2	6	4	0	15	0
Am cheese, Borden	1 slice	28		110	80	9	14	5	25	25	8	430	18	1	0	0	0	<1	6	4	0	15	0
Am cheese, Lucerne	1 slice	21		80	60	7	10	4	20	30	10	280	12	0	0	0	0	0	4	4	0	10	0
cheddar cheese soup, cnd cond, Campbell's	1/2 cup	124		130	70	8	12	3.5	18	20	7	1080	45	11	4	1	4	2	4	25	0	0	2
cheddar cheese, sharp, Lucerne	1 oz	28		110	80	9	14	5	27	30	9	180	8	1	0	0	0	0	7	6	0	20	0
cheese sauce, cnd, Franco-Am	1/4 cup	59		40	20	2	3	1	5	5	2	390	16	4	1	0	0	0	1	0	0	2	0
cheese soup w/broccoli, cnd cond, Campbell's	1/2 cup	124		110	60	7	11	3	15	10	3	860	36	9	3	2	8	2	3	30	2	2	4
cottage cheese, fat-free, Borden	1/2 cup	113		80	0	0	0	0	0	10	3	450	19	5	2	0	0	4	14	0	0	10	0
cottage cheese, low fat 1%, Borden	1/2 cup	113		80	10	1	2	0.5	3	10	3	430	18	5	2	0	0	4	12	0	0	8	0
cottage cheese, low fat 2%, Borden	1/2 cup	113		90	20	2	3	1.5	7	15	4	500	21	5	2	0	0	4	12	0	0	8	0
mozzarella cheese, low-moisture, part skim, Lucerne	1/4 cup	30		80	50	5	8	3	15	15	5	180	8	1	0	0	0	0	8	4	0	20	0
mozzarella cheese, part skim, Double H	1 oz	30		70	50	6	9	4	20	15	5	140	6	1	0	0	0	0	7	4	0	15	0
mozzarella nuggets, frzn, Banquet	6 pieces	81		210	100	11	16	4	20	10	4	1060	44	20	7	2	7	3	9	0	0	15	2
Muenster cheese, Lucerne	1 oz	28		100	70	8	13	5	24	30	9	170	7	1	0	0	0	0	7	6	0	20	0
nacho cheese soup/dip, cnd cond, Campbell's	1/2 cup	124		140	80	8	12	4	20	15	5	810	34	11	4	2	8	2	5	25	2	10	2
Neufchatel cheese, Lucerne	2 tbsp	30		70	60	6	10	4	21	20	7	100	4	2	1	0	0	2	2	4	0	2	0
Swiss cheese, Best Buy	1 oz	28		100	70	8	12	5	23	25	9	60	2	1	0	0	0	0	8	6	0	25	0

Food Name	Serving Size	gm	mL	Calories	Calories from Fat	Total Fat (g)	%DV	Saturated Fat (g)	%DV	Cholesterol (mg)	%DV	Sodium (mg)	%DV	Total Carbohydrates[5] (g)	%DV	Fiber[6] (g)	%DV	Sugars[8] (g)	Protein (g)	Vitamin A (%DV)	Vitamin C[7] (%DV)	Calcium (%DV)	Iron (%DV)
DAIRY-BASED DESSERTS																							
cheesecake, choc, mix not prepared, No-Bake Royal	1/6 package	56		220	30	4	6	1.5	6	<5	1	340	14	38	13	2	6	23	10	4	0	35	4
cheesecake, lite, mix not prepared, No-Bake Royal	1/8 package	29		120	30	4	6	1	6	<5	1	200	8	19	6	1	3	7	4	2	0	10	2
cheesecake, mix not prepared, No-Bake Royal	1/6 package	56		230	45	5	8	1.5	9	5	2	370	15	41	14	1	3	27	6	4	0	20	2
frzn yogurt, berry berry strawberry, fat-free, Borden	1/2 cup	71		100	0	0	0	0	0	0	0	45	2	21	7	0	0	16	3	6	4	10	0
frzn yogurt, black cherry, Borden	1/2 cup	72		110	25	3	5	2	10	10	3	40	2	19	6	0	0	16	2	0	0	8	0
frzn yogurt, blueberry, Borden	1/2 cup	72		110	25	2.5	4	1.5	8	10	3	40	2	19	6	0	0	16	2	2	0	8	0
frzn yogurt, cappuccino swirl, Lucerne	1/2 cup	68		130	30	3	5	2	10	15	5	65	3	22	7	0	0	20	2	0	0	10	0
frzn yogurt, caramel toffee crunch, fat-free, Borden	1/2 cup	71		120	0	0	0	0	0	0	0	70	3	27	9	0	0	20	3	6	0	10	0
frzn yogurt, choc amaretto nut, Lucerne	1/2 cup	68		130	45	5	7	2	9	15	5	90	4	19	6	0	0	18	3	0	0	10	0
frzn yogurt, choc cookie, fat-free, Borden	1/2 cup	71		110	0	0	0	0	0	0	0	65	3	25	8	0	0	18	3	6	0	10	2
frzn yogurt, choc, Borden	1/2 cup	72		110	25	3	5	2	10	10	3	55	2	18	6	0	0	15	3	0	0	8	2
frzn yogurt, choc, fat-free, Borden	1/2 cup	71		100	0	0	0	0	0	0	0	50	2	22	7	0	0	16	3	6	0	10	0
frzn yogurt, choc, Lucerne	1/2 cup	69		110	30	3	5	2	10	15	5	55	2	19	6	0	0	19	3	2	0	10	0
frzn yogurt, mint choc flake, Lucerne	1/2 cup	68		120	35	4	6	2	11	15	5	65	3	20	7	0	0	19	3	0	6	10	0
frzn yogurt, peach, Borden	1/2 cup	72		110	25	2.5	4	1.5	8	10	3	40	2	18	6	0	0	15	3	0	6	8	0
frzn yogurt, peach/van/van & choc, Lucerne	1/2 cup	68		110	25	3	4	2	9	15	5	55	2	18	6	0	0	18	3	2	0	10	0
frzn yogurt, peachy, fat-free, Borden	1/2 cup	71		100	0	0	0	0	0	0	0	50	2	22	7	0	0	17	3	6	2	10	0
frzn yogurt, pralines & cream, Lucerne	1/2 cup	68		120	25	3	5	1	7	10	4	75	3	22	7	0	0	21	2	2	0	8	0
frzn yogurt, raspberry, Borden	1/2 cup	72		110	25	3	5	2	10	10	3	40	2	18	6	0	0	15	3	0	0	8	0
frzn yogurt, strawberry, Borden	1/2 cup	72		100	25	2.5	4	1.5	8	10	3	40	2	18	6	0	0	15	2	4	4	8	0

Consult a similar product for brand names not listed.

Food Name	Serving Size	gm	mL	Calories	Calories from Fat	Total Fat (g)	%DV	Saturated Fat (g)	%DV	Cholesterol (mg)	%DV	Sodium (mg)	%DV	Total Carbohydrates[8] (g)	%DV	Fiber[8] (g)	%DV	Sugars[8] (g)	Protein (g)	Vitamin A (%DV)	Vitamin C[7] (%DV)	Calcium (%DV)	Iron (%DV)
frzn yogurt, strawberry, Lucerne	1/2 cup	68		110	25	3	4	2	9	15	5	50	2	19	6	0	0	19	3	2	6	10	0
frzn yogurt, van fudge sundae, fat-free, Borden	1/2 cup	71		110	0	0	0	0	0	0	0	55	2	24	8	0	0	18	3	6	0	10	2
frzn yogurt, van, Borden	1/2 cup	72		110	25	3	5	2	10	10	3	55	2	18	6	0	0	17	3	0	0	8	0
frzn yogurt, van, Edy's	1/2 cup	65		100	25	2.5	4	1.5	8	10	3	30	1	17	6	0	0	14	3	2	0	6	0
frzn yogurt, van, fat-free, Borden	1/2 cup	71		100	0	0	0	0	0	0	0	55	2	21	7	0	0	15	3	6	0	10	0
frzn yogurt, van, Kemps	1/2 cup	72		120	25	2.5	4	2	10	10	3	55	2	22	7	0	0	17	3	0	0	8	0
frzn yogurt, van, nonfat, Kemps	1/2 cup	72		100	0	0	0	0	0	0	0	70	3	21	7	0	0	17	3	0	0	10	0
frzn yogurt, van/raspberry, Lucerne	1/2 cup	68		110	25	3	5	2	9	15	5	55	2	18	6	0	0	18	3	2	0	10	0
ice cream, black cherry/choc/peach, fat-free, Borden	1/2 cup	64		90	0	0	0	0	0	0	0	45	2	19	6	0	0	14	3	6	0	10	0
ice cream, brownie sundae, fat-free, Borden	1/2 cup	64		100	0	0	0	0	0	0	0	45	2	21	7	0	0	16	3	6	0	10	0
ice cream, cherry cheesecake, fat-free, Borden	1/2 cup	64		90	0	0	0	0	0	0	0	45	2	20	7	0	0	15	3	6	0	10	0
ice cream, cherry van, low fat, Borden	1/2 cup	64		110	20	2	3	1	5	10	3	40	2	20	7	0	0	16	2	6	0	8	0
ice cream, choc chip cookie dough, low fat, Borden	1/2 cup	70		120	25	2.5	4	1.5	8	10	3	60	3	23	8	0	0	19	2	6	0	8	0
ice cream, choc marshmallow swirl, low fat, Borden	1/2 cup	70		110	20	2	3	1.5	8	10	3	50	2	21	7	0	0	16	2	6	0	8	0
ice cream, choc swirl, low fat, Borden	1/2 cup	70		110	20	2	3	1	5	10	3	45	2	20	7	0	0	15	2	6	0	8	0
ice cream, choc, low fat, Borden	1/2 cup	71		110	20	2	3	1	5	10	3	50	2	21	7	0	0	15	3	6	0	8	2
ice cream, choc, reduced fat, Viva	1/2 cup	67		120	35	4	6	2.5	13	15	5	60	3	18	6	0	0	17	2	4	0	6	2
ice cream, cookies'n crm, lowfat, Borden	1/2 cup	70		110	20	2	3	1	5	5	2	55	2	20	7	0	0	15	2	6	0	8	0
ice cream, cookies'n crm, reduced fat, Viva	1/2 cup	67		130	45	5	8	3	15	15	5	95	4	19	6	0	0	17	2	4	0	6	0

Food Name	Serving Size	gm	mL	Calories	Calories from Fat	Total Fat (g)	%DV	Saturated Fat (g)	%DV	Cholesterol (mg)	%DV	Sodium (mg)	%DV	Total Carbohydrates (g)	%DV	Fiber[g] (g)	%DV	Sugars[6] (g)	Protein (g)	Vitamin A (%DV)	Vitamin C[7] (%DV)	Calcium (%DV)	Iron (%DV)
ice cream, neapolitan, fat-free, Borden	½ cup	64		90	0	0	0	0	0	0	0	45	2	18	6	0	0	13	3	6	0	10	0
ice cream, neapolitan, low fat, Borden	½ cup	70		110	20	2	3	1	5	10	3	40	2	20	7	0	0	14	2	6	0	8	0
ice cream, neapolitan, reduced fat, Viva	½ cup	67		110	35	4	6	2.5	13	15	5	60	3	17	6	0	0	17	2	4	0	6	0
ice cream, orange sherbet 'n crm, lowfat, Borden	½ cup	70		100	20	2	3	1	5	10	3	35	1	19	6	0	0	14	2	6	0	8	0
ice cream, strawberry, low fat, Borden	½ cup	70		100	20	2	3	1	5	10	3	40	2	19	6	0	0	14	2	6	2	8	0
ice cream, strawberry/van, fat-free, Borden	½ cup	64		80	0	0	0	0	0	0	0	45	2	18	6	0	0	13	2	6	4	8	0
ice cream, van w/dark choc coating, Dove Bar	1 bar	98		330	200	21	32	14	70	35	12	40	2	32	11	0	0	30	4	6	<2	10	4
ice cream, van, low fat, Borden	½ cup	70		100	20	2	3	1	5	10	3	40	2	18	6	0	0	14	2	6	0	8	0
ice cream, van, low fat, Healthy Choice	½ cup	70		100	20	2	3	1	5	5	2	50	2	18	6	1	4	17	3	6	0	10	0
ice cream, van, reduced fat, Viva	½ cup	67		110	35	4	6	2.5	13	15	5	65	3	17	6	0	0	17	2	4	0	6	0
pudding/pie filling mix, choc mint, No-Bake Royal	dry mix for ⅙ pie	43		190	60	6	10	2	11	0	0	270	11	35	12	1	4	22	3	0	0	10	6
pudding/pie filling mix, choc mousse, No-Bake Royal	dry mix for ⅙ pie	45		190	50	6	9	2	10	0	0	290	12	36	12	1	6	22	4	0	0	15	8
pudding/pie filling mix, choc peanut butter, No-Bake Royal	dry mix for ⅙ pie	61		290	130	14	22	3	16	0	0	490	20	37	12	3	10	23	6	0	0	10	8
pudding/pie filling mix, lemon, Royal	dry mix for ⅙ pie	14		50	0	0	0	0	0	0	0	120	5	13	4	0	0	6	0	0	0	0	0
pudding, banana, Del Monte Pudding Cup	4 oz	113		140	35	4	6	1	5	0	0	190	8	25	8	0	0	19	1	0	0	6	0
pudding, bread w/apples, frzn, Stouffer's	½ cup	122		180	60	7	10	2	9	130	43	330	14	23	8	3	11	14	7	0	10	8	6
pudding, butterscotch, inst mix, Royal	dry mix for ½ cup	24		90	0	0	0	0	0	0	0	380	16	22	7	0	0	18	0	0	0	0	0

Consult a similar product for brand names not listed.

Food Name	Serving Size	gm	mL	Calories	Calories from Fat	Total Fat (g)	%DV	Saturated Fat (g)	%DV	Cholesterol (mg)	%DV	Sodium (mg)	%DV	Total Carbohydrates[6] (g)	%DV	Fiber[6] (g)	%DV	Sugars[6] (g)	Protein (g)	Vitamin A (%DV)	Vitamin C[7] (%DV)	Calcium (%DV)	Iron (%DV)
pudding, butterscotch, inst mix, sugar-free, Royal	dry mix for ½ cup	12		40	0	0	0	0	0	0	0	410	17	10	3	0	0	0	0	0	0	2	0
pudding, butterscotch, reg mix, Royal	dry mix for ½ cup	24		90	0	0	0	0	0	0	0	180	8	23	8	<1	0	17	<1	0	0	0	0
pudding, butterscotch, Del Monte Pudding Cup	4 oz	113		140	35	6	4	1	5	0	0	170	7	25	8	0	0	19	1	0	0	6	0
pudding, caramel custard (flan), reg mix, Royal	dry mix for ½ cup	21		80	0	0	0	0	0	0	0	25	1	20	7	<1	1	20	<1	0	0	0	0
pudding, choc fudge, Del Monte Pudding Cup	4 oz	113		150	35	4	6	1	5	0	0	190	8	25	8	0	0	19	2	0	0	6	2
pudding, choc fudge, reg mix, My-T-Fine	dry mix for ½ cup	24		90	0	0	0	0	0	0	0	140	6	21	7	3	1	13	<1	0	0	0	2
pudding, choc, inst mix, Royal	dry mix for ½ cup	24		100	0	0	0	0	0	0	0	390	16	24	8	2	<1	19	0	0	0	2	0
pudding, choc, inst mix, sugar-free, Royal	dry mix for ½ cup	15		45	0	0	0	0	0	0	0	430	18	12	4	3	1	0	1	0	0	4	2
pudding, choc, Del Monte Pudding Cup	4 oz	113		160	35	4	6	1	5	0	0	130	5	27	9	<1	0	20	2	0	0	6	2
pudding, choc, reg mix, My-T-Fine	dry mix for ½ cup	24		90	0	0	0	0	0	0	0	140	6	22	7	3	<1	14	0	0	0	0	2
pudding, choc, reg mix, Royal	dry mix for ½ cup	24		90	0	0	0	0	0	0	0	80	4	22	7	2	<1	16	1	0	0	0	0
pudding, coconut, toasted, reg mix, Royal	dry mix for ½ cup	24		100	15	1.5	3	1.5	8	0	0	360	15	21	7	0	0	17	0	0	0	0	0
pudding, pistachio, inst mix, sugar-free, Royal	dry mix for ½ cup	12		40	5	0.5	1	0	0	0	0	410	17	9	3	0	0	0	0	0	0	2	0
pudding, van, Del Monte Pudding Cup	4 oz	113		150	35	4	6	1	5	0	0	150	6	26	8	0	0	19	1	0	0	6	0
pudding, van, inst mix, Royal	dry mix for ½ cup	24		90	0	0	0	0	0	0	0	330	14	23	8	0	0	19	0	0	0	0	0
pudding, van, inst mix, sugar-free, Royal	dry mix for ½ cup	12		40	0	0	0	0	0	0	0	410	17	10	3	0	0	0	0	0	0	2	0

Food Name	Serving Size	gm	mL	Calories	Calories from Fat	Total Fat (g)	%DV	Saturated Fat (g)	%DV	Cholesterol (mg)	%DV	Sodium (mg)	%DV	Total Carbohydrates (g)	%DV	Fiber (g)	%DV	Sugars (g)	Protein (g)	Vitamin A (%DV)	Vitamin C (%DV)	Calcium (%DV)	Iron (%DV)
pudding, van, reg mix, Royal	dry mix for 1/2 cup	21		80	0	0	0	0	0	0	0	160	7	20	7	<1	<1	15	<1	0	0	0	0
sherbet, lemon/other flavors,[33] Borden	1/2 cup	86		130	20	2	3	1	5	5	2	30	1	27	9	0	0	23	0	0	0	2	0
sherbet, Triple Treat,[34] Lucerne Gourmet	1/2 cup	89		120	15	2	3	1	5	5	2	15	1	26	9	0	0	26	1	0	0	2	0

Consult a similar product for brand names not listed.

MILK, MILK BEVERAGES, AND SOYMILK

Food Name	Serving Size (gm)	Serving Size (mL)	Calories	Calories from Fat	Total Fat (g)	%DV	Saturated Fat (g)	%DV	Cholesterol (mg)	%DV	Sodium (mg)	%DV	Total Carbohydrates[8] (g)	%DV	Fiber[8] (g)	%DV	Sugars[8] (g)	Protein[8] (g)	Vitamin A (%DV)	Vitamin C[7] (%DV)	Calcium (%DV)	Iron (%DV)
acidophilus, low fat 1%, Borden		240	100	25	2.5	4	1.5	8	10	3	125	5	12	4	0	0	10	8	10	4	30	0
blueberry, low fat 2%, Borden		240	200	45	5	8	3	15	20	7	90	4	31	10	0	0	31	7	10	2	25	0
buttermilk, 1% fat, Borden		240	100	20	2.5	4	1.5	8	10	3	290	12	12	4	0	0	11	8	8	0	30	0
Choc Smash, low fat 2%, Borden		240	200	45	5	8	3	15	20	7	170	7	31	10	0	0	30	8	10	2	25	4
choc, low fat 1%, Borden		240	170	25	2.5	4	1.5	8	15	5	180	8	29	10	0	0	25	7	10	0	25	2
cond, sweetened, Borden	39		130	25	3	5	2	10	10	3	40	2	23	8	0	0	23	3	2	0	10	0
cond, sweetened, fat-free, Borden	39		110	0	0	0	0	0	<5	1	40	2	24	8	0	0	24	3	0	0	10	0
cond, sweetened, low fat, Borden	39		120	15	1.5	2	1	5	5	2	40	2	23	8	0	0	23	3	2	0	10	0
eggnog, light, Borden		120 (½ cup)	150	35	4	6	2.5	13	20	7	65	3	23	8	0	0	21	5	8	0	15	0
evaporated, Lucerne	30		45	20	2.5	4	1.5	7	10	3	35	1	3	1	0	0	3	2	0	0	6	0
evaporated, Nestlé	30		40	20	2.5	4	1.5	7	10	3	35	1	3	1	0	0	3	2	0	0	8	0
Inst Breakfast, cafe mocha, dry, Carnation	37		130	0	0.5	1	0	1	<5	1	100	4	28	9	<1	1	23	4	35	45	35	25
Inst Breakfast, classic choc malt, dry, Carnation	35		130	15	1.5	2	0.5	3	<5	1	130	5	26	9	<1	3	16	4	35	45	25	25
Inst Breakfast, creamy milk choc, dry, Carnation	37		130	10	1	1	0.5	2	<5	1	100	4	28	9	1	4	22	4	35	45	30	25
Inst Breakfast, French van, dry, Carnation	35		130	0	0	0	0	0	<5	1	110	4	27	9	0	0	17	4	35	45	35	25
Inst Breakfast, strawberry crm, dry, Carnation	36		130	0	0	0	0	0	<5	1	160	7	28	9	0	0	18	4	35	45	35	25
low fat 0.5%, Borden		240	90	10	1	2	0.5	4	5	2	125	5	12	4	0	0	11	8	10	4	30	0
low fat 2%, Lucerne		236	130	45	5	8	3	15	20	7	125	5	13	4	0	0	12	8	10	4	30	0
nonfat, Borden		240	80	0	0	0	0	0	5	2	125	5	12	4	0	0	11	8	10	4	30	0
soymilk, dry, Soyagen, Loma Linda	28		130	60	6	9	1	5	0	0	150	6	12	4	3	12	7	6	25	8	10	10
strawberry, low fat 2%, Borden		240	200	45	5	8	3	15	20	7	85	4	31	10	0	0	31	7	10	2	25	0
whole, Lucerne		236	160	70	8	12	5	25	35	11	125	5	13	4	0	0	12	8	6	4	30	0

YOGURT

Food Name	Serving Size	gm	mL	Calories	Calories from Fat	Total Fat (g)	%DV	Saturated Fat (g)	%DV	Cholesterol (mg)	%DV	Sodium (mg)	%DV	Total Carbohydrates (g)	%DV	Fiber (g)	%DV	Sugars (g)	Protein (g)	Vitamin A (%DV)	Vitamin C[7] (%DV)	Calcium (%DV)	Iron (%DV)
lemon/pina colada, low fat 1.5%, Borden	1 container	226		200	30	3.5	5	2	10	15	5	135	6	35	12	0	0	32	8	0	0	30	0
low fat 1.5%, Borden	1 container	226		160	30	3.5	5	2	10	20	7	135	6	20	7	0	0	15	11	0	0	35	0
low fat 1.5%, Lucerne	8 fl oz (1 cup)		227	170	35	3.5	6	2.5	11	20	6	180	8	18	6	0	0	17	13	2	2	45	0
orange, low fat 1.5%, Borden	1 container	226		200	30	3.5	5	2	10	15	5	120	5	35	12	0	0	32	8	0	0	30	0
van, low fat 1.5%, Borden	1 container	226		190	30	3.5	5	2	10	20	7	135	6	30	10	0	0	24	10	0	0	35	0
van, nonfat, Lucerne	8 fl oz (1 cup)		227	180	0	0	0	0	0	5	2	160	7	33	11	0	0	31	11	0	2	40	0
various flavors, low fat 1%, Borden	1 container	226		230	20	2.5	4	1.5	7	15	5	150	6	42	14	0	0	35	10	0	0	30	0
various flavors, mountain high, nonfat, Borden	1 container	226		150	0	0	0	0	0	5	2	90	4	29	10	0	0	28	8	0	2	30	0
various flavors, Swiss, low fat 1.5%, Borden	1 container	226		200	30	3	5	2	10	15	5	120	5	36	12	0	0	27	8	0	0	25	0
various flavors, Swiss, nonfat, Borden	1 container	226		100	0	0	0	0	0	5	2	105	4	17	6	0	0	11	8	0	0	25	0

Consult a similar product for brand names not listed.

Meat, Poultry, Fish, Beans, Eggs, and Nuts

BEANS,[3] BEAN DIPS, AND BEAN ENTREES[1]

Food Name	Serving Size gm mL	Calories	Calories from Fat	Total Fat (g)	%DV	Saturated Fat (g)	%DV	Cholesterol (mg)	%DV	Sodium (mg)	%DV	Total Carbohydrates (g)	%DV	Fiber (g)	%DV	Sugars (g)	Protein (g)	Vitamin A (%DV)	Vitamin C (%DV)	Calcium (%DV)	Iron (%DV)
baked beans, bbq, cnd, Campbell's	130	170	25	2.5	4	0.5	3	5	2	460	19	29	10	6	24	10	7	4	0	8	10
baked beans, brick oven, cnd, S&W	127	160	5	0.5	1	0	0	0	0	620	26	32	11	7	28	11	7	0	4	6	10
baked beans, brown sugar & bacon, cnd, Campbell's	130	170	25	3	5	1	5	5	2	490	20	29	10	7	28	13	5	0	0	10	8
baked beans, homestyle, cnd, Campbell's	130	150	20	2	3	0.5	3	5	2	490	20	27	9	7	28	10	7	4	4	6	10
baked beans, honey mustard, cnd, S&W	133	130	0	0	0	0	0	0	0	500	21	31	10	7	28	12	7	0	6	8	10
baked beans, maple sugar, cnd, S&W	130	150	5	0.5	1	0	0	0	0	580	24	29	10	6	24	15	7	0	10	10	8
baked beans, New Engl, cnd, Campbell's	130	180	30	3	5	1	5	5	2	460	19	32	11	6	24	14	5	0	2	8	10
baked beans, sweet bacon, cnd, S&W	134	140	10	1.5	2	0.5	3	0	0	530	22	31	10	6	24	11	7	0	4	8	10
bbq beans, Texas, cnd, S&W	128	140	10	1.5	2	0.5	3	0	0	640	27	25	8	8	33	9	6	0	8	4	8
bean dip, jalapeño, Frito-Lay	35	40	10	1	2	0	0	0	0	170	7	5	2	1	3	0	2	0	0	0	2
bean dip, Marie's Fiesta	28	140	130	14	22	2	10	10	3	160	7	2	1	<1	2	<1	<1	2	0	0	2
bean dip, Ortega	34	40	10	1	2	0	0	0	0	170	7	6	2	1	6	<1	2	4	10	0	4
beans w/franks in tomato sauce, cnd, Campbell's	213	330	120	13	20	5	25	25	8	1080	45	39	13	8	32	14	14	4	6	10	20
beans w/franks, cnd, Libby's Diner	213	330	150	16	25	5	26	40	14	840	35	36	12	9	37	15	13	25	0	10	15
black bean dip, mild, Guiltless Gourmet	30	30	0	0	0	0	0	0	0	100	4	5	2	1	4	1	2	0	2	2	2
black bean dip, spicy, Guiltless Gourmet	30	30	0	0	0	0	0	0	0	100	4	5	2	1	4	1	2	0	2	2	2
black beans, 50% less salt, cnd, S&W	127	70	0	0	0	0	0	0	0	260	11	17	6	6	24	1	5	0	4	4	10
black beans, cnd, S&W	127	70	0	0	0	0	0	0	0	520	22	17	6	6	24	1	5	0	4	4	10
black beans, cnd, Sun Vista	127	70	10	1	2	0	0	0	0	630	26	20	7	7	27	2	5	0	10	4	8

Food Name	Serving Size	gm	mL	Calories	Calories from Fat	Total Fat (g)	%DV	Saturated Fat (g)	%DV	Cholesterol (mg)	%DV	Sodium (mg)	%DV	Total Carbohydrates (g)	%DV	Fiber (g)	%DV	Sugars (g)	Protein (g)	Vitamin A (%DV)	Vitamin C (%DV)	Calcium (%DV)	Iron (%DV)
black-eyed peas, cnd, Sun Vista	1/2 cup	122		70	0	0	0	0	0	0	0	550	23	15	5	4	16	0	6	0	2	4	10
butter beans (lima beans), cnd, S&W	1/2 cup	124		70	0	0	0	0	0	0	0	440	18	18	6	5	20	1	6	0	4	4	10
chili beans, cnd, Campbell's	1/2 cup	130		130	30	3	5	1	5	5	2	490	20	21	7	6	24	4	6	6	2	6	8
chili beans, cnd, S&W	1/2 cup	129		110	10	1	2	0	0	0	0	580	24	23	8	6	25	4	7	6	6	4	8
chili beans, cnd, Sun Vista	1/2 cup	126		110	10	1	2	0.5	3	0	0	360	15	24	8	7	28	2	7	8	25	6	10
chili beans, hot chipotle, cnd, S&W	1/2 cup	129		90	0	0	0	0	0	0	0	570	24	21	7	6	24	1	7	20	4	8	10
chili con carne w/beans, frzn, Stouffer's	1 cup	257		290	100	11	16	5	23	50	16	840	35	28	9	8	32	5	19	20	4	8	20
Chili Makin's, black bean, cnd, S&W	1/2 cup	130		80	0	0	0	0	0	0	0	750	31	19	6	6	24	3	6	25	4	6	15
Chili Makin's, cnd, S&W	1/2 cup	126		80	5	0.5	1	0	0	0	0	790	33	20	7	5	20	4	5	15	20	4	8
Chili Makin's, homestyle, cnd, S&W	1/2 cup	130		80	0	0	0	0	0	0	0	630	26	19	6	6	24	3	7	30	8	6	10
Chili Makin's, Santa Fe, cnd, S&W	1/2 cup	130		80	0	0	0	0	0	0	0	870	36	18	6	5	20	3	6	20	6	4	10
chili, 3-bean, frzn, Lean Cuisine	1 cup	250		180	35	4	6	1	3	0	0	750	31	27	9	9	37	9	8	25	25	10	15
chili w/beans, cnd, Libby's	1 cup	255		420	240	27	42	13	63	50	17	1210	50	29	10	4	16	1	16	15	0	6	20
chili w/beans, cnd, Libby's Diner	1 container	194		320	200	22	34	8	40	40	14	1010	42	23	8	9	38	1	13	15	0	4	15
chili w/beans, reg/hot, cnd, Armour Star	1 cup	253		440	220	28	43	12	59	50	17	1270	53	34	11	10	40	2	14	10	0	8	20
chili w/beans, western, cnd, Armour Star	1 cup	252		460	290	32	49	15	72	60	20	1130	47	29	10	9	36	4	14	10	0	6	15
chili, Wendy's	1 small serving	227		210	60	7	11	2.5	13	30	10	800	33	21	7	5	20	5	15	8	6	8	15
great northern beans,[35] cnd, Sun Vista	1/2 cup	127		70	0	0	0	0	0	0	0	490	20	17	6	6	24	3	6	0	2	4	8
hummos w/tahini, Luxor Assoc.	2 tbsp	28		57	30	3	5	0	2	0	0	150	6	5	2	2	8	1	2	0	0	0	2
pinquito beans, cnd, S&W	1/2 cup	127		80	0	0.5	1	0	0	0	0	480	20	20	7	6	26	1	6	2	8	6	10
pinto bean dip, spicy, Guiltless Gourmet	2 tbsp	30		35	0	0	0	0	0	0	0	100	4	6	2	2	8	1	2	2	2	4	4
pinto beans, cnd, Sun Vista	1/2 cup	126		80	5	0.5	1	0	0	0	0	530	22	12	4	3	12	2	3	0	0	0	15

Consult a similar product for brand names not listed.

Food Name	Serving Size	gm	mL	Calories	Calories from Fat	Total Fat (g)	%DV	Saturated Fat (g)	%DV	Cholesterol (mg)	%DV	Sodium (mg)	%DV	Total Carbohydrates[6] (g)	%DV	Fiber[6] (g)	%DV	Sugars[6] (g)	Protein (g)	Vitamin A (%DV)	Vitamin C[7] (%DV)	Calcium (%DV)	Iron (%DV)
pork & beans in tomato sauce, cnd, Campbell's	½ cup	130		130	20	2	3	0.5	3	5	2	420	18	24	8	6	24	8	5	4	0	6	8
refried beans, cnd, Ortega	½ cup	136		140	20	2.5	4	0.5	3	0	0	590	25	23	8	5	22	1	7	0	4	4	10
refried beans, vegetarian, cnd, Old El Paso	½ cup	118		100	5	1	1	0	0	0	0	490	20	16	5	6	23	2	6	0	0	4	8
vegetarian beans in tomato sauce, cnd, Campbell's	½ cup	130		130	20	2	3	1	5	0	0	460	19	24	8	6	24	10	5	4	0	10	6
white beans, small, cnd, S&W	½ cup	122		80	5	0.5	1	0	0	0	0	440	18	19	6	6	24	1	7	0	0	6	8

BEANS:[3] BEAN-BASED SOUPS

Food Name	Serving Size	gm	mL	Calories	Calories from Fat	Total Fat (g)	%DV	Saturated Fat (g)	%DV	Cholesterol (mg)	%DV	Sodium (mg)	%DV	Total Carbohydrates[8] (g)	%DV	Fiber[9] (g)	%DV	Sugars[8] (g)	Protein (g)	Vitamin A (%DV)	Vitamin C[7] (%DV)	Calcium (%DV)	Iron (%DV)
bean & ham, cnd rts, Campbell's Home Cookin'	1 can	305		230	20	2	3	0.5	3	5	2	890	37	41	14	11	44	10	11	35	4	10	15
bean w/bacon, cnd cond, Campbell's	1/2 cup	128		180	45	5	8	2	10	<5	1	890	37	25	8	7	28	4	8	10	0	8	10
bean w/bacon'n ham, rts microwave, Campbell's	1 container	227		180	55	6	9	2	10	10	3	750	31	26	9	7	28	5	8	15	0	10	6
black bean, cnd cond, Campbell's	1/2 cup	126		120	20	2	3	0.5	3	0	0	1030	43	19	6	5	20	4	6	4	0	4	10
black bean, dry mix, Knorr	1 package	53		190	10	1	2	0	0	0	0	590	25	36	12	9	36	3	10	10	15	0	6
black bean, frzn conc, Stouffer's	1/2 cup	125		200	35	4	6	2	9	10	2	920	32	32	11	15	63	2	10	0	0	8	25
black bean, Santa Fe, dry mix, Campbell's	1 package	75		250	15	1.5	2	0.5	3	<5	1	1080	45	48	16	6	24	6	11	50	2	8	10
chili beef w/beans, chunky, cnd rts, Campbell's	1 can	312		300	60	7	11	2	10	20	7	1080	45	38	13	9	36	4	21	30	15	8	25
chili beef w/beans, cnd cond, Campbell's	1/2 cup	128		170	45	5	8	2.5	13	15	5	910	38	24	8	4	16	4	7	15	2	10	4
green pea, cnd cond, Campbell's	1/2 cup	128		180	25	3	5	1	5	5	1	890	37	29	10	5	20	6	9	4	0	8	2
ham'n bean, chunky, cnd rts, Campbell's	1 can	305		270	90	10	15	5	25	25	8	1160	48	34	11	8	32	4	13	60	6	4	15
lentil, cnd rts, Campbell's Home Cookin'	1 can	305		190	25	3	5	0	0	0	0	1070	45	33	11	6	24	5	8	100	6	6	20
lentil, dry mix, Campbell's	1 package	70		240	15	1.5	2	0.5	3	<5	1	990	41	42	14	7	28	6	15	25	0	10	30
lentil, dry, Knorr	1 package	57		220	0	0	0	0	0	0	0	900	38	40	13	6	30	1	13	15	6	4	4
Mexican bean & rice, dry mix, Campbell's	1 package	63		210	15	1.5	2	0.5	3	<5	1	930	39	41	14	6	24	9	9	15	8	6	10
navy bean, dry mix, Knorr	1 package	38		140	0	0	1	0	0	0	0	870	36	27	9	5	21	1	7	15	6	2	2
navy bean, frzn rts, Stouffer's	1 cup	240		140	30	4	5	1	2	10	3	1140	47	18	6	5	19	3	7	8	0	4	10
navy bean w/ham, frzn conc, Stouffer's	1/2 cup	125		140	30	3.5	5	1	6	10	2	1050	44	20	7	5	20	4	6	8	0	4	10
red beans & rice, Creole, chunky, cnd rts, Campbell's	1 can	305		260	90	10	15	3.5	18	15	5	890	37	33	11	7	28	4	12	10	0	8	10

Consult a similar product for brand names not listed.

Food Name	Serving Size	gm	mL	Calories	Calories from Fat	Total Fat (g)	%DV	Saturated Fat (g)	%DV	Cholesterol (mg)	%DV	Sodium (mg)	%DV	Total Carbohydrates[6] (g)	%DV	Fiber[6] (g)	%DV	Sugars[6] (g)	Protein (g)	Vitamin A (%DV)	Vitamin C[7] (%DV)	Calcium (%DV)	Iron (%DV)
salsa bean, cnd rts, Campbell's Home Cookin'	1 cup	245		160	10	1	2	0	0	0	0	730	30	31	10	7	28	13	7	10	10	8	10
split pea, cnd rts, Progresso	9.5 oz	269		160	30	3	5	1	5	0	0	1050	44	27	9	4.5	18	4	11	10	0	2	10
split pea 'n ham, chunky, cnd rts, Campbell's	1 can	305		240	30	4	5	1.5	8	20	7	1400	58	33	11	4	16	6	18	80	10	4	15
split pea w/ham & bacon, cnd cond, Campbell's	1/2 cup	128		180	30	4	5	2	10	<5	1	860	36	28	9	5	20	4	10	10	0	2	10
split pea w/ham, cnd rts, Campbell's Home Cookin'	1 can	305		210	20	2	3	0.5	3	5	2	1100	46	37	12	8	32	7	12	50	6	4	15
split pea w/ham, frzn conc, Stouffer's	1/2 cup	124		190	15	2	2	0.5	2	10	2	1200	49	32	10	7	29	6	12	6	0	2	10

Food Name	Serving Size	gm mL	Calories	Calories from Fat	Total Fat (g)	%DV	Saturated Fat (g)	%DV	Cholesterol (mg)	%DV	Sodium (mg)	%DV	Total Carbohydrates[6] (g)	%DV	Fiber[6] (g)	%DV	Sugars[6] (g)	Protein (g)	Vitamin A (%DV)	Vitamin C[7] (%DV)	Calcium (%DV)	Iron (%DV)
EGGS, EGG ENTREES,[1] AND EGG SUBSTITUTES																						
egg & cheese sandwich, frzn, Swanson	1 sandwich	119	360	170	19	29	8	40	170	57	950	40	35	12	1	4	4	12	0	0	10	15
egg patty & Canadian bacon, frzn, Swanson	1 entree	120	240	50	6	9	2.5	13	25	8	720	30	33	11	2	8	2	14	0	4	20	10
egg substitute, frzn, Better'n Eggs	¼ cup	57	20	0	0	0	0	0	0	0	90	4	0	0	0	0	0	5	15	0	2	4
egg substitute, frzn, Egg Beaters	¼ cup	60	30	0	0	0	0	0	0	0	100	4	1	0	0	0	<1	6	6	0	2	6
egg substitute, frzn, Scramblers	¼ cup	57	35	0	0	0	0	0	0	0	95	4	2	1	0	0	2	6	15	0	2	6
egg, raw	1 large	50	70	40	4	7	1.5	6	215	71	65	3	1	0	0	0	0	6	6	0	2	4
eggs & silver dollar pancakes, frzn, Swanson	1 entree	121	250	130	14	22	6	30	290	97	540	23	22	7	1	4	6	9	0	0	6	8
eggs, scrambled & bacon, frzn, Swanson	1 entree	149	290	170	19	29	9	45	240	80	700	29	17	6	1	4	2	11	0	0	6	8
eggs, scrambled & homefries, frzn, Swanson	1 entree	120	200	110	12	18	8	40	190	63	390	16	15	5	2	8	2	7	0	2	4	8
eggs, scrambled & sausage, frzn, Swanson	1 entree	177	360	230	26	40	10	50	280	93	800	33	21	7	3	12	2	12	0	0	10	6
eggs, scrambled, frzn, Swanson	1 entree	149	240	120	13	20	4	20	40	13	510	21	22	7	1	4	2	10	15	10	2	2
soufflé, broccoli cheese, frzn, Stouffer's	½ cup	125	150	80	9	14	4	18	140	46	560	23	10	3	2	7	2	8	6	0	10	6
soufflé, corn (corn pudding), frzn, Stouffer's	½ cup	127	170	70	8	12	1	5	70	22	560	23	20	7	2	8	5	5	0	0	6	4
soufflé, spinach, frzn, Stouffer's	½ cup	122	160	100	11	17	2.5	12	100	31	700	29	10	3	1	5	5	6	50	0	10	6
strada, bacon & cheddar cheese, frzn, Stouffer's	½ cup	124	230	140	15	23	4	20	140	46	540	23	12	4	1	4	3	11	0	0	15	8
strada, Swiss cheese, mushrooms, & spinach, frzn, Stouffer's	⅓ cup	87	140	80	9	13	3	14	95	30	280	12	8	2	1	3	2	7	2	0	10	4

Consult a similar product for brand names not listed.

FISH: FISH

Food Name	Serving Size	gm	mL	Calories	Calories from Fat	Total Fat (g)	%DV	Saturated Fat (g)	%DV	Cholesterol (mg)	%DV	Sodium (mg)	%DV	Total Carbohydrates (g)	%DV	Fiber (g)	%DV	Sugars (g)	Protein (g)	Vitamin A (%DV)	Vitamin C (%DV)	Calcium (%DV)	Iron (%DV)
catfish, ckd	3 oz	84		140	80	9	14	2	10	50	17	40	2	0	0	0	0	0	17	0	0	0	0
clam jce, cnd, S&W	1 can		248	30	0	0	0	0	0	0	0	740	31	0	0	0	0	0	8	0	0	0	0
clams, chopped, cnd, S&W	1/4 cup	55		20	0	0	0	0	0	10	3	360	15	1	0	0	0	0	4	0	0	0	4
clams, ckd	12 small (3 oz)	84		100	15	1.5	2	0	0	55	18	95	4	0	0	0	0	0	22	10	0	6	60
clams, fried, frzn, Mrs. Paul's	3 oz	85		280	140	23	15	3	15	10	3	480	20	28	9	1	4	2	8	0	0	2	8
clams, minced, cnd, S&W	1/4 cup	55		20	0	0	0	0	0	10	3	360	15	1	0	0	0	0	8	0	0	0	4
clams, smoked, baby, cnd, S&W	2 oz	56		130	90	15	10	2	10	20	7	220	9	2	1	0	0	0	9	2	0	4	110
clams, whole, baby, cnd, S&W	1/4 cup	50		50	15	2	1.5	0.5	3	40	13	260	11	2	1	0	0	0	8	4	0	6	70
cod, ckd	3 oz	84		90	0	0.5	1	0	0	45	15	60	3	0	0	0	0	0	20	0	0	2	2
cod premium fillets, frzn, Mrs. Paul's	1 fillet	120		240	100	17	11	2.5	13	40	13	440	18	23	8	2	8	3	14	0	0	2	4
crab, blue, ckd	3 oz	84		100	10	2	1	0	0	90	30	320	13	0	0	0	0	0	20	0	0	8	4
crab, deviled, frzn, Mrs. Paul's	1 piece (2.8 oz)	80		170	60	11	7	1.5	8	20	7	430	18	17	6	1	4	3	8	0	0	6	6
crab, deviled miniatures, frzn, Mrs. Paul's	6 minis	92		230	100	17	11	3	15	15	5	620	26	25	8	2	8	4	8	0	0	8	8
crab, dungeness, cnd, S&W	1/3 cup	85		80	10	1	2	0	0	60	20	310	13	0	0	0	0	0	18	0	0	6	2
fish fillets, battered, crunchy, frzn, Mrs. Paul's	2 fillets	113		250	120	13	20	3	15	25	8	680	28	23	8	2	8	5	10	0	0	2	6
fish fillets, battered, frzn, Mrs. Paul's	1 fillet	72		170	100	11	17	3	15	15	5	460	19	13	4	1	4	2	6	0	0	2	2
fish fillets, breaded, crunchy, frzn, Mrs. Paul's	2 fillets	107		240	110	12	18	3	15	25	8	390	16	20	7	1	4	2	13	0	0	2	4
fish fillets, breaded, frzn, Mrs. Paul's	1 fillet	113		170	25	3	5	1.5	8	30	10	290	12	21	7	2	8	3	14	2	6	4	8
fish fillets in sauce, frzn, Mrs. Paul's	1 fillet	116		120	45	5	8	1.5	8	25	8	450	19	4	1	1	4	0	16	0	0	2	2
fish portions, battered, frzn, Mrs. Paul's	2 fillets	114		280	150	17	26	5	25	30	10	760	32	22	7	2	8	4	9	0	0	2	2
fish portions, breaded, frzn, Mrs. Paul's	2 portions	85		190	90	10	15	3	15	15	5	280	12	16	5	1	4	2	9	0	0	2	4
fish shapes, breaded, frzn, Mrs. Paul's	5 pieces	82		190	80	9	14	2.5	13	20	7	320	13	18	6	1	4	2	9	0	0	2	4

Food Name	Serving Size	gm	mL	Calories	Calories from Fat	Total Fat (g)	%DV	Saturated Fat (g)	%DV	Cholesterol (mg)	%DV	Sodium (mg)	%DV	Total Carbohydrates[6] (g)	%DV	Fiber[6] (g)	%DV	Sugars[6] (g)	Protein (g)	Vitamin A (%DV)	Vitamin C[7] (%DV)	Calcium (%DV)	Iron (%DV)
fish sticks, battered, frzn, Mrs. Paul's	6 sticks	90		240	140	15	23	4	20	25	8	720	30	19	6	1	4	2	7	0	0	2	2
fish sticks, breaded, crunchy, frzn, Mrs. Paul's	5 sticks	90		200	80	9	14	2.5	13	20	7	510	21	20	7	2	8	3	10	0	0	2	6
fish sticks (minced fish), breaded, frzn, Mrs. Paul's	6 sticks	87		220	100	11	17	3.5	18	20	7	430	18	20	7	1	4	2	9	0	0	2	4
fish stick minis, breaded, frzn, Mrs. Paul's	12 mini sticks	94		220	100	11	17	2.5	13	30	10	330	14	20	7	2	8	2	11	0	0	2	2
flounder fillets, battered, crunchy, frzn, Mrs. Paul's	2 fillets	106		260	130	14	22	3	15	30	10	540	23	24	8	2	8	4	11	0	0	4	4
flounder premium fillets, frzn, Mrs. Paul's	1 fillet	120		240	110	12	18	3.5	18	35	12	530	22	23	8	2	8	2	12	0	0	4	4
flounder/sole, ckd	3 oz	84		100	14	1.5	2	0.5	3	60	20	90	4	0	0	0	0	0	21	0	0	2	2
haddock fillets, battered, crunchy, frzn, Mrs. Paul's	2 fillets	106		250	110	12	18	2.5	13	25	8	630	26	25	8	2	8	7	10	0	0	2	4
haddock premium fillets, frzn, Mrs. Paul's	1 fillet	120		230	100	11	17	2.5	13	35	12	390	16	17	6	2	8	0	16	0	0	2	4
haddock, ckd	3 oz	84		100	10	1	2	0	0	80	27	85	4	0	0	0	0	0	21	0	0	2	6
halibut, ckd	3 oz	84		110	20	2	3	0	0	35	12	60	3	0	0	0	0	0	23	2	0	4	4
lobster, ckd	3 oz	84		80	0	0.5	1	0	0	60	20	320	13	1	0	0	0	0	17	0	0	4	2
mackerel, Atlantic/Pacific, ckd	3 oz	84		210	120	13	20	1.5	8	60	20	100	4	0	0	0	0	0	21	0	0	0	5
ocean perch, ckd	3 oz	84		110	20	2	3	0	0	50	17	95	4	0	0	0	0	0	21	0	0	10	6
orange roughy, ckd	3 oz	84		80	10	1	2	0	0	20	7	70	3	0	0	0	0	0	16	0	0	0	0
oysters, ckd	12 medium (3 oz)	84		100	35	3.5	5	1	5	115	38	190	8	4	1	0	0	0	10	0	0	6	45
oysters, smoked, cnd, S&W	2 oz	56		100	50	6	9	2	10	40	13	210	9	6	2	4	16	0	10	8	0	0	50
oysters, whole, cnd, S&W	2 oz	56		70	30	3	5	0	0	20	7	160	7	2	1	2	8	0	8	4	0	0	30
pollock, ckd	3 oz	84		90	10	1	2	0	0	80	27	110	5	0	0	0	0	0	20	0	0	0	2
pollock fillets, Ital herb, grilled, frzn, Gorton's	1 fillet	108		130	50	6	9	1	5	60	20	250	15	2	1	0	0	2	18	0	0	0	2
rainbow trout, ckd	3 oz	84		140	50	6	9	2	10	60	20	35	1	0	0	0	0	0	21	4	4	6	2

Consult a similar product for brand names not listed.

Food Name	Serving Size	gm	mL	Calories	Calories from Fat	Total Fat (g)	%DV	Saturated Fat (g)	%DV	Cholesterol (mg)	%DV	Sodium (mg)	%DV	Total Carbohydrates (g)	%DV	Fiber (g)	%DV	Sugars (g)	Protein (g)	Vitamin A (%DV)	Vitamin C (%DV)	Calcium (%DV)	Iron (%DV)
rockfish, ckd	3 oz	84		100	20	2	3	0	0	40	13	70	3	0	0	0	0	0	21	4	0	0	2
salmon, Atlantic/coho, ckd	3 oz	84		160	60	7	11	1	5	50	17	50	2	0	0	0	0	0	22	0	0	0	4
salmon, chinook, cnd, Pillar Rock	1/4 cup	63		140	90	10	15	3	14	40	13	270	11	0	0	0	0	0	12	2	0	6	2
salmon, chum, cnd, Sound Beauty	1/4 cup	63		90	35	4	6	1	5	40	13	270	11	0	0	0	0	0	13	0	0	10	2
salmon, chum/pink, ckd	3 oz	84		130	35	4	6	1	5	70	23	65	3	0	0	0	0	0	22	2	0	0	2
salmon, keta, cnd, Pink Beauty	1/4 cup	63		90	35	4	6	1	5	40	13	270	11	0	0	0	0	0	13	0	0	10	2
salmon, med red, cnd, Icy Point	1/4 cup	63		90	45	5	8	1	6	40	13	270	11	0	0	0	0	0	12	0	0	10	2
salmon, pink, cnd, Bay Beauty	1/4 cup	63		90	45	5	8	1	6	40	13	270	11	0	0	0	0	0	12	0	0	10	2
salmon, pink, cnd, Libby's	1/4 cup	63		90	45	5	8	1	6	40	13	270	11	0	0	0	0	0	12	0	0	10	2
salmon, pink, w/o skin/bone, cnd, Libby's	1/3 cup	56		70	20	2	3	0	0	40	13	190	8	0	0	0	0	0	14	0	0	0	2
salmon, pink, w/o skin/bone, cnd, Pillar Rock	1/3 cup	56		60	20	2	3	0	0	40	13	190	8	0	0	0	0	0	14	0	0	0	2
salmon, red, cnd, Icy Point	1/4 cup	63		110	60	7	10	1.5	8	40	13	270	11	0	0	0	0	0	13	2	0	10	2
salmon, red, cnd, Libby's	1/4 cup	63		110	60	7	10	1.5	8	40	13	270	11	0	0	0	0	0	13	2	0	10	2
salmon, red sockeye, cnd, S&W	1/4 cup	63		110	60	7	11	1.5	8	40	13	270	11	0	0	0	0	0	13	2	0	10	2
salmon, red sockeye, cnd, S&W	1 can	106		190	100	11	17	2.5	13	70	23	460	19	0	0	0	0	0	22	4	0	15	4
salmon, sockeye, ckd	3 oz	84		180	80	9	14	1.5	8	75	25	55	2	0	0	0	0	0	23	4	0	0	2
sardines in Louisiana hot sauce, cnd	3.75 oz	106		170	80	9	14	1.5	7	105	35	610	25	1	0	0	0	0	19	8	0	20	10
sardines in mustard sauce, cnd	3.75 oz	106		150	80	9	14	1.5	7	110	37	450	19	0.5	0	2	2	0	18	4	0	25	8
sardines in soybean oil, cnd	3.3 oz	94		220	150	17	26	3.5	17	115	38	360	15	0	0	0	0	0	19	2	0	30	10
sardines in soybean oil w/hot Tabasco peppers	3.3 oz	94		220	135	15	23	2.5	12	85	28	360	15	0	0	0	0	0	22	4	0	30	10
sardines in tomato sauce, cnd	3.75 oz	106		150	85	9	14	1.5	7	100	33	480	20	0	0	0	0	0	17	4	0	25	8
sardines in tomato sauce, cnd, Del Monte	1/2 fish w/sauce	55		80	35	4	6	1.5	7	35	12	170	7	1	<1	2	2	0	10	0	10	20	10
sardines in water	3.3 oz	94		170	90	10	15	3.5	18	140	47	240	10	0	0	0	0	0	18	2	0	30	6

Food Name	Serving Size	gm	mL	Calories	Calories from Fat	Total Fat (g)	%DV	Saturated Fat (g)	%DV	Cholesterol (mg)	%DV	Sodium (mg)	%DV	Total Carbohydrates[6] (g)	%DV	Fiber[6] (g)	%DV	Sugars[6] (g)	Protein (g)	Vitamin A (%DV)	Vitamin C[7] (%DV)	Calcium (%DV)	Iron (%DV)
sardines, Norwegian Brisling in olive oil, cnd, S&W	1.9 oz tin	53		160	120	13	20	3.5	18	60	20	190	8	0	0	0	0	0	10	0	0	15	6
sardines w/o skin/bone, cnd, S&W	1.7 oz tin	48		100	50	6	9	1	5	20	7	250	10	0	0	0	0	0	12	2	2	6	6
scallops, ckd	6 large or 14 small	84		120	10	1	2	0	0	55	18	260	11	2	1	0	0	0	22	0	0	2	2
scallops, fried, frzn, Mrs. Paul's	12 scallops	98		200	70	8	12	2	10	10	3	360	15	20	7	1	4	3	10	0	0	4	6
sea legs supreme, Nichirei	½ cup	85		80	10	1	2	0	0	10	3	650	27	8	3	0	0	5	9	0	0	6	6
shrimp, breaded, garlic & herb, frzn, Mrs. Paul's	1 package	156		340	140	15	23	3	15	110	37	910	38	33	11	3	12	4	19	0	0	25	4
shrimp, breaded, special recipe, frzn, Mrs. Paul's	1 package	156		350	140	16	25	2.5	13	95	32	720	30	32	11	2	8	3	20	0	0	20	4
shrimp, ckd	3 oz	84		80	10	1	2	0	0	165	55	190	8	0	0	0	0	0	18	0	0	2	15
shrimp, small/med, deveined, cnd, S&W	¼ cup	55		45	0	0	0	0	0	115	38	650	27	0	0	0	0	1	10	0	0	4	0
sole premium fillets, frzn, Mrs. Paul's	1 fillet	127		250	120	13	20	3.5	18	40	13	510	21	22	7	2	8	4	14	0	0	4	4
swordfish, ckd	3 oz	84		130	35	4	7	1	5	40	13	100	4	0	0	0	0	0	22	2	2	0	4
tuna, chunk light in oil, cnd, S&W	2 oz	56		110	50	6	9	1	5	30	10	230	10	0	0	0	0	0	14	0	0	0	2
tuna, chunk light in water, cnd, S&W	2 oz	56		70	5	0	1	0	0	35	12	230	10	0	0	0	0	0	15	0	0	0	0
tuna, chunk light in water, cnd, Star Kist	¼ cup (2 oz)	56		60	5	0	1	0	0	30	10	250	10	0	0	0	0	0	13	0	0	0	2
tuna, chunk white in water, cnd, Bumble Bee	¼ cup (2 oz)	56		60	10	1	2	0	0	25	8	250	10	0	0	0	0	0	13	0	0	0	0
tuna, solid white in oil, cnd, Star Kist	¼ cup (2 oz)	56		95	45	5	8	2	10	35	12	250	10	0	0	0	0	0	12	0	0	0	0
tuna, solid white in water, cnd, S&W	2 oz	56		80	15	1.5	2	0	0	20	7	230	10	0	0	0	0	0	17	0	0	0	0
whiting, ckd	3 oz	84		110	25	3	5	0.5	3	70	23	95	4	0	0	0	0	0	19	2	0	6	0

Consult a similar product for brand names not listed.

FISH: FISH-BASED ENTREES[1]

Food Name	Serving Size	gm	mL	Calories	Calories from Fat	Total Fat (g)	%DV	Saturated Fat (g)	%DV	Cholesterol (mg)	%DV	Sodium (mg)	%DV	Total Carbohydrates (g)	%DV	Fiber[6] (g)	%DV	Sugars[6] (g)	Protein (g)	Vitamin A (%DV)	Vitamin C[7] (%DV)	Calcium (%DV)	Iron (%DV)
fish & cheddar shells, frzn, Lean Cuisine	1 entree	255		260	70	8	12	2	9	50	16	580	23	28	9	3	13	5	19	30	20	15	8
fish cakes, frzn, Mrs. Paul's	2 cakes	106		200	70	8	12	2	10	15	5	680	28	23	8	2	8	2	8	0	0	2	4
fish, mac, & cheese, frzn, Swanson Entree	1 entree	224		350	140	15	23	4.5	23	30	10	930	39	38	13	4	16	6	16	4	2	15	8
fish'n chips, frzn, Swanson Entree	1 entree	156		310	110	12	18	5	25	35	12	620	26	38	13	4	16	3	12	0	4	2	6
sandwich, Fish Filet Deluxe, McDonald's	1 sandwich	228		560	250	28	44	6	30	60	20	1060	44	54	18	4	16	5	23	6	4	8	15
sandwich, fish fillet w/cheese, frzn, Mrs. Paul's	1 sandwich	121		330	140	15	23	4.5	23	25	8	630	26	38	13	3	12	5	10	0	0	15	15
sandwich, Fisherman's Fillet, Hardee's	1 sandwich	237		560	240	27	42	7	35	65	22	1330	55	54	18	NA	NA	NA	26	NA	NA	NA	NA

Food Name	Serving Size gm	mL	Calories	Calories from Fat	Total Fat (g)	%DV	Saturated Fat (g)	%DV	Cholesterol (mg)	%DV	Sodium (mg)	%DV	Total Carbohydrates[6] (g)	%DV	Fiber[6] (g)	%DV	Sugars[6] (g)	Protein (g)	Vitamin A (%DV)	Vitamin C[7] (%DV)	Calcium (%DV)	Iron (%DV)
FISH: FISH-BASED MEALS/DINNERS[2]																						
fish sticks, breaded, frzn, Swanson Budget	1 meal	198	340	100	11	17	6	30	25	8	710	30	51	17	3	12	18	9	0	2	4	6
fish sticks, frzn, Swanson Children	1 meal	198	360	130	14	22	5	25	25	8	640	27	47	16	4	16	12	11	6	8	6	8
fish'n chips, fried, battered portions, frzn, Swanson	1 meal	284	480	180	20	31	4	20	45	15	1050	44	55	18	5	20	17	19	2	4	6	8
fisherman's platter, frzn, Swanson Hungry Man	1 meal	368	650	230	26	40	6	30	60	20	1720	72	82	27	5	20	20	23	90	0	10	20

Consult a similar product for brand names not listed.

FISH: FISH-BASED CHOWDERS, SOUPS, AND STEWS

Food Name	Serving Size gm	mL	Calories	Calories from Fat	Total Fat (g)	%DV	Saturated Fat (g)	%DV	Cholesterol (mg)	%DV	Sodium (mg)	%DV	Total Carbohydrates[6] (g)	%DV	Fiber[6] (g)	%DV	Sugars[8] (g)	Protein (g)	Vitamin A (%DV)	Vitamin C[7] (%DV)	Calcium (%DV)	Iron (%DV)
clam, Boston, frzn rts, Stouffer's	227		190	70	8	13	3	13	35	11	970	40	20	6	2	7	7	10	0	0	20	4
clam, Manhattan, chunky, cnd rts, Campbell's	305		170	35	4	6	1	5	5	2	1120	47	25	8	4	16	4	7	110	15	6	10
clam, Manhattan, cnd cond, Campbell's	126		60	5	0.5	1	0	0	<5	1	910	38	12	4	2	8	2	2	30	6	2	4
clam, Manhattan, frzn conc, Stouffer's	130		90	25	2.5	4	<0.5	0	10	3	940	39	12	4	2	10	4	5	20	4	2	6
clam, New Engl, cnd cond, Campbell's	126		100	25	2.5	4	1	4	<5	2	980	41	15	5	1	4	1	4	0	2	2	6
clam, New Engl, chunky, cnd rts, Campbell's	305		300	160	18	28	7	35	15	5	1210	50	26	9	3	12	1	9	0	0	6	10
clam, New Engl, chunky, rts microwave, Campbell's	298		290	150	17	26	8	40	20	7	1150	48	26	9	3	12	1	8	0	0	6	10
clam, New Engl, cnd rts, Campbell's Home Cookin'	245		210	140	16	25	5	25	5	2	1120	47	12	4	2	8	1	4	0	0	4	6
clam, New Engl, frzn rts, Stouffer's	235		190	50	6	9	2.5	12	25	8	900	37	24	8	2	7	10	11	0	0	20	4
clam, New Engl, rts microwave, Campbell's	220		200	130	14	22	4	20	15	5	950	40	14	5	3	12	1	5	0	2	8	2
crab, Maryland, soup, frzn conc, Stouffer's	128		90	25	3	4	1	3	20	6	850	34	11	4	4	17	4	4	20	2	4	4
harborside veg, cnd rts, Campbell's Home Cookin'	245		80	15	1.5	2	1	5	5	2	770	32	13	4	2	8	4	3	40	8	4	6
oyster, cnd cond, Campbell's	126		90	50	6	9	3.5	18	20	7	940	39	6	2	0	0	1	2	0	6	10	2
shrimp, crm of, cnd cond, Campbell's	124		100	60	7	11	2	10	20	7	890	37	8	3	1	4	1	2	0	0	2	2

FRANKFURTERS, LUNCHEON MEATS, AND MEAT SNACKS

Food Name	Serving Size	gm	mL	Calories	Calories from Fat	Total Fat (g)	%DV	Saturated Fat (g)	%DV	Cholesterol (mg)	%DV	Sodium (mg)	%DV	Total Carbohydrates (g)	%DV	Fiber (g)	%DV	Sugars (g)	Protein (g)	Vitamin A (%DV)	Vitamin C (%DV)	Calcium (%DV)	Iron (%DV)
beef, chopped, cnd, Armour Star	2 oz	56		170	140	15	23	7	35	40	13	810	34	2	1	0	0	2	7	0	0	0	4
beef, dried, sliced, Armour Star	7 slices	30		60	15	1.5	2	0.5	3	25	8	1370	57	2	1	0	0	2	8	0	0	0	4
beef jerky, hot kippered beefsteak, Lance	0.8 oz	23		50	5	0.5	1	0.5	3	50	17	560	23	2	1	0	0	1	9	0	0	0	6
beef jerky, hot sausage, Lance	1 sausage	25		60	45	5	7	2.5	13	15	5	540	23	1	0	0	0	1	4	0	0	0	6
beef jerky, jumbo, Lance	1 piece (9/16 oz)	16		70	35	4	6	2	9	10	3	360	15	2	1	0	0	0	5	0	0	0	4
beef jerky w/cheese, Lance	1 package (1 1/2 oz)	42		150	100	11	16	6	28	45	15	630	26	3	1	0	0	0	9	0	0	15	6
bologna, beef, Oscar Mayer	1 slice	28		90	70	8	13	4	18	15	6	300	12	1	0	0	0	<1	3	0	0	0	2
braunschweiger (liver sausage), Oscar Mayer	2 oz	56		190	150	17	26	6	30	90	30	630	26	2	1	0	0	<1	8	190	8	0	30
chicken breast, oven-roasted deluxe, Louis Rich	1 slice	28		30	5	0.5	1	0	0	15	5	330	14	1	0	0	0	0	5	0	0	0	0
cotto salami, beef, Oscar Mayer	1 slice	28		60	40	4.5	7	2	10	25	8	370	15	1	0	0	0	<1	4	0	0	0	4
deviled meat, Libby's	1 can (3 oz)	85		160	120	13	20	5	26	90	29	620	26	0	0	0	0	0	11	0	0	4	8
franks, beef, Oscar Mayer	1 link	45		140	120	13	20	6	30	30	10	460	19	1	0	0	0	<1	5	0	0	0	4
franks, turkey and chicken, bun-length, Louis Rich	1 link	57		110	70	8	12	2.5	13	55	18	650	27	3	1	0	0	1	6	0	0	8	6
ham, chopped, cnd, Armour Star	2 oz	56		120	80	9	14	3	15	35	12	880	37	2	1	0	0	1	8	0	0	0	2
ham, deviled, cnd, Armour Star	1 can (3 oz)	85		200	140	16	25	6	30	60	20	800	33	0	0	0	0	0	14	0	0	0	4
head cheese, Oscar Mayer	1 slice	28		50	35	4	6	1.5	8	25	8	360	15	0	0	0	0	0	5	0	0	0	2
honey loaf, Oscar Mayer	1 slice	28		35	10	1	2	0	0	15	5	380	16	1	1	0	0	1	5	0	0	0	2
luncheon loaf, spiced, Oscar Mayer	1 slice	28		70	45	5	8	1.5	8	20	7	340	14	2	1	0	0	1	4	0	0	4	2
old-fashioned loaf, Oscar Mayer	1 slice	28		70	40	4.5	7	1.5	8	15	5	330	14	2	1	0	0	1	4	0	0	4	2
pepperoni, Oscar Mayer	15 slices	30		140	120	13	20	5	25	25	8	550	23	0	0	0	0	0	6	0	0	0	4
potted meat, cnd, Armour Star	1 can (3 oz)	85		120	70	8	12	4	20	80	27	820	34	0	0	0	0	0	11	0	0	2	6
potted meat, cnd, Libby's	1 can (3 oz)	85		160	120	13	20	5	26	90	29	620	26	0	0	0	0	0	11	0	0	4	8

Consult a similar product for brand names not listed.

Food Name	Serving Size	gm	mL	Calories	Calories from Fat	Total Fat (g)	%DV	Saturated Fat (g)	%DV	Cholesterol (mg)	%DV	Sodium (mg)	%DV	Total Carbohydrates[4] (g)	%DV	Fiber[5] (g)	%DV	Sugars[6] (g)	Protein (g)	Vitamin A (%DV)	Vitamin C[7] (%DV)	Calcium (%DV)	Iron (%DV)
salami, hard, Oscar Mayer	3 slices	27		100	80	9	13	3	18	25	9	510	21	0	0	0	0	0	6	0	0	0	2
Spreadables, chicken, Libby	1/3 cup	80		140	80	9	14	1.5	9	25	8	340	14	7	2	2	11	2	7	0	0	2	2
Spreadables, ham, Libby	1/3 cup	81		110	40	4.5	7	1	5	20	7	620	26	8	2	4	16	2	8	0	0	0	4
Spreadables, tuna, Libby	1/3 cup	81		130	70	8	12	1	6	15	5	370	15	6	2	3	12	3	7	0	0	0	2
Spreadables, turkey, Libby	1/3 cup	82		150	90	10	15	1.5	9	25	8	310	13	7	2	2	8	3	7	0	0	2	2
summer sausage (thuringer cervelat), Oscar Mayer	2 slices	46		140	110	13	20	5	25	40	13	650	27	0	0	0	0	0	7	0	0	0	6
Treet, cnd, Armour Star	2 oz	56		150	110	12	18	4	20	50	17	770	32	4	1	0	0	3	6	0	0	8	4
turkey bologna, Louis Rich	1 slice	28		50	35	3.5	5	1	5	20	7	270	11	1	0	0	0	0	3	0	0	4	2
turkey ham, Louis Rich	1 slice	28		30	10	1	2	0	0	20	7	350	15	0	0	0	0	0	5	0	0	0	2
Vienna sausage, cnd, Armour Star	3 sausages	53		170	140	16	25	6	30	50	17	420	18	1	0	0	0	0	5	0	0	4	4
Vienna sausage, cnd, Libby's	3 sausages	48		130	100	12	18	2.5	12	50	16	300	13	1	0	0	0	0	5	0	0	2	4
Vienna sausage, chicken, cnd, Libby's	3 links	48		100	70	8	12	2.5	13	50	17	450	19	0	0	0	0	0	6	0	0	2	4
Vienna sausage in bbq sauce, cnd, Armour Star	3 sausages	61		160	130	14	22	5	25	45	15	550	23	4	1	0	0	3	5	0	0	4	4
Vienna sausage in bbq sauce, cnd, Libby's	3 sausages w/sauce	60		130	110	12	18	2.5	12	50	16	330	14	1	0	0	0	<1	5	2	0	2	4
Vienna sausage in hot sauce, cnd, Armour Star	3 sausages	61		170	140	15	23	6	30	50	17	630	27	3	1	0	0	0	5	0	0	4	4

MEAT: MEAT

Food Name	Serving Size	gm	mL	Calories	Calories from Fat	Total Fat (g)	%DV	Saturated Fat (g)	%DV	Cholesterol (mg)	%DV	Sodium (mg)	%DV	Total Carbohydrates (g)	%DV	Fiber (g)	%DV	Sugars (g)	Protein (g)	Vitamin A (%DV)	Vitamin C (%DV)	Calcium (%DV)	Iron (%DV)
beef brisket, whole, braised	3 oz	85		290	190	21	32	8	40	80	27	55	2	0	0	0	0	0	22	0	0	0	10
beef chuck arm pot roast, braised	3 oz	85		260	160	18	28	7	35	85	28	50	2	0	0	0	0	0	24	0	0	0	15
beef chuck blade roast, braised	3 oz	85		290	190	21	32	9	45	90	30	55	2	0	0	0	0	0	23	0	0	0	15
beef rib, large end roast, roasted	3 oz	85		300	220	24	37	10	50	70	23	55	2	0	0	0	0	0	20	0	0	0	10
beef rib, small end steak, broiled	3 oz	85		280	190	21	32	9	45	70	23	55	2	0	0	0	0	0	20	0	0	0	10
beef round, bottom steak, braised	3 oz	85		220	110	12	18	5	25	80	27	40	2	0	0	0	0	0	25	0	0	0	15
beef round, eye, roasted	3 oz	85		170	60	7	11	3	15	60	20	50	2	0	0	0	0	0	24	0	0	0	10
beef round, tip roast, roasted	3 oz	85		190	90	10	15	4	20	70	23	55	2	0	0	0	0	0	23	0	0	0	15
beef round, top steak, broiled	3 oz	85		180	70	7	11	3	15	70	23	50	2	0	0	0	0	0	26	0	0	0	15
beef sirloin steak, broiled	3 oz	85		210	110	12	18	5	25	75	25	55	2	0	0	0	0	0	24	0	0	0	15
beef tenderloin steak, broiled	3 oz	85		240	150	16	25	6	30	75	25	50	2	0	0	0	0	0	22	0	0	0	15
beef top loin, broiled	3 oz	85		230	130	15	23	6	30	65	22	55	2	0	0	0	0	0	22	0	0	0	10
beef tripe, cnd, Armour Star	3 oz	84		90	15	1.5	2	1	5	125	42	100	4	0	0	0	0	0	18	0	0	0	0
beef, grnd, lean (10% fat), broiled	3 oz	85		210	100	11	17	4	20	85	28	70	3	0	0	0	0	0	27	0	0	0	15
beef, grnd, regular (27% fat), broiled	3 oz	85		230	120	13	20	5	25	85	28	70	3	0	0	0	0	0	24	0	0	0	15
lamb foreshank, braised	3 oz	85		210	100	11	17	5	25	90	30	60	3	0	0	0	0	0	24	0	0	0	10
lamb leg, whole, roasted	3 oz	85		210	110	12	18	5	25	80	27	55	2	0	0	0	0	0	22	0	0	0	10
lamb loin chop, broiled	3 oz	85		250	160	18	28	7	35	85	28	65	3	0	0	0	0	0	22	0	0	0	10
lamb rib roast, roasted	3 oz	85		290	210	23	35	10	50	80	27	65	3	0	0	0	0	0	19	0	0	0	8
lamb shoulder arm chop, broiled	3 oz	85		230	140	15	23	7	35	80	27	65	3	0	0	0	0	0	21	0	0	0	10
lamb shoulder blade chop, broiled	3 oz	85		230	140	16	25	6	30	80	27	70	3	0	0	0	0	0	20	0	0	0	8
pork bacon, cooked, Oscar Mayer	2 slices	14		70	50	6	9	2	10	15	5	290	12	0	0	0	0	0	4	0	0	0	0
pork, ground, broiled	3 oz	85		250	160	18	28	7	35	80	27	60	3	0	0	0	0	0	22	0	0	0	6
pork loin, center chop, broiled	3 oz	85		200	100	11	17	4	20	70	23	50	2	0	0	0	0	0	24	0	0	0	4
pork loin, country style ribs, roasted	3 oz	85		280	190	22	34	8	40	80	27	45	2	0	0	0	0	0	20	0	0	0	6
pork loin, rib chop, broiled	3 oz	85		220	120	13	20	5	25	70	23	55	2	0	0	0	0	0	24	0	0	0	4
pork loin, top chop, boneless, roasted	3 oz	85		200	90	10	15	3	15	70	23	55	2	0	0	0	0	0	25	0	0	0	4

Consult a similar product for brand names not listed.

Food Name	Serving Size	gm	mL	Calories	Calories from Fat	Total Fat (g)	%DV	Saturated Fat (g)	%DV	Cholesterol (mg)	%DV	Sodium (mg)	%DV	Total Carbohydrates (g)	%DV	Fiber[8] (g)	%DV	Sugars[8] (g)	Protein (g)	Vitamin A (%DV)	Vitamin C[7] (%DV)	Calcium (%DV)	Iron (%DV)
pork loin, top roast, roasted	3 oz	85		190	90	10	15	4	20	65	22	40	2	0	0	0	0	0	24	0	0	0	4
pork sausage links, cooked, Oscar Mayer	2 links	48		170	130	15	23	5	25	40	13	410	17	1	0	0	0	0	9	0	0	0	4
pork shoulder blade steak, broiled	3 oz	85		220	130	14	22	5	25	80	27	60	3	0	0	0	0	0	22	0	0	0	6
pork sirloin roast, roasted	3 oz	85		220	120	14	22	5	25	75	25	50	2	0	0	0	0	0	23	0	0	0	4
pork spareribs, braised	3 oz	85		340	230	26	40	9	45	105	35	80	3	0	0	0	0	0	25	0	0	0	8
pork, tenderloin, broiled	3 oz	85		150	45	5	8	2	10	65	22	45	2	0	0	0	0	0	24	0	0	0	6
veal cutlet, unbreaded, pan fried	3 oz	85		140	35	4	6	2	10	85	28	60	3	0	0	0	0	0	24	0	0	0	4
veal loin chop, roasted	3 oz	85		180	100	10	15	4	20	85	28	80	3	0	0	0	0	0	21	0	0	0	4
veal rib roast, roasted	3 oz	85		190	110	12	18	5	25	95	32	80	3	0	0	0	0	0	20	0	0	0	4
veal shoulder arm steak, braised	3 oz	85		200	80	9	14	3	15	125	42	75	3	0	0	0	0	0	29	0	0	0	6
veal shoulder blade steak, braised	3 oz	85		190	80	9	14	3	15	130	43	85	4	0	0	0	0	0	27	0	0	0	6

MEAT: MEAT-BASED ENTREES[1]

Food Name	Serving Size	gm	mL	Calories	Calories from Fat	Total Fat (g)	%DV	Saturated Fat (g)	%DV	Cholesterol (mg)	%DV	Sodium (mg)	%DV	Total Carbohydrates (g)	%DV	Fiber[6] (g)	%DV	Sugars[6] (g)	Protein (g)	Vitamin A (%DV)	Vitamin C[7] (%DV)	Calcium (%DV)	Iron (%DV)
beef chop suey, frzn, Lean Cuisine	1/2 cup	149		90	30	3	4	1	3	20	7	470	18	8	3	1	5	4	8	15	0	2	4
beef sirloin tips frzn, Budget Gourmet[38]	1 entree	255		300	110	13	20	7	35	65	22	850	35	32	11	3	12	1	16	6	2	2	20
beef stew, cnd, Armour Star	1 cup	244		220	110	12	19	5	25	30	10	1250	52	21	7	2	8	0	8	8	0	2	6
beef stew, cnd, Libby's Diner	1 container	322		290	180	20	30	5	25	40	12	850	35	19	6	5	22	1	12	25	0	2	8
beef stew, frzn, Banquet Family	1 cup	246		160	35	4	6	2	10	25	8	1110	46	16	5	4	16	3	14	10	15	2	8
beef stew, frzn, Stouffer's	1 cup	248		210	80	9	13	3	11	45	13	890	37	16	5	3	12	2	15	20	4	2	6
beef stroganoff, frzn, Stouffer's	2/3 cup (w/o pasta)	159		230	130	15	23	6	29	55	19	650	26	7	2	1	4	2	17	0	0	4	8
chili w/o beans, cnd, Armour Star	1 cup	249		470	340	38	59	17	85	85	28	1200	50	18	6	0	0	0	14	25	0	4	10
chili w/o beans, cnd, Libby's	1 cup	253		480	330	37	57	17	86	75	24	1580	66	16	5	1	5	2	21	25	0	8	20
corned beef, cnd, Armour Star	2 oz	56		120	50	7	11	3	15	45	15	490	20	1	0	0	0	1	15	0	0	0	8
corned beef, cnd, Libby's	2 oz	56		120	60	7	11	3	14	50	16	490	20	0	0	0	0	0	15	0	0	0	8
corned beef hash, cnd, Armour Star	1 cup	236		440	270	30	46	14	70	100	33	840	35	23	8	2	8	1	19	2	0	2	10
corned beef hash, cnd, Libby's	1 cup	252		490	320	36	55	17	84	95	32	1250	52	26	8	9	36	1	22	0	0	2	10
creamed chipped beef, frzn, Banquet	1 entree	113		100	35	4	6	1.5	8	25	8	700	29	8	3	0	0	1	9	0	0	8	4
creamed chipped beef, frzn, Stouffer's	1/2 cup	129		180	110	13	19	3	13	40	13	660	27	5	2	1	4	5	11	0	0	10	6
gravy & charbroiled beef, frzn, Banquet Family	1 patty w/gravy	132		180	120	13	20	6	30	25	8	640	27	7	2	2	8	0	8	0	0	2	6
gravy & sliced beef, frzn, Banquet	1 entree	255		240	60	7	10	3	14	70	23	660	27	19	6	4	16	12	26	4	10	4	20
hamburger, Big Bacon Classic, Wendy's	1 sandwich	287		610	290	33	51	13	65	105	35	1510	63	45	15	3	12	11	36	15	25	25	35
hamburger, Big Mac, McDonald's	1 sandwich	216		560	280	31	48	10	51	85	28	1070	45	45	15	3	12	8	26	6	6	20	25
hamburger, grilled sourdough, Jack in the Box	1 sandwich	223		670	390	43	66	16	80	110	37	1180	49	39	13	0	0	4	32	15	10	20	25
hamburger, Jr. Deluxe w/cheese, Wendy's	1 sandwich	179		360	150	16	25	6	30	45	15	840	35	36	12	3	12	9	18	10	10	15	20

Consult a similar product for brand names not listed.

Food Name	Serving Size (gm)	Serving Size (mL)	Calories	Calories from Fat	Total Fat (g)	%DV	Saturated Fat (g)	%DV	Cholesterol (mg)	%DV	Sodium (mg)	%DV	Total Carbohydrates (g)	%DV	Fiber (g)	%DV	Sugars (g)	Protein (g)	Vitamin A (%DV)	Vitamin C (%DV)	Calcium (%DV)	Iron (%DV)
hamburger, Jr. w/bacon & cheese, Wendy's	170	1 sandwich	410	190	21	32	8	40	60	20	910	38	34	11	2	8	7	22	8	15	15	20
hamburger, Jumbo Jack w/cheese, Jack in the Box	246	1 sandwich	650	390	43	67	16	82	105	34	1090	45	32	11	4	14	5	32	10	15	25	30
hamburger, McDonald's	106	1 sandwich	260	80	9	14	3.5	17	30	10	580	24	34	11	2	9	7	13	0	4	15	15
hamburger, mushroom 'n Swiss, Hardee's	193	1 sandwich	490	220	25	38	12	60	80	27	1100	46	39	13	NA	NA	NA	28	NA	NA	NA	NA
hamburger, Quarter Pounder w/cheese, McDonald's	200	1 sandwich	530	270	30	46	13	63	95	32	1290	54	38	13	2	8	9	28	10	4	15	25
hamburger, single w/everything, Wendy's	219	1 sandwich	420	180	20	31	7	35	70	23	810	34	37	12	3	12	9	26	6	10	10	30
hamburger w/bacon & cheese, Hardee's	231	1 sandwich	690	410	46	71	15	75	95	32	1150	48	38	13	NA	NA	NA	30	NA	NA	NA	NA
meatloaf & gravy, frzn, Stouffer's	164	1 entree	220	120	13	20	4	19	60	20	540	23	10	3	1	5	2	16	2	0	4	10
meatloaf, tomato sauce, & veg in sauce, frzn, Swanson Entree	224	1 entree	260	110	12	18	6	30	50	17	860	36	20	7	7	28	10	17	80	35	6	15
pepper steak, Chinese style, frzn, Stouffer's	144	½ cup	130	60	6	9	2	7	35	10	650	27	7	2	2	7	2	12	2	25	2	6
pepper steak, rice, green peppers, & onions, frzn, Budget Gourmet	203	1 entree	290	70	8	12	3	15	40	13	1060	44	38	13	4	16	6	18	15	15	4	10
pork brains in milk gravy, cnd, Armour Star	156	⅔ cup	150	45	5	8	2.5	13	3500	1170	550	23	10	3	0	0	0	16	0	10	0	10
pork patty w/bbq sauce, frzn, Swanson Entree	215	1 entree	460	200	22	34	7	35	45	15	1060	44	48	16	6	24	18	17	6	2	10	8
pork, turkey, & egg patty, frzn, Swanson	142	1 entree	280	80	9	14	3.5	18	45	15	800	33	32	11	3	12	3	18	0	0	20	10
roast beef hash, cnd, Armour Star	240	1 cup	400	230	25	38	12	60	95	32	1460	61	23	8	3	12	0	20	0	0	4	15
roast beef hash, cnd, Libby's	234	1 cup	460	300	33	51	13	63	80	27	1390	58	23	8	3	14	<1	19	0	0	2	10
roast beef in gravy, cnd, Armour Star	56	2 oz	60	15	2	2	1	5	35	12	280	12	1	0	0	0	0	11	0	0	0	6
roast beef in gravy, cnd, Libby's	152	⅔ cup	140	30	3	5	1.5	8	70	24	800	34	2	1	0	0	0	26	0	2	0	8
roast beef sandwich, frzn, Swanson	291	1 sandwich	350	100	11	17	4	20	30	10	590	25	46	15	5	20	15	17	0	20	6	10

Food Name	Serving Size	gm	mL	Calories	Calories from Fat	Total Fat (g)	%DV	Saturated Fat (g)	%DV	Cholesterol (mg)	%DV	Sodium (mg)	%DV	Total Carbohydrates (g)	%DV	Fiber (g)	%DV	Sugars (g)	Protein (g)	Vitamin A (%DV)	Vitamin C (%DV)	Calcium (%DV)	Iron (%DV)
roast beef sandwich, Hardee's	1 sandwich	123		320	140	16	25	6	30	43	14	820	34	26	9	NA	NA	NA	17	NA	NA	NA	NA
salisbury steak & gravy, frzn, Banquet	1 entree	269		340	170	19	29	7	35	60	20	1040	43	28	9	4	16	4	15	0	0	4	10
salisbury steak & gravy, frzn, Lean Cuisine	1 steak w/gravy	151		180	70	8	11	3	15	50	17	560	23	10	3	2	8	2	18	0	0	4	15
salisbury steak & gravy, frzn, Stouffer's	1 steak w/gravy	163		210	110	12	19	4	20	75	24	830	34	10	3	0	1	0	15	0	0	2	10
salisbury steak, gravy, & mashed potatoes, frzn, Swanson Entree	1 entree	255		310	150	17	26	11	55	30	10	1070	45	23	8	2	8	3	17	0	4	4	15
salisbury steak, gravy, mac & cheese, frzn, Wt Watchers	1 entree	240		250	80	9	14	3	15	30	10	590	25	24	8	4	16	7	19	6	0	10	15
sloppy joe, frzn, Banquet	1 entree	136		140	60	7	11	3	15	25	8	530	22	12	4	1	4	1	7	6	0	2	4
Swedish meatballs & gravy, frzn, Stouffer's	½ cup	140		240	140	16	24	7	30	40	12	740	30	11	3	1	4	2	12	0	0	4	8
veal parmigiana, frzn, Banquet	1 entree	255		360	170	19	29	6	31	25	9	960	40	35	12	7	26	15	13	4	45	6	10
veal parmigiana, frzn, Swanson	1 entree	284		310	110	12	18	5	25	60	20	970	40	33	11	4	16	8	18	8	10	10	15

Consult a similar product for brand names not listed.

MEAT: MEAT-BASED MEALS/DINNERS[2]

Food Name	Serving Size		Calories	Calories from Fat	Total Fat (g)	%DV	Saturated Fat (g)	%DV	Cholesterol (mg)	%DV	Sodium (mg)	%DV	Total Carbohydrates (g)	%DV	Fiber (g)	%DV	Sugars[5] (g)	Protein (g)	Vitamin A (%DV)	Vitamin C[7] (%DV)	Calcium (%DV)	Iron (%DV)
	gm	mL																				
beef & broccoli, frzn, Swanson	284		340	90	10	15	5	5	30	10	770	32	51	17	4	16	24	11	35	25	6	10
beef & gravy, frzn, Swanson	312		310	60	7	11	5	5	40	13	760	32	37	12	5	20	15	25	10	10	2	25
beef, broccoli, sauce, & rice, frzn, Swanson Hungry Man	439		500	140	16	25	7	7	50	17	1200	50	73	24	6	24	29	17	70	35	10	15
beef, mesquite, frzn, Healthy Choice[27]	312		310	40	4	7	1.5	7	45	14	490	21	45	15	6	24	5	23	4	0	4	10
beef patties, frzn, Swanson Children	227		470	170	19	29	7	35	40	13	490	20	54	18	5	20	5	21	0	6	4	20
beef sirloin & gravy, frzn, Swanson	298		310	80	9	14	4	20	30	10	840	35	34	11	5	20	14	23	60	4	8	20
beef steak, chicken-fried, & gravy, frzn, Swanson	305		450	210	23	35	10	50	50	17	1320	55	44	15	3	12	14	17	0	10	8	20
meatloaf, frzn, Healthy Choice[38]	340		320	80	8	13	4	21	35	12	460	19	46	15	7	26	24	16	15	90	4	10
meatloaf, frzn, Swanson	319		380	140	16	25	9	45	35	12	1160	48	44	15	5	20	13	16	20	25	8	15
meatloaf, frzn, Swanson Budget	262		330	170	19	29	10	50	25	8	970	40	29	10	4	16	8	10	4	25	4	10
meatloaf, frzn, Swanson Hungry Man	468		610	250	28	43	13	65	45	15	1950	81	65	22	6	24	24	24	6	30	15	30
pork patty w/bbq sauce, frzn, Swanson Hungry Man	400		770	340	38	58	13	65	90	30	1540	64	78	26	9	36	44	29	0	15	15	20
pork patty, frzn, Swanson	284		510	210	23	35	8	40	50	17	1150	48	57	19	6	24	33	17	0	10	10	15
ribs w/bbq sauce, frzn, Swanson Children	204		450	220	24	37	8	40	45	15	1060	44	44	15	3	12	14	15	4	10	8	10
salisbury steak, frzn, Budget Gourmet[39]	193		260	70	8	12	3	15	35	12	430	18	31	10	6	24	5	19	20	25	4	15
salisbury steak, frzn, Swanson	312		420	180	20	31	8	40	60	20	980	41	40	13	5	20	12	19	2	2	4	15
salisbury steak, frzn, Swanson Hungry Man	461		590	290	32	49	17	85	80	27	1610	61	45	15	11	44	12	30	15	8	10	30
sirloin beef tips, frzn, Swanson Hungry Man	447		450	140	16	25	6	30	120	40	870	36	49	16	9	36	19	28	100	8	8	25
sirloin beef tips, noodles, & gravy, frzn, Swanson	198		200	70	8	12	3	15	35	12	380	16	20	7	2	8	4	13	110	15	4	10
veal parmigiana, frzn, Swanson	326		400	160	18	28	8	40	85	28	1060	44	40	13	5	20	14	19	10	15	15	15

Food Name	Serving Size	gm	mL	Calories	Calories from Fat	Total Fat (g)	%DV	Saturated Fat (g)	%DV	Cholesterol (mg)	%DV	Sodium (mg)	%DV	Total Carbohydrates[8] (g)	%DV	Fiber[8] (g)	%DV	Sugars[8] (g)	Protein (g)	Vitamin A (%DV)	Vitamin C[7] (%DV)	Calcium (%DV)	Iron (%DV)
veal parmigiana, frzn, Swanson Hungry Man	1 meal	517		640	210	23	35	12	60	75	25	2070	86	74	25	7	28	26	35	10	40	30	35
yankee pot roast, frzn, Swanson	1 meal	326		260	50	5	8	3	15	40	13	770	32	36	12	6	24	14	17	45	6	4	15
yankee pot roast, frzn, Swanson Hungry Man	1 meal	454		380	70	8	12	2	10	45	15	1090	45	48	16	6	24	16	28	70	10	8	25

Consult a similar product for brand names not listed.

MEAT: MEAT-BASED SOUPS

Food Name	Serving Size	gm	mL	Calories	Calories from Fat	Total Fat (g)	%DV	Saturated Fat (g)	%DV	Cholesterol (mg)	%DV	Sodium (mg)	%DV	Total Carbohydrates[8] (g)	%DV	Fiber[d] (g)	%DV	Sugars[8] (g)	Protein (g)	Vitamin A (%DV)	Vitamin C[7] (%DV)	Calcium (%DV)	Iron (%DV)
beef, chunky, rts microwave, Campbell's	1 container	298		210	45	5	8	1	5	35	12	1120	47	24	8	3	12	2	16	200	4	4	15
beef, veg, & barley, cnd cond, Campbell's	½ cup	126		80	20	2	3	1	5	15	5	920	38	11	4	2	8	1	5	25	2	4	2
beefy mushroom, cnd cond, Campbell's	½ cup	126		70	25	3	5	1	5	10	3	1000	42	6	2	1	4	1	5	0	0	4	0
chili beef, rts microwave, Campbell's	1 container	227		180	45	5	8	2	10	10	3	790	33	28	9	7	28	4	8	15	2	10	6
pepper steak, chunky, cnd rts, Campbell's	1 can	305		180	30	3.5	5	1.5	8	25	8	1040	43	22	7	3	12	5	14	60	8	4	10
sirloin burger w/veg, cnd rts, Campbell's	1 can	305		230	100	11	17	4.5	23	25	8	1160	48	25	8	5	20	3	12	120	0	4	15
sirloin burger, chunky, rts microwave, Campbell's	1 container	298		210	70	8	12	3	15	15	5	1090	45	24	8	5	20	3	10	130	2	4	10

MEAT SUBSTITUTES

Food Name	Serving Size	gm	mL	Calories	Calories from Fat	Total Fat (g)	%DV	Saturated Fat (g)	%DV	Cholesterol (mg)	%DV	Sodium (mg)	%DV	Total Carbohydrates (g)	%DV	Fiber (g)	%DV	Sugars (g)	Protein (g)	Vitamin A (%DV)	Vitamin C (%DV)	Calcium (%DV)	Iron (%DV)
Better'n Burgers, frzn, Morningstar	1 patty	78		70	0	0	0	0	0	0	0	360	15	6	2	3	12	0	11	0	0	6	10
Big Franks, cnd, Loma Linda	1 frank	51		110	60	7	11	1	5	0	0	240	10	2	1	2	8	0	10	0	0	0	4
Breakfast Links, frzn, Morningstar	2 links	45		60	20	2.5	4	0.5	3	0	0	340	14	2	1	2	8	0	8	0	0	0	8
Breakfast Patties, frzn, Morningstar	1 patty	38		70	25	3	5	0.5	3	0	0	270	11	2	1	2	8	0	8	0	0	0	10
Breakfast Strips, frzn, Morningstar	2 strips	16		60	40	4.5	7	0.5	3	0	0	220	9	2	1	<1	2	0	2	0	0	0	2
Chik Patties, frzn, Morningstar	1 patty	71		170	90	10	15	1.5	8	0	0	570	24	13	4	2	8	3	7	0	0	0	4
Choplets, cnd, Worthington	2 slices	92		90	15	1.5	2	1	5	0	0	500	21	3	1	2	8	0	17	0	0	0	2
Deli Franks, frzn, Morningstar	1 frank	45		110	60	7	11	1	5	0	0	520	22	3	1	2	8	0	10	0	0	0	0
Frichik, cnd, Worthington	2 pieces	90		120	70	8	12	1	5	0	0	430	18	1	0	1	4	0	10	0	0	0	6
Fripats, frzn, Worthington	1 patty	64		130	60	6	9	1	5	0	0	320	13	4	1	3	12	0	14	0	0	6	6
Garden Grain Pattie, frzn, Morningstar	1 patty	71		120	25	2.5	4	1	5	<5	1	280	12	18	6	4	16	0	6	0	0	6	6
Garden Vege Pattie, frzn, Morningstar	1 patty	67		110	35	4	6	0.5	3	0	0	350	15	8	3	4	16	1	10	4	0	4	6
Garden Vege Pattie, frzn, Natural Touch	1 patty	67		110	35	4	6	1	5	0	0	280	12	8	3	3	12	0	10	4	0	4	6
Grillers, frzn, Morningstar	1 patty	64		140	60	7	11	1.5	8	0	0	260	11	5	2	3	12	<1	14	0	0	4	6
Lentil Rice Loaf, frzn, Natural Touch	1 slice	90		170	80	9	14	2.5	13	0	0	370	15	14	5	4	16	<1	8	15	0	2	6
Linketts, cnd, Loma Linda	1 link	35		70	40	4.5	7	0.5	3	0	0	160	7	1	0	1	4	0	7	0	0	0	2
Multigrain Cutlets, cnd, Worthington	2 slices	92		100	15	2	3	0.5	3	0	0	390	16	5	2	4	16	0	15	0	0	0	4
Nine Bean Loaf, frzn, Natural Touch	1 slice	85		160	70	8	12	1.5	8	<5	1	350	15	13	4	5	20	<1	8	30	2	4	4
Okara Pattie, frzn, Natural Touch	1 patty	64		110	45	5	8	1	5	0	0	360	15	4	1	3	12	0	11	0	0	4	6
Prime Pattie, frzn, Morningstar	1 patty	64		130	50	5	8	1.5	8	0	0	240	10	4	1	3	12	0	16	0	8	4	10
Prime Stakes, cnd, Worthington	1 piece	92		140	80	9	14	1.5	8	0	0	440	18	4	1	4	16	0	9	0	0	0	2
Spicy Black Bean Burger, frzn, Morningstar	1 patty	78		100	10	1	2	0	0	0	0	470	20	16	5	5	20	2	8	0	0	4	10
Stakelets, frzn, Worthington	1 piece	71		140	70	8	12	1.5	8	0	0	480	20	6	2	2	8	0	12	0	0	4	6
Stripples, frzn, Worthington	2 strips	17		60	45	5	8	0.5	3	0	0	260	11	2	1	0	0	0	2	0	0	0	2
Super Links, cnd, Worthington	1 link	48		110	70	8	12	1	5	0	0	350	15	2	1	1	4	0	7	0	0	0	0

Consult a similar product for brand names not listed.

Food Name	Serving Size	gm	mL	Calories	Calories from Fat	Total Fat (g)	%DV	Saturated Fat (g)	%DV	Cholesterol (mg)	%DV	Sodium (mg)	%DV	Total Carbohydrates[δ] (g)	%DV	Fiber[δ] (g)	%DV	Sugars[δ] (g)	Protein (g)	Vitamin A (%DV)	Vitamin C[γ] (%DV)	Calcium (%DV)	Iron (%DV)
Swiss Stake w/gravy, cnd, Loma Linda	1 piece	92		120	50	6	9	1	5	0	0	430	18	8	3	4	16	<1	9	0	0	2	2
Vegan Burger, frzn, Natural Touch	1 patty	78		70	0	0	0	0	0	0	0	370	15	6	2	3	12	0	11	0	0	6	10
Vege-Burger, cnd, Loma Linda	1/4 cup	55		70	15	1.5	2	0.5	3	0	0	115	5	2	1	2	8	0	11	0	0	0	2
Vege Frank, frzn, Natural Touch	1 frank	45		100	50	6	9	1	5	0	0	470	20	2	1	2	8	0	10	0	0	0	2
Vegetable Skallops, cnd, Worthington	1 cup	85		90	15	1.5	2	0.5	3	0	0	410	17	3	1	3	12	0	15	0	0	0	4
Vegetarian Burger, cnd, Worthington	1/4 cup	55		60	15	2	3	0	0	0	0	270	11	2	1	1	4	0	9	0	0	0	10
Veja-Links, cnd, Worthington	1 link	31		50	25	3	5	0.5	3	0	0	190	8	1	0	0	0	0	5	0	0	0	4

Food Name	Serving Size	gm	mL	Calories	Calories from Fat	Total Fat (g)	%DV	Saturated Fat (g)	%DV	Cholesterol (mg)	%DV	Sodium (mg)	%DV	Total Carbohydrates (g)	%DV	Fiber (g)	%DV	Sugars (g)	Protein (g)	Vitamin A (%DV)	Vitamin C (%DV)	Calcium (%DV)	Iron (%DV)
NUT BUTTERS/PASTES, NUTS, AND SEEDS																							
almond paste, Blue Diamond	2 tbsp	30		150	90	10	15	1	5	0	0	0	0	11	4	2	8	9	4	0	0	4	4
almonds, bbq, Blue Diamond	3 tbsp	30		190	140	16	25	1.5	8	0	0	260	11	5	2	4	16	1	7	0	0	10	6
almonds, Blue Diamond	3 tbsp	32		200	150	16	25	1.5	8	0	0	0	0	7	2	4	16	1	7	0	0	8	6
almonds, dry-roasted, Blue Diamond	3 tbsp	30		200	150	16	25	1	5	0	0	130	5	6	2	3	12	1	7	0	0	10	6
almonds, honey-roasted, Blue Diamond	3 tbsp	30		180	140	13	20	1	5	0	0	40	2	10	3	3	12	0	6	0	0	8	4
almonds, oil-roasted, Blue Diamond	3 tbsp	30		200	150	16	25	1.5	8	0	0	0	0	4	1	4	16	1	7	0	0	10	6
almonds, smoked, Lance	1 package	21		130	90	10	15	1	5	0	0	125	5	4	1	3	12	0	6	0	0	6	4
cashews, Frito-Lay	3 tbsp	29		180	130	15	23	3	14	0	0	190	8	7	2	1	5	2	5	0	0	0	8
cashews, Lance	1 package	32		200	150	16	25	3	15	0	0	90	4	8	3	3	12	3	6	0	0	0	10
cashews, oil-roasted, Fisher	1/4 cup	28		170	130	15	22	2.5	13	0	0	160	7	8	3	0	3	2	5	0	0	0	10
mixed nuts, deluxe, oil-roasted, Fisher	1/4 cup	28		180	140	16	25	2.5	12	0	0	95	4	5	2	2	5	2	6	0	0	4	6
mixed nuts, dry-roasted, TownHouse	28 nuts	28		170	130	15	23	2	10	0	0	220	9	7	2	3	12	1	5	0	0	2	6
peanut butter & jelly, Smucker's	3 tbsp	53		230	120	13	20	2	10	0	0	160	6	24	8	2	8	16	7	0	0	0	3
peanut butter, creamy, Jif	2 tbsp	32		190	130	16	25	3	16	0	0	150	6	7	2	2	9	3	8	0	0	0	4
peanut butter, creamy, reduced fat, Skippy	2 tbsp	36		190	100	12	19	2.5	12	0	0	200	8	13	4	1	6	3	9	0	0	0	4
peanut butter, creamy/super chunk, Skippy	2 tbsp	32		190	140	17	26	3.5	17	0	0	150	6	5	2	2	8	2	8	0	0	0	2
peanut butter, extra crunchy, Jif	2 tbsp	32		190	130	16	25	3	15	0	0	130	5	7	2	2	8	3	8	0	0	0	4
peanut butter, natural (no stabilizers), Smucker's	2 tbsp	32		200	150	16	25	2	10	0	0	120	5	7	2	2	9	2	7	0	0	0	4
peanut butter, reduced fat, Jif	2 tbsp	36		190	110	12	18	2.5	12	0	0	220	9	15	5	2	8	4	8	0	0	0	4
peanut butter, Smucker's	2 tbsp	30		190	130	15	23	3	15	0	0	160	7	6	2	2	8	3	7	0	0	0	3
peanut butter, super chunk, reduced fat, Skippy	2 tbsp	35		190	110	12	19	2.5	13	0	0	170	7	12	4	1	6	3	9	0	0	0	4
peanuts & cashews, honey-roasted, Fisher	1/4 cup	28		170	120	13	20	2	9	0	0	110	5	8	3	1	5	5	6	0	0	0	4

Consult a similar product for brand names not listed.

Food Name	Serving Size	gm	mL	Calories	Calories from Fat	Total Fat (g)	%DV	Saturated Fat (g)	%DV	Cholesterol (mg)	%DV	Sodium (mg)	%DV	Total Carbohydrates (g)	%DV	Fiber[6] (g)	%DV	Sugars[6] (g)	Protein (g)	Vitamin A (%DV)	Vitamin C[7] (%DV)	Calcium (%DV)	Iron (%DV)
peanuts, honey-roasted, Fisher	1/4 cup	28		160	110	14	21	2.5	12	0	0	120	5	7	2	1	5	4	6	0	0	0	2
peanuts, honey-roasted, Planters	39 nuts	28		150	90	11	17	1.5	7	0	0	115	5	10	3	2	7	7	6	0	0	0	2
peanuts, honey-toasted, Lance	1/4 cup	35		200	130	14	22	2.5	13	0	0	150	6	11	4	3	12	5	8	0	0	0	2
peanuts, hot, Frito-Lay	3 tbsp	31		190	140	16	24	2.5	13	0	0	250	10	6	2	2	9	2*	7	0	0	2	2
peanuts, oil-roasted, Fisher	1/4 cup	28		170	120	15	23	2.5	13	0	0	130	5	5	2	2	7	1	7	0	0	0	2
peanuts, roasted in shell, Lance	3/4 cup (22 peanuts)	50		190	130	14	22	2.5	10	0	0	0	0	6	2	4	14	1	9	0	0	2	2
peanuts, salted, Frito-Lay	3 tbsp	30		200	150	16	25	4	20	0	0	180	8	5	2	2	8	1	7	0	0	0	2
peanuts, salted, Lance	1/4 cup	28		180	120	14	22	2.5	12	0	0	135	6	5	2	3	12	0	8	0	0	0	2
peanuts, Spanish, roasted, Fisher	1/4 cup	28		180	130	16	25	2.5	12	0	0	130	5	6	2	2	8	2	5	0	0	0	2
pistachios, Lance	1 package	32		90	60	7	11	1	5	0	0	105	4	4	1	2	8	0	4	0	0	2	4
sunflower seeds w/shells, Lance	2/3 cup	51		160	120	13	20	3	15	0	0	30	1	5	2	2	7	1	6	0	0	2	6
sunflower seeds, Frito-Lay	1/3 cup	29		140	70	8	13	1	6	0	0	1350	56	12	4	12	49	<1	4	0	0	4	4
sunflower seeds, oil-roasted, Fisher	1/4 cup	28		170	120	15	23	2	8	0	0	170	7	6	2	2	8	1	8	0	0	2	6
sunflower seeds, roasted, Lance	1/4 cup	35		210	160	17	27	2.5	12	0	0	110	5	6	2	2	9	1	7	0	0	2	10
trail mix w/nuts and dried fruit, Del Monte	1 oz	28		120	50	6	9	2	10	0	0	50	2	16	5	2	10	13	3	0	4	4	2

POULTRY: POULTRY

Food Name	Serving Size (gm / mL)	Calories	Calories from Fat	Total Fat (g)	%DV	Saturated Fat (g)	%DV	Cholesterol (mg)	%DV	Sodium (mg)	%DV	Total Carbohydrates (g)	%DV	Fiber (g)	%DV	Sugars (g)	Protein (g)	Vitamin A (%DV)	Vitamin C (%DV)	Calcium (%DV)	Iron (%DV)
chicken & cheddar nuggets, frzn, Banquet	2.5 oz	280	180	19	29	6	30	25	8	560	23	13	4	1	4	2	12	0	0	8	4
chicken breast & wing, rotisserie, KFC	176 / 1 each	335	168	19	29	5	27	157	52	1104	46	1	0	0	0	<1	40	<2	<2	<2	<2
chicken breast, baked, Louis Rich	45 / 2 slices	45	5	0.5	1	0	0	25	8	510	21	2	1	0	0	0	9	0	0	0	4
chicken breast, fried, frzn, Banquet	155 / 1 piece	410	240	26	41	13	66	85	28	600	25	18	6	4	14	2	23	0	8	6	4
chicken breast, fried, KFC	137 / 1 breast	360	180	20	31	5	27	115	38	870	36	12	4	1	4	0	33	0	0	6	6
chicken breast, skinless, baked	85 / 3 oz	120	15	1.5	2	0.5	3	70	23	65	3	0	0	0	0	0	24	0	0	0	4
chicken, chunk, cnd, Swanson	62 / ¼ cup	90	30	3	5	1	5	35	12	200	8	2	1	0	0	0	16	0	0	0	2
chicken, chunk, white, cnd, Swanson	68 / 1 can	80	20	2	3	1	5	40	13	240	10	1	0	0	0	0	15	0	0	0	0
chicken, country fried, frzn, Banquet	84 / 3 oz	270	160	18	27	5	23	65	22	620	26	13	4	1	5	1	14	0	6	8	4
chicken, drum & thigh, fried, frzn, Banquet	84 / 3 oz	260	160	18	28	5	23	65	21	540	22	10	3	2	8	1	15	0	8	2	2
chicken drumstick, fried, KFC	51 / 1 drumstick	130	60	7	11	2	9	70	24	210	9	4	1	0	0	0	13	0	0	0	2
chicken drumstick, skinless, baked	85 / 3 oz	130	35	4	6	1	5	80	27	80	3	0	0	0	0	0	23	0	0	0	6
chicken, fried, frzn, Banquet	255 / 1 meal	470	240	27	42	9	46	105	35	1040	43	35	12	3	12	3	21	0	8	8	6
chicken, fried, hot & spicy, frzn, Banquet	84 / 3 oz	260	160	18	27	5	23	65	22	590	25	13	4	1	5	1	14	0	6	8	4
chicken McNuggets, McDonald's	106 / 6 pieces	290	150	17	26	3.5	18	60	21	510	21	15	5	0	0	0	18	0	0	2	6
chicken, mixin' in broth, cnd, Swanson	62 / ¼ cup	110	60	7	11	3	15	45	15	190	8	1	0	0	0	0	12	0	0	4	2
chicken nibbles, frzn, Swanson	121 / 1 package	340	180	20	31	9	45	90	30	730	30	31	10	2	8	3	10	0	4	2	8
chicken nuggets, KFC	95 / 6 pieces	284	162	18	28	4	20	66	22	865	36	15	5	<1	4	0	16	0	0	2	4
chicken nuggets, southern fried, frzn, Banquet	81 / 9 nuggets	230	140	15	23	3	15	30	10	500	21	14	5	1	4	3	10	0	0	0	6
chicken nuggets, sweet & sour, frzn, Banquet	113 / 6 nuggets	320	160	18	28	4	20	45	15	670	28	25	8	2	8	0	16	0	2	2	6
chicken nuggets, Wendy's	94 / 6 pieces	280	180	20	31	5	25	50	17	600	25	12	4	0	0	0	14	0	0	2	4
chicken patty, fried, frzn, Banquet	64 / 1 patty	190	130	14	22	3	15	30	10	440	18	10	3	1	4	2	7	0	0	0	4

Consult a similar product for brand names not listed.

Food Name	Serving Size	gm	mL	Calories	Calories from Fat	Total Fat (g)	Total Fat %DV	Saturated Fat (g)	Saturated Fat %DV	Cholesterol (mg)	Cholesterol %DV	Sodium (mg)	Sodium %DV	Total Carbohydrates[δ] (g)	Total Carbohydrates %DV	Fiber[δ] (g)	Fiber %DV	Sugars[δ] (g)	Protein (g)	Vitamin A (%DV)	Vitamin C[7] (%DV)	Calcium (%DV)	Iron (%DV)
chicken patty strips, breaded, frzn, Swanson	1 package	150		340	170	19	29	3.5	18	30	10	560	23	31	10	3	12	2	11	2	10	2	8
chicken patty, Southern fried, frzn, Banquet	1 patty	64		170	90	10	15	2	11	20	7	430	18	10	3	1	3	1	10	0	2	0	4
chicken, skinless, fried, frzn, Banquet	3 oz	84		210	120	13	21	3	15	55	18	480	20	7	2	2	8	1	18	0	10	2	2
chicken, southern fried, frzn, Banquet	3 oz	84		270	160	18	27	5	23	65	22	590	25	13	4	1	5	1	14	0	6	8	4
chicken tenders, frzn, Banquet	3 tenders	85		240	140	15	23	3.5	18	40	13	480	20	15	5	<1	3	1	12	0	2	0	4
chicken tenders, southern fried, frzn, Banquet	3 tenders	89		210	90	10	15	2	10	20	7	490	20	14	5	2	8	0	16	0	2	2	8
chicken thigh & leg, rotisserie, KFC	1 each	146		333	213	24	36	6.6	33	163	54	980	41	1	0	0	0	0	30	0	0	0	0
chicken thigh, fried, KFC	1 thigh	92		260	150	17	26	5	23	110	36	570	24	9	3	1	5	0	19	0	0	4	6
chicken thigh, skinless, baked	3 oz	85		150	60	7	11	2	10	80	27	75	3	0	0	0	0	0	21	0	0	0	6
chicken, whole, skinless, roasted	3 oz	85		130	35	4	6	1	5	75	25	75	3	0	0	0	0	0	23	0	0	0	6
chicken wings, bbq, frzn, Banquet	4 pieces	113		230	140	16	25	5	25	85	28	280	12	5	2	1	4	0	15	0	8	2	4
chicken wings, fried, KFC	1 wing	48		150	80	8	13	3	12	40	13	380	16	7	2	0	0	0	11	0	0	2	2
chicken wings, hot & spicy, frzn, Banquet	4 pieces	112		260	160	18	28	5	25	85	28	400	17	7	2	<1	3	0	18	0	2	2	4
chicken wings, skinless, baked	3 oz	85		150	50	6	9	1.5	8	70	23	80	3	0	0	0	0	0	23	0	0	0	6
turkey bacon, Louis Rich	1 slice	14		35	25	2.5	4	1	5	15	5	180	8	0	0	0	0	0	2	0	0	0	0
turkey breast, roasted, Louis Rich	1 slice	28		25	0	0	0	0	0	10	3	330	14	1	0	0	0	<1	4	0	0	0	0
turkey breast, skinless, baked	3 oz	85		120	10	1	2	0	0	55	18	45	2	0	0	0	0	0	26	0	0	0	8
turkey, chunk, cnd, Swanson	1/4 cup	62		100	35	4	6	1	5	50	17	230	10	2	1	0	0	0	15	0	0	0	4
turkey, chunk, white, cnd, Swanson	1/4 cup	62		90	20	2	3	0.5	3	35	12	220	9	4	1	1	4	0	16	0	0	0	0
turkey drumstick, skinless, baked	3 oz	85		140	40	4	6	1	5	65	22	80	3	0	0	0	0	0	24	0	0	0	15
turkey, ground, Louis Rich	4 oz	112		190	110	12	18	3.5	18	90	30	140	6	0	0	0	0	0	20	0	0	2	10
turkey sausage links, Louis Rich	2.5 oz	70		120	70	8	12	2.5	13	55	18	430	18	1	0	0	0	0	12	0	0	4	6
turkey thigh, skinless, baked	3 oz	85		140	40	5	8	1.5	8	65	22	70	3	0	0	0	0	0	23	0	0	0	15
turkey whole, skinless, roasted	3 oz	85		130	25	3	5	1	5	65	22	60	3	0	0	0	0	0	25	0	0	0	8
turkey wing, skinless, baked	3 oz	85		140	25	3	5	1	5	60	20	75	3	0	0	0	0	0	26	0	0	0	8

POULTRY: POULTRY-BASED ENTREES[1]

Food Name	Serving Size	gm	mL	Calories	Calories from Fat	Total Fat (g)	%DV	Saturated Fat (g)	%DV	Cholesterol (mg)	%DV	Sodium (mg)	%DV	Total Carbohydrates[6] (g)	%DV	Fiber[6] (g)	%DV	Sugars[6] (g)	Protein (g)	Vitamin A (%DV)	Vitamin C[7] (%DV)	Calcium (%DV)	Iron (%DV)
chicken & dumplings in broth, frzn, Stouffer's	1 cup	248		230	90	10	15	3	12	100	31	900	37	17	6	2	10	0	18	0	2	2	8
chicken & dumplings, cnd, Swanson	1 cup	247		260	120	13	20	5	25	65	22	1120	47	22	7	0	0	1	13	8	0	4	6
chicken & dumplings, frzn, Banquet Family	1 entree	283		270	80	9	14	3	16	40	14	780	33	35	12	3	12	16	13	40	0	4	6
chicken & dumplings, frzn, Stouffer's	1 cup	255		350	180	20	31	5	20	85	28	980	41	24	8	2	10	8	18	0	2	15	10
chicken a la king, cnd, Swanson	1 cup	245		320	200	22	34	8	40	60	20	1080	45	17	6	0	0	2	15	0	0	8	6
chicken a la king, frzn, Banquet	1 entree	77		100	40	4	6	1.5	8	40	13	480	20	7	2	1	4	3	9	10	2	6	2
chicken chow mein, frzn, Lean Cuisine	1/2 cup	122		70	15	2	3	0.5	3	20	6	260	11	8	3	1	6	2	5	2	20	2	2
chicken classica,[40] frzn, Lean Cuisine	1 cup	240		190	60	6	10	2.0	8	45	15	570	24	20	6	2	7	9	14	35	35	10	4
chicken, creamed, frzn, Lean Cuisine	1/2 cup	139		220	160	18	27	8	40	60	18	520	22	6	2	1	3	3	9	0	0	6	2
chicken fajita pita, Jack in the Box	1 sandwich	187		280	80	9	14	4	18	75	25	840	35	25	8	3	11	5	24	10	0	15	15
chicken, fried, & whipped potatoes, frzn, Swanson Entree	1 entree	198		400	190	21	32	8	40	80	27	1120	47	34	11	2	8	3	19	0	6	6	10
chicken, glazed in sauce, frzn, Lean Cuisine	2 pieces w/sauce	116		100	40	5	7	1	4	35	12	410	17	4	1	0	0	2	12	0	2	0	2
chicken, honey mustard sauce, & veg rice, frzn, Lean Cuisine	1 entree	212		250	40	4.5	7	1	5	50	16	460	19	32	11	4	16	12	20	20	4	4	8
chicken italienne,[41] frzn, Lean Cuisine	1/2 cup	129		90	35	4	6	1	4	30	10	550	23	6	2	2	7	3	7	8	15	4	4
chicken kung pao w/rice, frzn, Yu Sing	1 container	234		310	80	9	14	2	10	35	11	630	26	44	15	4	17	6	13	2	0	4	6
chicken lo mein, broccoli, carrots, & sauce, frzn, Banquet	1 entree	297		270	60	6	10	1	6	20	7	1060	44	43	14	5	22	8	11	70	15	4	10
chicken lo mein, frzn, Yu Sing	1 container	241		240	35	4	7	2	9	15	6	880	37	37	12	4	14	1	14	4	0	8	8
chicken, Mexicali-style,[42] frzn, Lean Cuisine	1/2 cup	150		100	35	4	6	1	4	30	10	260	11	9	3	3	13	5	8	15	30	4	4

Consult a similar product for brand names not listed.

Food Name	Serving Size	gm	mL	Calories	Calories from Fat	Total Fat (g)	%DV	Saturated Fat (g)	%DV	Cholesterol (mg)	%DV	Sodium (mg)	%DV	Total Carbohydrates (g)	%DV	Fiber[6] (g)	%DV	Sugars[6] (g)	Protein (g)	Vitamin A (%DV)	Vitamin C[7] (%DV)	Calcium (%DV)	Iron (%DV)
chicken parmesan, frzn, Banquet Family	1 entree	269		320	160	18	28	4.5	22	50	17	900	38	29	10	3	12	4	10	6	50	6	10
chicken parmigiana, frzn, Contadina	1 patty & sauce	176		270	130	14	22	4	18	40	13	780	33	21	7	2	10	5	15	8	10	10	8
chicken, peanut sauce, linguini, & veg, frzn, Lean Cuisine	1 entree	255		280	60	6	9	1	5	45	14	590	25	33	11	3	11	5	23	8	8	8	8
chicken primavera, frzn, Lean Cuisine[3]	1/2 cup	145		80	30	4	5	0.5	3	25	8	420	17	6	2	2	9	2	7	15	15	2	2
chicken sandwich, bbq, KFC	1 sandwich	149		256	74	8	12	1	5	57	19	782	33	28	9	2	7	18	17	<1	6	6	23
chicken sandwich, breaded, Wendy's	1 sandwich	208		440	160	18	28	3	15	60	20	840	35	44	15	2	8	6	28	4	10	10	15
chicken sandwich, club, Wendy's	1 sandwich	220		500	200	23	35	5	25	70	23	1090	45	44	15	2	8	7	32	4	15	10	20
chicken sandwich, grilled, Wendy's	1 sandwich	177		290	60	7	11	1.5	8	55	18	720	30	35	12	2	8	8	24	4	10	10	15
chicken sandwich, KFC	1 sandwich	166		482	243	27	42	6	30	47	16	1060	44	39	13	3	12	2	21	0	0	5	7
chicken sandwich, supreme, Jack in the Box	1 sandwich	234		680	400	45	69	11	53	85	28	1500	63	46	15	4	17	8	23	15	15	25	15
chicken stew, cnd, Swanson	1 cup	245		180	70	8	12	3	15	35	12	1110	46	17	6	2	8	2	11	70	4	4	6
chicken, sweet & sour, frzn, Lean Cuisine	1/2 cup	145		110	20	2.5	4	0.5	2	20	6	200	8	15	5	2	9	11	8	15	25	2	2
chicken, sweet & sour w/rice, frzn, Yu Sing	1 container	241		350	80	9	14	4	18	25	8	640	27	53	18	2	10	15	13	8	0	6	6
chicken teriyaki bowl, Jack in the Box	1 serving	502		670	40	4	6	1	5	15	5	1620	68	128	43	5	18	24	29	60	0	15	0
chicken, turkey bacon, mushrooms, & pasta, frzn, Lean Cuisine	1 entree	255		290	70	8	11	2	8	40	13	540	22	32	11	4	15	6	22	0	0	15	10
chicken, veg, & crm sauce, frzn, Stouffer's	1/2 cup	125		140	80	9	13	2.5	10	35	11	490	20	8	3	1	5	2	7	15	4	4	2
gravy & turkey, frzn, Banquet Family	1 entree	262		280	90	10	15	2.5	13	55	18	1060	44	34	11	3	11	7	14	0	0	4	6
gravy, turkey, & dressing, cnd, Libby's Diner	1 container	167		180	70	7	11	1.5	8	35	11	830	35	17	5	2	9	2	11	25	0	2	6
turkey roast, white meat & gravy, frzn, Jennie-O	4 oz & 2 tbsp gravy	140		150	60	7	10	1.5	8	55	18	780	32	3	1	0	0	2	19	0	2	2	4

Food Name	Serving Size	gm	mL	Calories	Calories from Fat	Total Fat (g)	%DV	Saturated Fat (g)	%DV	Cholesterol (mg)	%DV	Sodium (mg)	%DV	Total Carbohydrates[a] (g)	%DV	Fiber[a] (g)	%DV	Sugars[a] (g)	Protein (g)	Vitamin A (%DV)	Vitamin C[a] (%DV)	Calcium (%DV)	Iron (%DV)
turkey, sauce, & rice w/veg., frzn, Smart Ones	1 entree	240		190	15	2	3	0.5	3	20	7	530	22	34	11	4	16	3	10	10	8	2	10
turkey, white meat, gravy, & dressing, frzn, Swanson	1 entree	255		230	45	5	8	2	10	30	10	1040	43	30	10	3	12	3	15	0	8	4	8

Consult a similar product for brand names not listed.

POULTRY: POULTRY-BASED MEALS/DINNERS[2]

Food Name	Serving Size	gm mL	Calories	Calories from Fat	Total Fat (g)	%DV	Saturated Fat (g)	%DV	Cholesterol (mg)	%DV	Sodium (mg)	%DV	Total Carbohydrates (g)	%DV	Fiber (g)	%DV	Sugars (g)	Protein (g)	Vitamin A (%DV)	Vitamin C (%DV)	Calcium (%DV)	Iron (%DV)
chicken, dark meat, fried, frzn, Swanson	1 meal	281	550	250	28	45	7	35	110	37	1530	64	50	17	4	16	16	24	2	4	4	15
chicken, dark meat, fried, frzn, Swanson Hungry Man	1 meal	404	810	370	41	63	14	70	120	40	1710	71	76	25	9	36	16	34	0	6	6	20
chicken, dark meat, fried, frzn, Swanson Budget	1 meal	240	460	190	21	32	6	30	85	28	1480	62	46	15	4	16	2	21	0	2	4	10
chicken drumlets, frzn, Swanson Children	1 meal	255	470	210	23	35	10	50	60	20	1110	46	50	17	3	12	19	16	0	8	4	10
chicken, fried, frzn, Swanson Children	1 meal	312	570	270	30	46	7	35	110	37	1430	60	50	17	4	16	16	25	2	4	4	15
chicken, frzn, Budget Gourmet[44]	1 meal	311	240	60	7	11	2	10	35	12	660	28	29	10	4	16	6	16	10	20	10	10
chicken, frzn, Swanson Hungry Man	1 meal	489	690	240	27	42	11	55	105	35	1390	58	76	25	7	28	23	35	25	8	8	25
chicken, herb-roasted, frzn, Swanson	1 meal	291	290	50	6	9	2.5	13	30	10	750	31	42	14	3	12	11	16	110	2	2	8
chicken nuggets, frzn, Banquet	1 meal	191	430	210	23	35	8	40	50	17	650	27	42	14	4	16	11	14	0	10	2	8
chicken nuggets, frzn, Swanson	1 meal	269	440	170	19	29	7	35	35	12	980	41	48	16	4	16	14	18	2	4	4	8
chicken parmigiana, frzn, Swanson	1 meal	326	400	170	19	29	7	35	35	12	1160	48	43	14	4	16	14	15	20	45	15	10
chicken parmigiana, frzn, Swanson Budget	1 meal	284	340	160	18	28	8	40	40	13	760	32	33	11	4	16	8	11	170	30	8	6
chicken patties, grilled, frzn, Swanson Hungry Man	1 meal	482	580	170	19	29	8	40	90	30	1360	57	67	22	13	52	50	35	10	15	10	25
chicken tenders platter, frzn, Swanson	1 meal	227	320	110	12	18	3	15	25	8	790	33	39	13	3	12	13	14	70	8	4	6
chicken, white meat, fried, frzn, Swanson	1 meal	294	560	230	26	40	7	35	70	23	1710	71	54	18	5	20	17	27	2	4	6	15
chicken, white meat, fried, frzn, Swanson Hungry Man	1 meal	468	810	360	40	62	14	70	120	40	2060	86	77	26	7	28	17	35	0	6	8	20
chicken, white meat, grilled in garlic sauce, frzn, Swanson	1 meal	284	260	50	6	9	3	15	30	10	660	28	35	12	5	20	17	17	110	30	10	10
turkey breast meat & pasta, frzn, Swanson	1 meal	319	270	60	7	11	4	20	35	12	720	30	31	10	6	24	11	20	140	60	15	10

Food Name	Serving Size	gm	mL	Calories	Calories from Fat	Total Fat (g)	%DV	Saturated Fat (g)	%DV	Cholesterol (mg)	%DV	Sodium (mg)	%DV	Total Carbohydrates[6] (g)	%DV	Fiber[6] (g)	%DV	Sugars[5] (g)	Protein (g)	Vitamin A (%DV)	Vitamin C[7] (%DV)	Calcium (%DV)	Iron (%DV)
turkey, frzn, Bel-Air[45]	1 meal	533		560	180	20	30	5	24	75	25	1910	80	63	21	7	28	26	32	0	0	10	20
turkey, white meat, frzn, Swanson	1 meal	333		300	50	6	9	3	15	35	12	1130	47	42	14	4	16	15	20	10	15	4	10
turkey, white meat, frzn, Swanson Hungry Man	1 meal	475		510	130	15	23	6	30	45	15	1660	69	59	20	9	36	18	35	10	10	6	20

Consult a similar product for brand names not listed.

POULTRY: POULTRY-BASED CHOWDERS AND SOUPS

Food Name	Serving Size	gm	mL	Calories	Calories from Fat	Total Fat (g)	Total Fat %DV	Saturated Fat (g)	Saturated Fat %DV	Cholesterol (mg)	Cholesterol %DV	Sodium (mg)	Sodium %DV	Total Carbohydrates (g)	Total Carbohydrates %DV	Fiber (g)	Fiber %DV	Sugars (g)	Protein (g)	Vitamin A (%DV)	Vitamin C (%DV)	Calcium (%DV)	Iron (%DV)
chicken & broccoli, crm of, cnd cond, Campbell's	½ cup	124		120	70	12	8	2.5	13	15	5	860	36	9	3	1	4	1	4	15	2	2	2
chicken broccoli cheese, chunky, cnd rts, Campbell's	1 can	305		250	140	23	15	6	30	30	10	1400	58	17	6	1	4	1	11	25	0	4	4
chicken, chunky, cnd rts, Campbell's	1 can	305		160	45	5	8	1.5	8	25	8	1180	49	19	6	3	12	3	12	110	0	4	8
chicken corn, chunky, cnd rts, Campbell's	1 can	305		310	170	19	29	9	45	30	10	1080	45	22	7	4	16	5	12	90	6	4	8
chicken, creamy w/mushroom soup, chunky, cnd rts, Campbell's	1 can	305		270	180	20	31	9	45	25	8	1270	53	14	5	1	4	2	12	30	0	2	4
chicken, crm of, cnd cond, Campbell's	½ cup	124		130	70	8	12	3	15	10	3	890	37	11	4	1	4	1	3	10	0	2	2
chicken, crm of, cnd rts, Campbell's Home Cookin'	1 can	305		260	200	22	34	8	40	20	7	1460	61	11	4	3	12	2	4	0	6	2	4
chicken dumplings, cnd cond, Campbell's	½ cup	126		80	25	3	5	1	5	25	8	1050	44	10	3	2	8	1	4	8	0	2	2
chicken, grilled, southwest, frzn conc, Stouffer's	½ cup	131		110	45	5	5	1	5	20	5	630	25	13	4	2	9	4	5	15	6	2	2
chicken gumbo, cnd cond, Campbell's	½ cup	126		60	15	1.5	3	0.5	3	10	3	990	41	9	3	1	4	1	2	4	0	2	2
chicken gumbo, frzn conc, Stouffer's	½ cup	106		100	40	5	7	1	6	15	5	1040	43	11	4	1	3	2	3	4	15	2	2
chicken mushroom, chunky, cnd rts, Campbell's	1 cup	245		210	110	12	18	4	20	10	3	970	40	15	5	3	12	1	10	0	8	2	8
chicken mushroom, cnd cond, Campbell's	½ cup	124		130	80	9	14	2.5	13	15	5	1000	42	9	3	1	4	1	3	15	0	2	2
chicken nuggets w/veg, chunky, cnd rts, Campbell's	1 can	305		190	60	7	11	2	10	15	5	1030	43	24	8	4	16	5	10	50	8	4	8
chicken veg, chunky, cnd rts, Campbell's	1 cup	245		90	10	1	2	0	0	10	3	870	36	13	4	3	12	2	7	35	6	2	10
chicken veg, cnd cond, Campbell's	½ cup	126		80	20	2	3	0.5	3	10	3	940	39	12	4	2	8	4	3	50	0	2	4
chicken veg, cnd rts, Campbell's Home Cookin'	1 can	305		170	35	4	6	1	5	10	3	1020	43	24	8	4	16	7	8	90	4	6	6

Food Name	Serving Size		Calories	Calories from Fat	Total Fat		Saturated Fat		Cholesterol		Sodium		Total Carbohydrates⁶		Fiber⁸		Sugars⁸	Protein	Vitamin A	Vitamin C⁷	Calcium	Iron
	gm	mL			(g)	%DV	(g)	%DV	(mg)	%DV	(mg)	%DV	(g)	%DV	(g)	%DV	(g)	(g)	(%DV)	(%DV)	(%DV)	(%DV)
chicken veg, southwest, cnd cond, Campbell's	126		110	15	1.5	2	0.5	3	10	3	900	38	18	6	4	16	4	7	10	40	4	6
chicken won ton, cnd cond, Campbell's	126		45	10	1	2	0	0	15	5	940	39	5	2	1	4	1	4	2	0	2	2
turkey veg, cnd cond, Campbell's	126		80	25	2.5	4	1	5	10	3	840	35	11	4	2	8	2	3	50	0	2	4

Consult a similar product for brand names not listed.

Fats, Oils,

and

Sweets

(and Alcohol)

Food Name	Serving Size	gm	mL	Calories	Calories from Fat	Total Fat (g)	%DV	Saturated Fat (g)	%DV	Cholesterol (mg)	%DV	Sodium (mg)	%DV	Total Carbohydrates[δ] (g)	%DV	Fiber[δ] (g)	%DV	Sugars[δ] (g)	Protein (g)	Vitamin A (%DV)	Vitamin C[7] (%DV)	Calcium (%DV)	Iron (%DV)
ALCOHOLIC BEVERAGES																							
beer	12 fl oz	356		146	0	0	0	0	0	0	0	9	0	13	4	0	0	0	1	0	0	0	0
beer, light	12 fl oz	354		99	0	0	0	0	0	0	0	9	0	5	2	0	0	0	1	0	0	0	0
vodka, 80 proof	1.5 fl oz	42		97	0	0	0	0	0	0	0	0	0	0	0	0	0	0	0	0	0	0	0
whiskey, 86 proof	1.5 fl oz	42		105	0	0	0	0	0	0	0	0	0	0	0	0	0	0	0	0	0	0	0
wine, red	3.5 fl oz	103		74	0	0	0	0	0	0	0	5	0	2	0	0	0	0	0	0	0	0	0
wine, white	3.5 fl oz	103		70	0	0	0	0	0	0	0	5	0	1	0	0	0	0	0	0	0	0	0

FAT- AND OIL-BASED PRODUCTS

Food Name	Serving Size	gm	mL	Calories	Calories from Fat	Total Fat (g)	%DV	Saturated Fat (g)	%DV	Cholesterol (mg)	%DV	Sodium (mg)	%DV	Total Carbohydrates (g)	%DV	Fiber (g)	%DV	Sugars (g)	Protein (g)	Vitamin A (%DV)	Vitamin C (%DV)	Calcium (%DV)	Iron (%DV)
butter, sweet crm, Lucerne	1 tbsp	14		100	100	11	17	7	36	30	10	90	4	0	0	0		0	0	8	0	0	0
creamer, nondairy, Cremora, Borden	1 tsp	2		10	10	1	1	0.5	3	0	0	0	0	1	0	0	0	0	0	0	0	0	0
Dijonnaise, Hellmann's/Best Foods[45]	1 tsp	5		10	10	1	1	0	0	0	0	60	3	1	0	0	0	0	0	0	0	0	0
dip, bacon ranch, Marie's	2 tbsp	28		150	144	16	25	2	10	15	5	200	8	3	1	0	0	0	1	0	2	0	0
dip, parmesan garlic, Marie's	2 tbsp	28		140	130	14	22	2	10	10	3	140	6	2	1	<1	1	<1	1	2	2	0	2
dip, ranch, Marie's	2 tbsp	28		150	140	15	22	2	10	15	5	140	6	3	1	0	0	1	0	2	0	0	2
dip, spinach, Marie's	2 tbsp	28		140	130	14	22	2	10	10	3	200	8	3	1	0	0	<1	0	8	0	0	2
dressing, blue cheese, Best Foods	1 1/3 tbsp	19		80	70	8	12	2	10	10	3	230	10	1	1	0	0	0	0	0	0	0	0
dressing, blue cheese, chunky, reduced cal, Marie's	2 tbsp	32		100	60	7	11	1.5	8	10	3	260	11	7	2	0	0	2	1	0	0	4	0
dressing, coleslaw, Hellmann's/Best Foods	2 tbsp	30		160	140	16	25	2.5	12	5	2	180	8	4	1	0	0	4	0	0	0	0	0
dressing, coleslaw, Marie's	2 tbsp	30		150	120	13	20	2	10	10	3	210	9	6	2	0	0	6	0	0	0	0	0
dressing/dip, buttermilk spice ranch, Marie's	2 tbsp	30		180	160	18	28	3	15	15	5	230	10	4	1	0	0	2	0	0	0	0	0
dressing/dip, French, tangy, Marie's	2 tbsp	30		130	100	11	17	1.5	8	0	0	260	11	8	3	0	0	7	0	0	0	0	0
dressing/dip, honey mustard, Marie's	2 tbsp	30		160	140	15	23	2	10	5	2	160	7	8	3	<1	2	10	0	0	0	0	0
dressing/dip, Ital, creamy garlic, reduced cal, Marie's	2 tbsp	32		90	60	7	11	0.5	3	5	2	240	10	6	2	1	4	3	<1	0	0	2	0
dressing/dip, parmesan ranch, Marie's	2 tbsp	30		180	170	19	29	3	15	15	5	160	7	3	1	0	0	<1	<1	0	0	0	0
dressing/dip, poppyseed, Marie's	2 tbsp	30		150	110	12	18	1.5	8	10	3	200	8	8	3	0	0	6	0	0	0	0	0
dressing/dip, ranch, Marie's	2 tbsp	30		190	180	20	31	3	15	15	5	170	7	3	1	0	0	<1	<1	0	0	0	0
dressing/dip, ranch, reduced cal, Marie's	2 tbsp	30		100	70	8	12	0.5	3	10	3	280	12	7	2	<1	2	3	1	0	0	2	0
dressing/dip, sour crm & dill, Marie's	2 tbsp	30		190	180	20	31	3	15	15	5	160	7	3	1	0	0	<1	0	0	0	0	0
dressing/dip, thousand island, Marie's	2 tbsp	30		240	210	23	35	4	20	20	7	320	13	7	2	0	0	5	0	0	0	0	0
dressing, Ital, creamy, Best Foods	1 1/3 tbsp	19		110	110	12	18	2	10	5	2	210	9	1	1	0	0	0	0	0	0	0	0

Consult a similar product for brand names not listed.

Food Name	Serving Size	gm	mL	Calories	Calories from Fat	Total Fat (g)	%DV	Saturated Fat (g)	%DV	Cholesterol (mg)	%DV	Sodium (mg)	%DV	Total Carbohydrates (g)	%DV	Fiber (g)	%DV	Sugars (g)	Protein (g)	Vitamin A (%DV)	Vitamin C (%DV)	Calcium (%DV)	Iron (%DV)
dressing, Ital, creamy garlic, Marie's	2 tbsp	30		180	170	19	29	3	15	15	5	220	9	3	1	0	0	<1	0	0	0	0	0
dressing, ranch, Best Foods	1 1/3 tbsp	19		120	110	13	20	2	10	10	3	220	9	1	1	0	0	0	0	0	0	0	0
dressing, ranch, light, Best Foods	1 1/3 tbsp	20		70	60	7	11	1	6	0	0	200	8	2	1	0	0	1	0	0	0	0	0
dressing, thousand island, Best Foods	1 1/3 tbsp	20		80	70	8	12	1	5	0	0	200	8	3	1	0	0	2	0	0	0	0	0
gravy, au jus, cnd, Franco-Am	1/4 cup	59		10	5	0.5	1	0	0	<5	1	310	13	2	1	0	0	2	0	0	0	0	0
gravy, beef w/beef pieces, cnd, Pepperidge	1/4 cup	59		25	10	1	2	0	0	<5	1	360	15	4	1	0	0	0	1	0	0	0	0
gravy, beef, cnd, Franco-Am	1/4 cup	59		30	20	2	3	1	5	<5	1	300	13	4	1	0	0	0	1	0	0	0	0
gravy, brown, & onion, dry mix, Knorr	1/5 package	6		20	5	0.5	1	0	0	0	0	320	13	4	1	0	0	0	0	0	0	0	0
gravy, brown, dry mix, Knorr	1/6 package	6		20		0.5	1	0	0	0	0	400	17	3	1	0	0	0	0	0	0	0	0
gravy, brown w/onions, cnd, Franco-Am	1/4 cup	59		25	10	1	2	0	0	<5	1	340	14	4	1	0	0	2	0	0	0	0	0
gravy, chicken giblet, cnd, Franco-Am	1/4 cup	59		30	20	2	3	0	0	10	3	310	13	3	1	0	0	0	1	0	0	0	0
gravy, chicken w/chicken pieces, cnd, Pepperidge	1/4 cup	59		25	10	1	2	0	0	<5	1	270	11	3	1	0	0	0	1	0	0	0	0
gravy, chicken, cnd, Franco-Am	1/4 cup	59		45	35	4	6	1	5	5	2	270	11	3	1	0	0	1	1	0	0	0	0
gravy, chicken, cnd, Libby's	1/4 cup	61		60	35	4	6	0.5	3	5	2	330	14	3	1	0	0	0	1	0	0	0	0
gravy, chicken, dry mix, Knorr	1/5 package	7		30	10	1	2	0	0	5	1	330	13	3	1	0	0	0	2	0	0	0	0
gravy, chicken, rotisserie, cnd, Pepperidge	1/4 cup	59		25	10	1	2	0	0	5	2	280	12	3	1	0	0	0	1	0	0	0	0
gravy, creamy mushroom, cnd, Franco-Am	1/4 cup	59		20	10	1	2	0	0	<5	1	310	13	4	1	0	0	0	1	0	0	0	0
gravy, crm of chicken, cnd, Pepperidge	1/4 cup	59		30	10	1	2	0.5	3	5	2	280	12	3	1	0	0	0	1	0	0	0	0
gravy, mushroom & wine, cnd, Pepperidge	1/4 cup	59		30	5	0	1	0	0	<5	1	300	13	4	1	0	0	0	1	0	0	0	0
gravy, mushroom, cnd, Franco-Am	1/4 cup	59		20	10	1	2	0	0	5	1	300	15	3	1	0	0	0	1	0	0	0	0
gravy, mushroom, dry mix, Knorr	1/5 package	6		25	10	1	1	0	0	0	0	270	11	4	1	0	0	0	1	0	0	0	0

Food Name	Serving Size	gm	mL	Calories	Calories from Fat	Total Fat (g)	%DV	Saturated Fat (g)	%DV	Cholesterol (mg)	%DV	Sodium (mg)	%DV	Total Carbohydrates (g)	%DV	Fiber (g)	%DV	Sugars (g)	Protein (g)	Vitamin A (%DV)	Vitamin C (%DV)	Calcium (%DV)	Iron (%DV)
gravy, onion & garlic, cnd, Pepperidge	1/4 cup	59		25	10	1	2	0.5	3	<5	1	350	15	4	1	0	0	0	0	0	0	0	0
gravy, pork, cnd, Franco-Am	1/4 cup	59		45	35	4	6	1.5	8	4	1	340	14	3	1	1	4	0	1	0	0	0	0
gravy, sausage, cnd, Libby's	1/4 cup	64		90	60	7	11	1.5	8	5	2	280	12	3	1	0	0	0	1	0	0	0	0
gravy, stroganoff w/mushrooms, cnd, Pepperidge	1/4 cup	59		30	10	1	2	0.5	3	<5	1	240	10	4	1	0	0	0	<1	0	0	0	0
gravy, turkey, cnd, Franco-Am	1/4 cup	59		25	10	1	2	0	0	<5	1	290	12	3	1	0	0	0	<1	0	0	0	0
gravy, turkey, dry mix, Knorr	1/5 package	7		25	5	0.5	1	0	0	5	1	290	12	4	1	0	0	0	2	0	0	0	0
gravy, turkey w/turkey pieces, cnd, Pepperidge	1/4 cup	59		30	10	1	2	0	0	<5	1	330	14	4	1	0	0	0	2	0	0	0	0
margarine, 40% corn oil, Diet Mazola	1 tbsp	14		50	50	6	9	1	5	0	0	130	5	0	0	0	0	0	0	10	0	0	0
margarine, Land O Lakes	1 tbsp	14		100	100	11	17	2	11	0	0	115	5	0	0	0	0	0	0	10	0	0	0
margarine, Mazola	1 tbsp	14		100	100	11	17	2	10	0	0	100	4	0	0	0	0	0	0	10	0	0	0
mayonnaise, Hellmann's	1 tbsp	14		100	100	11	17	1.5	9	5	2	80	3	0	0	0	0	0	0	0	0	0	0
mayonnaise, light, Hellmann's	1 tbsp	15		50	45	5	8	1	4	5	2	115	5	1	0	0	0	0	0	0	0	0	0
oil, canola & corn, Rightblend, Mazola	1 tbsp	14		120	120	14	22	1	5	0	0	0	0	0	0	0	0	0	0	0	0	0	0
oil, canola, Puritan	1 tbsp	14		120	120	14	21	1	5	0	0	0	0	0	0	0	0	0	0	0	0	0	0
oil, corn canola, Crisco	1 tbsp	14		120	120	14	21	1.5	7	0	0	0	0	0	0	0	0	0	0	0	0	0	0
oil, corn, Mazola	1 tbsp	14		120	120	14	22	2	9	0	0	0	0	0	0	0	0	0	0	0	0	0	0
oil, Crisco	1 tbsp	14		120	120	14	21	2	10	0	0	0	0	0	0	0	0	0	0	0	0	0	0
Sandwich Spread, Hellmann's	1 tbsp	15		50	45	5	8	1	4	<5	1	170	7	3	1	0	0	2	0	0	0	0	0
sauce, alfredo, Contadina	1/2 cup	125		290	220	25	37	7	35	50	16	620	26	12	3	0	0	5	5	0	0	20	0
sauce, demi-glacé, dry mix, Knorr	1/5 package	7		30	10	1	1	0	0	0	0	380	16	4	1	0	0	1	1	0	0	0	0
sauce, peppercorn, dry mix, Knorr	1/5 package	6		25	5	1	1	0	0	0	0	350	15	3	1	0	0	1	1	0	0	0	0
sauce, pesto, Contadina	1/4 cup	61		150	100	12	18	3	13	15	5	230	10	4	1	2	11	1	6	25	4	15	4
shortening, butter flavor, Crisco	1 tbsp	12		110	110	12	18	3	15	0	0	0	0	0	0	0	0	0	0	4	0	0	0
shortening, Crisco	1 tbsp	12		110	110	12	18	3	15	0	0	0	0	0	0	0	0	0	0	0	0	0	0
sour cream	1 tbsp	12		30	20	2.5	4	1.5	8	5	2	0	0	0	0	0	0	0	0	2	0	0	0

Consult a similar product for brand names not listed.

Food Name	Serving Size	gm	mL	Calories	Calories from Fat	Total Fat (g)	%DV	Saturated Fat (g)	%DV	Cholesterol (mg)	%DV	Sodium (mg)	%DV	Total Carbohydrates (g)	%DV	Fiber (g)	%DV	Sugars (g)	Protein (g)	Vitamin A (%DV)	Vitamin C (%DV)	Calcium (%DV)	Iron (%DV)
spread, corn oil, Mazola Light 40%	1 tbsp	14		50	50	6	9	1	5	0	0	100	4	0	0	0	0	0	0	10	0	0	0
tartar sauce, Hellmann's	2 tbsp	28		80	60	7	11	1	5	10	4	300	12	3	0	0	0	2	0	0	0	0	0
tartar sauce, low fat, Hellmann's	2 tbsp	32		40	15	2	2	0	0	0	0	360	15	7	2	0	0	5	0	0	0	0	0
Vegetable oil cooking spray, Pam spray	1/3 second	0.26		0	0	0	0	0	0	0	0	0	0	0	0	0	0	0	0	0	0	0	0

SWEETS: BEVERAGES, SWEETENED

Food Name	Serving Size	gm	mL	Calories	Calories from Fat	Total Fat (g)	%DV	Saturated Fat (g)	%DV	Cholesterol (mg)	%DV	Sodium (mg)	%DV	Total Carbohydrates (g)	%DV	Fiber (g)	%DV	Sugars (g)	Protein (g)	Vitamin A (%DV)	Vitamin C (%DV)	Calcium (%DV)	Iron (%DV)
Cherry Royal Crown Cola	8 fl oz		240	110	0	0	0	0	0	0	0	35	1	29	10	0	0	29	0	0	0	0	0
Cherry 7UP	12 fl oz		355	140	0	0	0	0	0	0	0	35	1	39	13	0	0	39	0	0	0	0	0
Coca Cola	12 fl oz		360	140	0	0	0	0	0	0	0	50	2	39	13	0	0	39	0	0	0	0	0
Dr Pepper	12 fl oz		355	150	0	0	0	0	0	0	0	55	2	40	13	0	0	40	0	0	0	0	0
Fruit Punch Nehi	8 fl oz		240	120	0	0	0	0	0	0	0	35	1	34	11	0	0	34	0	0	0	0	0
Grape Nehi	8 fl oz		240	120	0	0	0	0	0	0	0	35	1	32	11	0	0	32	0	0	0	0	0
Kick Citrus Soda	8 fl oz		240	120	0	0	0	0	0	0	0	35	1	32	11	0	0	32	0	0	0	0	0
Mountain Dew	8 fl oz		240	110	0	0	0	0	0	0	0	50	2	31	10	0	0	31	0	0	0	0	0
Nehi Ginger Ale	8 fl oz		240	90	0	0	0	0	0	0	0	35	1	24	8	0	0	24	0	0	0	0	0
Orange Nehi	8 fl oz		240	130	0	0	0	0	0	0	0	35	1	35	12	0	0	35	0	0	0	0	0
Pepsi	8 fl oz		240	100	0	0	0	0	0	0	0	25	1	27	9	0	0	27	0	0	0	0	0
Pineapple Nehi	8 fl oz		240	130	0	0	0	0	0	0	0	35	1	36	12	0	0	36	0	0	0	0	0
Royal Crown Cola	8 fl oz		240	110	0	0	0	0	0	0	0	35	1	29	10	0	0	29	0	0	0	0	0
7UP	12 fl oz		355	140	0	0	0	0	0	0	0	75	3	39	13	0	0	39	0	0	0	0	0
Slice Lemon Lime	12 fl oz		360	150	0	0	0	0	0	0	0	55	2	40	13	0	0	39	0	0	0	0	0
Strawberry Nehi	8 fl oz		240	120	0	0	0	0	0	0	0	35	1	32	11	0	0	32	0	0	0	0	0
tea, iced, inst powder w/sugar, Tetley	1 ½ tbsp	23		90	0	0	0	0	0	0	0	10	1	21	7	0	0	21	0	0	0	0	0
Upper 10	8 fl oz		240	110	0	0	0	0	0	0	0	0	0	29	10	0	0	29	0	0	0	0	0

Consult a similar product for brand names not listed.

SWEETS: CANDY

Food Name	Serving Size	gm	mL	Calories	Calories from Fat	Total Fat (g)	%DV	Saturated Fat (g)	%DV	Cholesterol (mg)	%DV	Sodium (mg)	%DV	Total Carbohydrates (g)	%DV	Fiber (g)	%DV	Sugars (g)	Protein (g)	Vitamin A (%DV)	Vitamin C (%DV)	Calcium (%DV)	Iron (%DV)
After Dinner Mint	1.4 oz	40		160	5	0.5	1	0	0	0	0	0	0	38	13	0	0	38	0	0	0	0	0
Almond Joy, Peter Paul	1 package	49		240	120	13	21	9	45	0	0	65	3	28	9	2	8	20	2	0	0	2	2
Aplets & Cotlets, Liberty Orchards	3 pieces	42		150	30	4	6	0	0	0	0	45	2	31	10	0	0	24	<1	0	0	0	0
Baby Ruth, Nestlé	1 bar (2.1 oz)	60		280	110	12	19	7	36	0	0	135	6	38	13	2	7	25	4	0	0	2	0
Bordeaux Egg, See's Candies	240	56		240	90	11	17	7	35	20	7	65	3	38	13	0	0	36	2	4	0	4	2
Butterfinger, Nestlé	1 bar (2.1 oz)	60		280	100	11	17	6	31	0	0	120	5	41	14	1	6	40	4	0	0	0	2
butterscotch discs	3 pieces	15		60	0	0	0	0	0	0	0	40	2	14	5	0	0	14	0	0	0	0	0
candied citron, S&W	39 pieces	30		90	0	0	0	0	0	0	0	25	1	23	8	1	4	17	0	0	0	0	0
candied lemon peel, S&W	58 pieces	30		80	0	0	0	0	0	0	0	25	1	23	8	2	8	18	0	0	0	4	0
candied orange peel, S&W	58 pieces	30		80	0	0	0	0	0	0	0	35	1	23	8	2	8	18	0	0	0	4	0
Candy Corn	36 pieces	40		160	0	0	0	0	0	0	0	15	1	38	13	0	0	38	0	0	0	0	0
caramel fudge egg, Fanny Farmer	1/6 egg	40		212	120	13	20	5	25	10	3	55	2	22	7	2	8	16	2	0	0	2	2
caramels	4 pieces	40		160	15	2	3	0.5	3	0	0	5	0	32	11	0	0	27	0	0	0	0	0
Charleston Chew	1 bar	53		230	60	7	11	6	32	0	0	50	2	40	13	1	5	30	2	0	0	4	2
chewing gum	1 stick	3		10	0	0	0	0	0	0	0	0	0	3	1	0	0	3	0	0	0	0	0
chewing gum, Big Red, Wrigley's	1 stick	3		10	0	0	0	0	0	0	0	0	0	2	1	0	0	2	0	0	0	0	0
chewing gum, bubble, Lance	1 piece	7		25	0	0	0	0	0	0	0	0	0	6	2	0	0	5	0	0	0	0	0
chewing gum, Doublemint, Wrigley's	1 piece	3		10	0	0	0	0	0	0	0	0	0	2	1	0	0	2	0	0	0	0	0
Chews, all flavors, Lance	11 pieces	30		120	5	0.5	1	0.5	3	0	0	0	0	28	9	0	0	22	0	0	0	0	0
choc caramels, Riesen	5 pieces	40		180	60	7	10	3	17	<5	1	30	1	29	10	3	12	20	2	0	0	4	6
choc, dark	1.4 oz	40		200	100	11	17	7	35	0	0	0	0	25	8	4	16	21	1	0	0	0	12
choc, dark w/almonds, Trader Joe's	5 squares	40		230	140	16	24	7	35	0	0	0	0	19	6	6	26	7	4	0	0	0	20
choc, dark, chips	30 pieces	15		70	35	4	6	2.5	12	0	0	0	0	27	9	1	4	8	1	0	0	0	4
choc, dark, Dove	1 bar	37		200	110	12	19	7	36	5	1	0	0	22	7	2	9	19	2	0	0	0	4
choc, dark, Dove Miniatures	7 pieces	42		220	120	14	21	8	41	5	1	0	0	26	9	2	10	21	2	0	0	0	6
choc, dark, Hershey's	1 bar	73		410	220	24	36	15	74	0	0	5	0	44	15	4	15	34	4	0	0	2	10
choc, dark, Trader Joe's	4 squares	40		230	130	15	23	9	45	0	0	5	0	21	7	6	26	14	3	0	0	0	2

Food Name	Serving Size	gm	mL	Calories	Calories from Fat	Total Fat (g)	%DV	Saturated Fat (g)	%DV	Cholesterol (mg)	%DV	Sodium (mg)	%DV	Total Carbohydrates (g)	%DV	Fiber (g)	%DV	Sugars (g)	Protein (g)	Vitamin A (%DV)	Vitamin C (%DV)	Calcium (%DV)	Iron (%DV)
choc, milk	1.4 oz	40		210	120	20	13	7	35	11	4	35	2	23	8	1	4	22	3	0	0	10	2
choc, milk, malted milk balls	17 pieces	40		180	50	6	9	3	15	2	1	55	2	28	9	0	0	26	0	0	0	6	0
choc, milk, Nestlé	1 bar (1.45 oz)	41		220	110	13	20	7	37	10	3	30	1	23	8	2	6	21	4	0	0	0	8
choc, milk w/almonds	1.4 oz	40		210	130	14	22	7	35	7	2	30	2	21	7	2	8	20	4	0	0	8	4
choc, milk w/almonds, Hershey's	1.3 oz	37		210	120	13	20	6	31	5	2	30	1	19	6	1	5	16	4	0	0	8	2
chocolates,[47] assorted, See's	3 pieces	44		200	100	12	18	6	30	10	3	45	2	25	8	1	4	22	2	2	0	4	4
chocolates,[47] choc & variety, See's	3 pieces	45		220	110	13	20	6	30	15	5	60	3	24	8	1	4	20	3	4	0	4	2
chocolates,[47] crisp & chewy, Fannie May	3 pieces	47		239	120	13	20	10	50	10	3	125	5	29	10	0	0	22	2	2	2	4	2
chocolates,[47] dark, Fanny May	2 pieces	35		164	70	7	11	6	30	<5	0	40	2	23	8	1	4	19	1	0	0	2	2
chocolates,[47] dark, See's	3 pieces	47		210	100	13	20	6	30	10	3	40	2	27	9	2	8	22	2	2	0	2	4
chocolates,[47] milk choc, Russell Stover	1.5 oz	40		220	130	14	22	7	35	5	2	30	1	22	7	1	4	20	3	0	0	6	2
chocolates,[47] milk choc, See's	3 pieces	45		210	110	12	18	6	30	15	5	50	2	27	9	<1	4	23	2	4	0	4	2
chocolates,[47] nuts & chews, See's	3 pieces	47		240	130	16	25	6	30	10	3	55	2	24	8	2	8	19	4	2	0	4	6
chocolates,[47] soft centers, See's	2 pieces	38		170	70	8	12	5	25	10	3	35	1	24	8	<1	3	22	1	2	0	2	0
Chuckles jelly rings	4 pieces	45		150	0	0	0	0	0	0	0	15	1	37	12	0	0	27	0	0	0	0	0
Chunky, Nestlé	1 bar (1.4 oz)	40		200	100	11	17	6	29	<5	1	20	1	22	7	2	7	20	3	0	0	6	2
Crunch, Nestlé	1 bar (1.55 oz)	44		230	110	12	18	7	34	5	2	60	2	28	9	1	4	23	3	0	0	8	0
Dunking Sticks, Lance	1 piece	39		180	80	9	14	3	15	<5	1	130	5	22	7	<1	3	15	2	0	0	0	2
Fruit Bunch Jellies, Brach's	3 pieces	44		150	0	0	0	0	0	0	0	15	1	37	12	0	0	26	0	0	0	0	0
Gum Ball Pop, Lance	1 candy	12		45	0	0	0	0	0	0	0	0	0	12	4	0	0	12	0	0	0	0	0
Gummy Bears	28 pieces	40		130	0	0	0	0	0	0	0	15	1	30	10	0	0	30	3	0	0	0	0
jelly beans	11 pieces	40		160	0	0	0	0	0	0	0	5	0	37	12	0	0	25	0	0	0	0	0
jelly beans, Starburst	1/4 cup	42		140	0	0	0	0	0	0	0	10	0	36	12	0	0	30	0	0	0	0	0
Lemon Drops, Brach's	4 pieces	17		70	0	0	0	0	0	0	0	5	0	16	5	0	0	10	0	0	0	0	0

Consult a similar product for brand names not listed.

Food Name	Serving Size gm	mL	Calories	Calories from Fat	Total Fat (g)	%DV	Saturated Fat (g)	%DV	Cholesterol (mg)	%DV	Sodium (mg)	%DV	Total Carbohydrates (g)	%DV	Fiber (g)	%DV	Sugars (g)	Protein (g)	Vitamin A (%DV)	Vitamin C (%DV)	Calcium (%DV)	Iron (%DV)
Licorice Twists	1.4 oz	40	140	0	0	0	0	0	0	0	115	5	37	12	0	0	16	0	0	0	2	0
Life Savers, 5 flavors	4 pieces	16	60	0	0	0	0	0	0	0	0	0	16	5	0	0	15	0	0	0	0	0
lollipop/sucker	0.5 oz	15	60	0	0	0	0	0	0	0	20	1	15	5	0	0	15	0	0	0	0	0
lollipop/sucker, Lance	3 pieces	14	50	0	0	0	0	0	0	0	6	0	13	4	0	0	10	0	0	0	0	0
marshmallow eggs, choc-covered, Fanny Farmer	3 pieces	42	191	70	8	12	5	25	0	0	50	2	29	10	2	8	24	2	0	0	2	4
Milk Duds	1 box	52	230	70	8	12	6	30	0	0	115	5	38	13	0	0	27	1	0	0	2	2
Momints, Lance	4 pieces	44	180	60	6	9	4	20	0	0	10	1	32	11	0	0	30	1	0	0	0	0
Mounds, Peter Paul	2 bars	39	190	90	10	15	8	40	0	0	60	3	23	8	2	8	15	1	0	0	0	4
Nestlé Crunch	1 bar	46	230	110	12	18	7	34	5	2	60	2	28	9	1	4	23	3	0	0	8	0
Nestlé Quik Bar	1 bar	47	180	30	3.5	6	3	15	<5	2	20	1	36	12	<1	3	23	2	0	0	4	0
Oh Henry!, Nestlé	1 bar (1.8 oz)	51	230	80	9	14	4	20	<5	1	125	5	32	11	2	8	30	6	0	0	4	0
100 Grand, Nestlé	1 bar (1.5 oz)	43	200	70	8	12	5	25	10	3	75	3	30	10	<1	2	27	2	0	0	4	0
peanut bar, choc-covered, Lance	1 bar	57	290	130	15	23	4	21	0	0	90	4	32	11	2	8	23	9	0	0	2	4
peanut bar, Lance	1 bar	50	270	130	15	23	2.5	13	0	0	80	3	23	8	2	8	15	10	0	0	0	2
peanut brittle	1.4 oz	40	180	50	6	9	3	15	0	0	210	9	30	10	1	4	22	3	0	0	0	2
peanuts, choc-covered	16 pieces	40	210	120	13	20	4	20	2	1	15	1	21	7	2	8	18	6	0	0	6	2
peanuts, choc-covered, Goobers	1 bag (1.38 oz)	39	210	120	13	20	5	25	<5	1	20	1	19	6	3	12	16	5	0	0	4	2
peanuts, choc-covered, Lance K Nuts	4 pieces	43	240	140	15	23	5	25	5	2	130	5	23	8	0	0	17	4	0	0	0	0
pectin slices	3 pieces	40	140	0	0	0	0	0	0	0	35	2	34	11	NA	NA	NA	0	0	0	0	0
Peppermint Patties, York	3 pieces	41	170	35	4	6	2.5	12	0	0	10	1	32	11	0	0	24	1	0	0	0	0
Pop-A-Lance, Lance	1 pop	12	45	0	0	0	0	0	0	0	0	0	11	4	0	0	10	0	0	0	0	0
raisins, choc-covered, Brach's	34 pieces	40	170	60	7	10	5	23	5	1	20	1	27	9	2	6	25	2	0	0	0	2
raisins, choc-covered, Raisinets	1 bag	45	200	70	8	12	4	22	<5	1	15	1	31	10	2	10	28	2	0	0	4	2
Sno Caps, Nestlé	1 box (2.3 oz)	62	300	110	13	19	8	38	0	0	0	0	48	16	3	14	38	2	0	0	0	6
Sour Balls, Brach's	3 pieces	18	70	0	0	0	0	0	0	0	10	0	17	6	0	0	11	0	0	0	0	0

Food Name	Serving Size gm	mL	Calories	Calories from Fat	Total Fat (g)	%DV	Saturated Fat (g)	%DV	Cholesterol (mg)	%DV	Sodium (mg)	%DV	Total Carbohydrates (g)	%DV	Fiber (g)	%DV	Sugars (g)	Protein (g)	Vitamin A (%DV)	Vitamin C (%DV)	Calcium (%DV)	Iron (%DV)
Spice Drops, Brach's	39		130	0	0	0	0	0	0	0	15	1	33	11	0	0	23	0	0	0	0	0
Starlight Mints, Lance	15		60	0	0	0	0	0	0	0	0	0	15	5	0	0	11	0	0	0	0	0
taffy	40	1.4 oz	160	15	2	1.5	0	0	0	0	50	2	34	11	0	0	32	0	0	0	0	0
toffee	15		60	5	0.5	1	0	0	0	0	50	2	15	4	0	0	14	0	0	0	2	0
Turtles, Nestlé	33		160	80	9	14	3	15	<5	1	30	1	20	7	1	6	13	2	0	0	4	0
Twizzlers, cherry bites	34		110	10	1	2	0	0	0	0	80	3	23	8	0	0	13	1	0	0	0	0
Twizzlers, cherry, pull-n-peel	40		140	10	1	2	0.5	2	0	0	120	5	31	10	0	0	16	1	0	0	0	0
Whistle Pops, all flavors, Lance	19		70	0	0	0	0	0	0	0	0	0	19	6	0	0	17	0	0	0	0	0

Consult a similar product for brand names not listed.

SWEETS: GELATIN DESSERTS, SUGARS, SYRUPS, AND TOPPINGS

Food Name	Serving Size	gm	mL	Calories	Calories from Fat	Total Fat (g)	%DV	Saturated Fat (g)	%DV	Cholesterol (mg)	%DV	Sodium (mg)	%DV	Total Carbohydrates[6] (g)	%DV	Fiber[6] (g)	%DV	Sugars[6] (g)	Protein (g)	Vitamin A (%DV)	Vitamin C[7] (%DV)	Calcium (%DV)	Iron (%DV)
dip, caramel fruit, fat-free, Smucker's	2 tbsp	41		130	0	0	0	0	0	0	0	85	4	30	10	0	0	22	1	0	0	4	0
dip, caramel, low fat, Marie's	2 tbsp	35		140	20	2	3	1.5	8	5	2	90	4	29	10	0	0	23	1	0	0	2	0
dip, caramel, Marie's	2 tbsp	35		150	45	5	8	4	20	5	2	75	3	24	8	1	4	18	<1	0	0	2	0
dip, choc fruit, fat-free, Smucker's	2 tbsp	40		130	5	1	0	0	0	0	0	75	3	31	10	<1	3	19	2	0	0	4	0
gelatin dessert, all flavors, Del Monte Gel Cups	1 cup	99		100	0	0	0	0	0	0	0	80	3	25	8	<1	2	24	0	0	0	2	0
gelatin dessert, all flavors, dry mix, Royal	dry mix for ½ cup	21		80	0	0	0	0	0	0	0	105	4	19	6	0	0	18	2	0	0	0	0
glaze for blueberries, Marie's	2 tbsp	30		40	0	0	0	0	0	0	0	30	1	10	3	0	0	8	0	0	0	0	0
glaze for peaches, Marie's	2 tbsp	30		40	0	0	0	0	0	0	0	50	2	10	3	0	0	8	0	0	0	0	0
glaze for strawberries, Marie's	2 tbsp	30		40	0	0	0	0	0	0	0	30	1	9	3	0	0	9	0	0	0	0	0
glaze, creamy for bananas, Marie's	2 tbsp	30		60	20	2.5	4	0.5	3	0	0	50	2	8	3	0	0	7	0	0	0	0	0
molasses, Brer Rabbit	1 tbsp	21		90	0	0	0	0	0	0	0	10	0	14	5	0	0	14	0	0	0	8	10
sugar, brown	1 tsp	4		15	0	0	0	0	0	0	0	0	0	4	1	0	0	4	0	0	0	0	0
sugar, granulated	1 tsp	4		15	0	0	0	0	0	0	0	0	0	4	1	0	0	4	0	0	0	0	0
sugar, raw	1 packet	5		20	0	0	0	0	0	0	0	0	0	5	2	0	0	5	0	0	0	0	0
syrup, corn, dark w/refiners' syrup, Karo	2 tbsp	30	30	120	0	0	0	0	0	0	0	45	2	30	10	0	0	30	0	0	0	0	0
syrup, corn, light, Karo	2 tbsp	30	30	120	0	0	0	0	0	0	0	35	1	30	10	0	0	30	0	0	0	0	0
syrup, fruit, light, Smucker's	¼ cup	60	60	130	0	0	0	0	0	0	0	0	0	33	11	0	0	33	0	0	0	0	0
syrup, fruit, natural, Smucker's	¼ cup	60	60	210	0	0	0	0	0	0	0	0	0	52	17	0	0	52	0	0	0	0	0
syrup, pancake, Golden Griddle	¼ cup (4 tbsp)	60	60	220	0	0	0	0	0	0	0	55	2	57	19	0	0	57	0	0	0	0	0
syrup, pancake, Karo	¼ cup (4 tbsp)	60	60	240	0	0	0	0	0	0	0	85	4	60	20	0	0	60	0	0	0	0	0
syrup, pancake, Vermont Maid	¼ cup	60	60	210	0	0	0	0	0	0	0	25	1	53	18	0	0	41	0	0	0	0	0
syrup, 70% cal-reduced, S&W[48]	¼ cup	60	60	60	0	0	0	0	0	0	0	105	4	15	5	0	0	15	0	0	0	0	0

Food Name	Serving Size	gm	mL	Calories	Calories from Fat	Total Fat (g)	%DV	Saturated Fat (g)	%DV	Cholesterol (mg)	%DV	Sodium (mg)	%DV	Total Carbohydrates (g)	%DV	Fiber (g)	%DV	Sugars (g)	Protein (g)	Vitamin A (%DV)	Vitamin C (%DV)	Calcium (%DV)	Iron (%DV)
syrup, sundae, choc/butterscotch/caramel, Smucker's	2 tbsp	40		110	0	0	0	0	0	0	0	70	3	27	9	1	4	26	0	0	0	0	0
syrup w/pecans, Smucker's	2 tbsp	40		190	100	11	17	1	5	0	0	0	0	22	7	0	0	14	1	0	0	1	2
syrup w/walnuts, Smucker's	2 tbsp	40		190	90	10	15	1	5	0	0	0	0	23	8	0	0	15	2	0	0	1	2
topping, butterscotch caramel, fat-free, Smucker's	2 tbsp	41		130	0	0	0	0	0	0	0	110	5	31	10	<1	2	21	0	0	0	2	0
topping, butterscotch caramel, Smucker's	2 tbsp	42		130	10	1	2	0.5	3	5	1	70	3	30	10	<1	2	28	1	0	0	4	0
topping, caramel, Smucker's	2 tbsp	41		120	25	3	4	0.5	3	0	0	60	3	29	10	0	0	23	1	0	0	5	0
topping, choc fudge, Smucker's	2 tbsp	40		130	15	1.5	3	0.5	3	0	0	60	3	28	9	1	4	18	0	0	0	0	2
topping, hot fudge, light, Smucker's	2 tbsp	39		90	0	0	0	0	0	0	0	90	4	23	8	2	8	15	2	0	0	4	5
topping, hot fudge, Smucker's	2 tbsp	39		140	35	4	6	1	5	0	0	60	2	24	8	1	3	16	2	0	0	6	4
topping, Magic Shell, Smucker's	2 tbsp	34		220	150	16	25	6	30	0	0	25	1	16	5	0	0	16	1	0	0	0	7
topping, marshmallow, Smucker's	2 tbsp	40		120	0	0	0	0	0	0	0	0	0	29	10	0	0	28	0	0	0	0	0
topping, peanut butter caramel, Smucker's	2 tbsp	41		150	40	4.5	7	0.5	3	0	0	125	5	24	8	<1	2	16	3	0	0	2	0
topping, pineapple, Smucker's	2 tbsp	40		110	0	0	0	0	0	0	0	0	0	28	9	0	0	28	0	0	0	0	0
topping, strawberry, Smucker's	2 tbsp	40		100	0	0	0	0	0	0	0	0	0	26	9	0	0	26	0	0	0	0	0

Consult a similar product for brand names not listed.

Extra Foods[4]

EXTRA FOODS[1]

Food Name	Serving Size	gm	mL	Calories	Calories from Fat	Total Fat (g)	%DV	Saturated Fat (g)	%DV	Cholesterol (mg)	%DV	Sodium (mg)	%DV	Total Carbohydrates[8] (g)	%DV	Fiber[8] (g)	%DV	Sugars[8] (g)	Protein (g)	Vitamin A (%DV)	Vitamin C[7] (%DV)	Calcium (%DV)	Iron (%DV)
bouillon cube, beef, Armour Star	1 cube	4		5	0	0	0	0	0	0	0	920	38	1	0	0	0	0	0	0	0	0	0
bouillon cube, beef, Knorr	½ cube	6		20	15	1.5	2	0.5	2	NA	NA	1290	54	<1	0	0	0	0	1	0	0	0	0
bouillon cube, beef, Wyler's	1 cube	3.5		5	0	0	0	0	0	0	0	930	39	1	0	0	0	0	0	0	0	0	0
bouillon cube, chicken, Armour Star	1 cube	4		5	0	0	0	0	0	0	0	910	38	1	0	0	0	0	0	0	0	0	0
bouillon cube, chicken, Knorr	½ cube	6		20	15	1.5	2	0.5	2	NA	NA	1200	50	1	0	0	0	0	1	0	0	0	0
bouillon cube, chicken, Wyler's	1 cube	3.5		5	0	0	0	0	0	NA	NA	900	38	1	0	0	0	0	0	0	0	0	0
bouillon cube, fish, Knorr	½ cube	4.5		10	10	1	2	NA	NA	NA	NA	960	40	0	0	0	0	0	1	0	0	0	0
bouillon cube, vegetarian veg, Knorr	½ cube	5		15	10	1	2	NA	NA	0	0	910	38	1	0	0	0	0	1	0	0	0	0
bouillon, veg, dry mix, Wyler's	1 tsp	3.5		5	0	0	0	0	0	0	0	870	36	1	0	0	0	0	0	0	0	0	0
broth, beef, cnd rts, College Inn	1 cup		240	20	0	0	0	0	0	0	0	1140	48	0	0	0	0	0	4	0	0	0	0
broth, beef, cnd rts, Swanson	1 cup	235		20	10	1	2	0.5	3	<5	1	820	34	2	1	0	0	1	2	0	0	0	2
broth, beef double-rich, cnd cond, Campbell's	½ cup	124		15	0	0	0	0	0	<5	1	900	38	1	0	0	0	0	3	0	0	2	0
broth, chicken, cnd cond, Campbell's	½ cup	124		30	20	2	3	0.5	3	<5	1	770	32	2	1	0	0	1	2	0	0	0	0
broth, chicken, cnd rts, College Inn	1 cup		240	25	15	1.5	2	0.5	2	<5	0	1050	44	1	0	0	0	1	1	0	0	0	0
broth, chicken, cnd rts, Swanson	1 cup	235		30	20	2	3	0.5	3	0	0	1000	42	1	0	0	0	2	2	0	0	0	0
broth, Scotch, cnd cond, Campbell's	½ cup	124		80	25	3	5	1.5	8	10	3	870	36	9	3	1	4	1	4	40	0	4	2
broth, vegetable, cnd rts, Swanson	1 cup	235		20	15	2	2	0	0	0	0	1000	42	3	2	0	0	3	2	0	0	0	0
Butter Buds	1 tsp	2		5	0	0	0	0	0	0	0	75	3	2	1	0	0	0	0	0	0	0	0
coffee, inst powder, reg/decaf	8 fl oz (1 cup)		240	0	0	0	0	0	0	0	0	0	0	0	0	0	0	0	0	0	0	0	0
consomme, beef, cnd cond, Campbell's	½ cup	124		25	0	0	0	0	0	5	1	820	34	2	1	0	0	2	4	0	0	2	0
creamer, nondairy, Cremora Lite, Borden	1 tsp	2		10	0	0	0	0	0	0	0	0	0	2	1	0	0	0	0	0	0	0	0
Diet Cherry 7UP	12 fl oz		355	0	0	0	0	0	0	0	0	35	1	0	0	0	0	0	0	0	0	0	0
Diet Dr Pepper	12 fl oz		355	0	0	0	0	0	0	0	0	55	2	0	0	0	0	0	0	0	0	0	0
Diet Mountain Dew	8 fl oz		240	0	0	0	0	0	0	0	0	25	1	0	0	0	0	0	0	0	0	0	0

Food Name	Serving Size	gm	mL	Calories	Calories from Fat	Total Fat (g)	%DV	Saturated Fat (g)	%DV	Cholesterol (mg)	%DV	Sodium (mg)	%DV	Total Carbohydrates (g)	%DV	Fiber (g)	%DV	Sugars (g)	Protein (g)	Vitamin A (%DV)	Vitamin C (%DV)	Calcium (%DV)	Iron (%DV)
Diet Pepsi	8 fl oz		240	0	0	0	0	0	0	0	0	25	1	0	0	0	0	0	0	0	0	0	0
Diet Rite cola	8 fl oz		240	0	0	0	0	0	0	0	0	0	0	0	0	0	0	0	0	0	0	0	0
Diet Rite fruit flavors	8 fl oz		240	0	0	0	0	0	0	0	0	0	0	0	0	0	0	0	0	0	0	0	0
Diet Royal Crown cola	8 fl oz		240	0	0	0	0	0	0	0	0	35	1	0	0	0	0	0	0	0	0	0	0
Diet 7UP	12 fl oz		355	0	0	0	0	0	0	0	0	35	1	0	0	0	0	0	0	0	0	0	0
Diet Slice Lemon Lime	12 fl oz		355	0	0	0	0	0	0	0	0	35	1	1	0	0	0	0	0	0	0	0	0
dip, garlic & onion, fat-free, Marie's	2 tbsp	30		35	0	0	0	0	0	0	0	350	15	7	2	1	4	0	0	0	0	2	0
dip, peppercorn ranch, fat-free, Marie's	2 tbsp	30		35	0	0	0	0	0	0	0	260	11	7	2	1	4	2	1	0	0	2	0
dip, sour crm, French onion, fat-free, Borden	2 tbsp	32		25	0	0	0	0	0	0	0	170	7	4	1	0	0	3	2	2	0	6	0
dressing, blue cheese, creamy, low fat, Marie's	2 tbsp	33		30	0	0	0	0	0	0	0	340	14	6	2	0	0	2	0	0	0	0	0
dressing/dip, Ital, creamy herb, low fat, Marie's	2 tbsp	33		30	0	0	0	0	0	0	0	340	14	7	2	0	0	3	<1	0	0	0	0
dressing, parmesan, creamy, low fat, Marie's	2 tbsp	33		35	0	0	0	0	0	0	0	280	12	7	2	0	0	2	<1	0	0	2	0
dressing, ranch, zesty, low fat, Marie's	2 tbsp	33		30	0	0	0	0	0	0	0	310	13	7	2	0	0	2	0	0	0	0	0
Equal	1 packet	1		0	0	0	0	0	0	0	0	0	0	<1	0	0	0	<1	0	0	0	0	0
gelatin dessert, all flavors, sugar-free, dry mix, Royal	dry mix for ½ cup	2.5		10	0	0	0	0	0	0	0	80	3	1	0	0	0	0	1	0	0	0	0
gravy, au jus, dry mix, Knorr	⅕ package	3.5		15	0	0	0	0	0	0	0	310	13	3	1	0	0	0	0	0	0	0	0
Natra Taste	1 packet	1		0	0	0	0	0	0	0	0	0	0	0	0	0	0	0	0	0	0	0	0
Natra Taste	1 packet	1		0	0	0	0	0	0	0	0	0	0	1	0	0	0	1	0	0	0	0	0
NutraSweet Spoonful	1 tsp	<1		0	0	0	0	0	0	0	0	0	0	<1	0	0	0	<1	0	0	0	0	0
Roma, dry, Natural Touch Kaffree[49]	1 tsp (makes 1 cup)	2		10	0	0	0	0	0	0	0	0	0	2	1	0	0	2	0	0	0	0	0
salt sub, Morton	¼ tsp	1.2		0	0	0	0	0	0	0	0	0	0	0	0	0	0	0	0	0	0	0	0
salt sub, seasoned, Morton	¼ tsp	1.1		0	0	0	0	0	0	0	0	0	0	0	0	0	0	0	0	0	0	0	0

Consult a similar product for brand names not listed.

Food Name	Serving Size	gm	mL	Calories	Calories from Fat	Total Fat (g)	%DV	Saturated Fat (g)	%DV	Cholesterol (mg)	%DV	Sodium (mg)	%DV	Total Carbohydrates (g)	%DV	Fiber (g)	%DV	Sugars (g)	Protein (g)	Vitamin A (%DV)	Vitamin C (%DV)	Calcium (%DV)	Iron (%DV)
salt, coarse Kosher, Morton	¼ tsp	1.2		0	0	0	0	0	0	0	0	480	20	0	0	0	0	0	0	0	0	0	0
salt, garlic, Morton	¼ tsp	1.2		0	0	0	0	0	0	0	0	370	15	0	0	0	0	0	0	0	0	0	0
salt, lite, Morton	¼ tsp	1.4		0	0	0	0	0	0	0	0	290	12	0	0	0	0	0	0	0	0	0	0
salt, Morton	¼ tsp	1.5		0	0	0	0	0	0	0	0	590	25	0	0	0	0	0	0	0	0	0	0
salt, popcorn, Morton	¼ tsp	1.5		0	0	0	0	0	0	0	0	580	24	0	0	0	0	0	0	0	0	0	0
salt, seasoned, Morton	¼ tsp	1.3		0	0	0	0	0	0	0	0	400	17	0	0	0	0	0	0	0	0	0	0
sauce/marinade, mesquite, S&W	1 tbsp	17		10	0	0	0	0	0	0	0	400	40	3	3	0	1	3	0	0	3	0	0
sauce/marinade, teriyaki, S&W	1 tbsp	18		25	0	0	0	0	0	0	0	480	18	5	2	0	0	6	1	0	5	0	0
sauce/marinade, teriyaki, lite, S&W	1 tbsp	18		25	0	0	0	0	0	0	0	220	9	5	2	0	0	3	1	0	0	0	0
sauce, oriental stir fry, S&W	1 tbsp	17		20	0	0	0	0	0	0	0	390	16	5	2	0	0	3	1	0	2	0	0
sauce, southwest fajita, S&W	1 tbsp	17		10	0	0	0	0	0	0	0	230	10	2	1	1	2	3	0	0	4	0	0
sauce, steak, A1	1 tbsp	17		15	0	0	0	0	0	0	0	250	10	3	0	0	0	2	0	0	0	0	0
seasoning blend, Nature's Seasons, Morton	¼ tsp	1.2		0	0	0	0	0	0	0	0	380	16	0	0	0	0	0	0	0	0	0	0
seltzer water, regular/flavored, Vintage	8 fl oz		240	0	0	0	0	0	0	0	0	0	0	0	0	0	0	0	0	0	0	0	0
soup, herb, dry mix, Knorr	⅓ package	24		100	40	5	7	1.5	8	<5	1	1010	42	13	4	0	0	0	3	2	0	4	4
soup, hot & sour, dry mix, Knorr	⅓ package	13		50	15	2	2	0.5	2	0	0	810	34	8	3	0	0	0	1	0	0	0	0
soup, oxtail, dry mix, Knorr	⅓ package	17		60	20	2	3	1	5	<5	1	910	38	9	3	0	0	1	2	4	20	0	2
sour crm, fat-free, Borden	2 tbsp	31		20	0	0	0	0	0	0	0	45	2	3	1	0	0	2	2	4	0	6	0
soy sauce, Kikkoman	1 tbsp	15	15	10	0	0	0	0	0	0	0	920	38	0	0	0	0	0	2	0	0	0	0
Sugar Twin	1 tsp	0.4		0	0	0	0	0	0	0	0	0	0	0	0	0	0	0	0	0	0	0	0
Sweet One	1 packet	1		0	0	0	0	0	0	0	0	0	0	1	0	0	0	1	0	0	0	0	0
Sweet'n Low	1 packet	1		0	0	0	0	0	0	0	0	0	0	1	0	0	0	1	0	0	0	0	0
Tabasco sauce, McIlhenny	1 tsp	5		0	0	0	0	0	0	0	0	30	1	0	0	0	0	0	0	4	0	0	0
tea, brewed, reg/decaf, Lipton	1 tea bag	1.9		0	0	0	0	0	0	0	0	0	0	0	0	0	0	0	0	0	0	0	0
vinaigrette, balsamic, fat-free, S&W Lites	2 tbsp	34		35	0	0	0	0	0	0	0	460	19	8	3	0	0	8	0	0	0	0	0

Food Name	Serving Size gm	mL	Calories	Calories from Fat	Total Fat (g)	%DV	Saturated Fat (g)	%DV	Cholesterol (mg)	%DV	Sodium (mg)	%DV	Total Carbohydrates[6] (g)	%DV	Fiber[6] (g)	%DV	Sugars[6] (g)	Protein (g)	Vitamin A (%DV)	Vitamin C[7] (%DV)	Calcium (%DV)	Iron (%DV)
vinaigrette, classic herb, fat-free, Marie's	35	2 tbsp	30	0	0	0	0	0	0	0	250	10	7	2	0	0	3	0	0	0	0	0
vinaigrette, honey dijon, fat-free, Marie's	35	2 tbsp	50	0	0	0	0	0	0	0	125	5	11	4	0	0	8	0	0	0	0	0
vinaigrette, ital, fat-free, Marie's	35	2 tbsp	35	0	0	0	0	0	0	0	280	12	8	3	0	0	4	0	0	0	0	0
vinaigrette, mango key lime, fat-free, S&W Lites	33	2 tbsp	30	0	0	0	0	0	0	0	390	16	7	2	0	0	7	0	0	0	0	0
vinaigrette, oriental rice wine, fat-free, S&W Lites	34	2 tbsp	30	0	0	0	0	0	0	0	280	12	8	3	0	0	7	0	0	0	0	0
vinaigrette, raspberry blush, fat-free, S&W Lites	34	2 tbsp	40	0	0	0	0	0	0	0	410	17	10	3	0	0	10	0	0	0	0	0
vinaigrette, raspberry, fat-free, Marie's	35	2 tbsp	35	0	0	0	0	0	0	0	35	1	8	3	0	0	5	0	0	0	0	0
vinaigrette, red wine, fat-free, Marie's	35	2 tbsp	40	0	0	0	0	0	0	0	300	13	10	3	0	0	6	0	0	0	0	0
vinaigrette, red wine w/herbs, fat-free, S&W Lites	34	2 tbsp	40	0	0	0	0	0	0	0	440	18	8	3	0	0	10	0	0	0	0	0
vinaigrette, white wine, fat-free, Marie's	35	2 tbsp	40	0	0	0	0	0	0	0	310	13	10	3	0	0	6	0	0	0	0	0
vinaigrette, white wine w/herbs, fat-free, S&W Lites	34	2 tbsp	40	0	0	0	0	0	0	0	450	19	10	3	0	0	10	0	0	0	0	0
vinegar, cider/other flavors,[50] S&W	15	1 tbsp	0	0	0	0	0	0	0	0	0	0	0	0	0	0	0	0	0	0	0	0
vinegar, malt ale, S&W	16	1 tbsp	0	0	0	0	0	0	0	0	0	0	0	0	0	0	0	0	0	0	0	0

Consult a similar product for brand names not listed.

Notes

1. "Entrees" are items (usually canned, frozen, or fast-food items) intended to be a main or side dish, but not a full meal.

2. "Meals/dinners" refers to items (usually frozen meals) intended to be full meals. They usually consist of a main dish and one or more side dishes.

3. "Beans" refers to mature legumes (beans and peas) that serve as sources of protein and carbohydrate. String/snap beans, snow peas, and wax beans are included in the vegetable group.

4. "Extra foods" are products with few or no calories or nutrients. These products are not easily classified into the other groups. Extra foods include broth, coffee, tea, and artificially sweetened beverages and gelatin desserts.

5. Values listed as "not significant" on food labels are listed as zeros on the tables.

6. Total carbohydrate includes starches, sugars, and dietary fiber. The values you see for sugars and dietary fiber in foods are usually less than the total carbohydrate. However,

you will find some foods for which the value for sugars (or the value for sugars plus dietary fiber) is slightly higher than that for total carbohydrate. This is because the nutrient values are rounded and adjusted to be in compliance with FDA and USDA nutrition labeling regulations.

7. High levels of vitamin C (e.g., 100% DV) in some canned fruits and in some juices and juice drinks may be due to added ascorbic acid (the chemical name for vitamin C). This accounts for inconsistencies in the vitamin C of similar products (i.e., the same product with a different brand name).

8. Enchanadas are corn-filled pasta with sauce.

9. The bean and beef burritos are garnished with salsa and cheese; the dinner includes rice and creamed corn with red peppers.

10. The bean and cheese enchiladas are garnished with sauce; the dinner includes refried beans and vegetables.

11. "Frank on bun" is the same as "hot dog."

12. The other pastas are macaroni, ruffles, shells, and twists.

13. The other pastas are angel hair, fettuccine, linguine, and vermicelli.

14. The other pastas are capellini, fettuccine, linguine, and vermicelli.

15. Beefaroni is a mixture of macaroni, beef, and tomato sauce.

16. Beefogetti is a mixture of pasta, mini meatballs, and tomato sauce.

17. Chili Mac is a mixture of macaroni, beef, and chili gravy.

18. The "lasagna al forno" contains lasagna pasta with marinara and bechamel sauces, sausage, and cheese.

19. The vegetables are broccoli, carrots, and zucchini.

20. The vegetables are carrots, onions, and zucchini.

21. The cheese manicotti contains ricotta and mozzarella cheeses and marinara sauce.

22. The Florentine manicotti contains ricotta cheese, spinach, and marinara sauce.

23. Mexi-Mac is a mixture of tomato sauce, macaroni, and beef.

24. Rigatoni is macaroni with a tomato meat sauce.

25. The beef stroganoff dinner consists of beef on egg noodles with side dishes of green beans and carrots.

26. The rice entree contains rice, pasta, chicken, tomatoes, and broccoli in a cheese sauce.

27. Water is required to prepare the mashed potatoes.

28. Milk and margarine are required to prepare the mashed potatoes.

29. The heartland medley contains gravy, vegetables, and beef.

30. Black olives are also referred to as "ripe" olives.

31. Green olives are also referred to as "Spanish" olives.

32. The other flavors are pineapple, raspberry, seedless blackberry, seedless raspberry, seedless strawberry, and strawberry.

33. The other flavors are lime, orange, pineapple, rainbow, raspberry, and triple fruit.

34. The flavor is a mixture of orange, pineapple, and raspberry.

35. Great northern beans are also referred to as "white" beans.

36. The beef sirloin tips entree includes beef and noodles with cream sauce and a vegetable.

37. The mesquite beef dinner includes mesquite beef with barbecue sauce, mashed potatoes, and corn.

38. The meat loaf dinner includes meat loaf with tomato sauce, potatoes with parsley, vegetable medley, and apple crisp.

39. The salisbury steak dinner includes salisbury steak with mushroom sauce, red skinned potatoes, broccoli, red peppers, and corn.

40. Chicken classica includes chicken with herb sauce, vegetables, and pasta.

41. Chicken Italienne is chicken with tomato sauce.

42. The Mexicali-style chicken includes chicken with tomato sauce and vegetables.

43. Chicken primavera is vegetables and chicken with an herb sauce.

44. This chicken dinner includes chicken with herb gravy, corn bread stuffing, creamed potatoes, green beans, and mushrooms.

45. This turkey dinner includes turkey with gravy, dressing, mashed potatoes, and corn.

46. Dijonnaise is a commercial blend of mayonnaise and Dijon mustard sold under the brand names of Hellmann's and Best Foods.

47. "Chocolates" refers to chocolate-covered centers, usually available as boxed candy.

48. The flavors include blueberry, butter flavor, maple flavor, and strawberry.

49. Roma is a barley beverage powder.

50. Other vinegar flavors include garlic wine, Italian herb, red wine, tarragon, and white distilled.

Abbreviations

&	and
Am	American
bbq	barbecue/barbeque
cal	calorie
Calif	California
choc	chocolate
cinn	cinnamon
ckd	cooked
cnd	canned
conc	concentrate/concentrated
cond	condensed
crm	cream/crème
decaf	decaffeinated
enr	enriched
fl	fluid

frzn	frozen
grnd	ground
inst	instant
Ital	Italian/Italiano
jce	juice
mac	macaroni
med	medium
NA	not available
orig	original
oz	ounce
% DV	percent Daily Value
prep	prepared
reg	regular
rts	ready-to-serve
sce	sauce
spagh	spaghetti
sub	substitute
tom	tomato(es)
tbsp	tablespoon
tsp	teaspoon
van	vanilla
veg	vegetable(s)
w/	with
w/o	without
/	or

MANUFACTURERS

Banquet Family	Banquet Family Entrees
Borden	Borden/Meadow Gold (for ice cream)
Boyardee	Chef Boyardee
Chompsalot	Sir Chompsalot
Franco-Am	Franco-American
Hellmann's	Hellmann's/Best Foods
KFC	Kentucky Fried Chicken
Morningstar	Morningstar Farms
New Engl	New England
Pepperidge	Pepperidge Farm
S&W Lites	S&W Vintage Lites
Swanson	Swanson Great Starts (breakfast entrees)
Swanson Children	Swanson Meals for Children
Swanson Kids	Swanson Kids Breakfast
Worthington	Worthington Foods
Wt Watchers	Weight Watchers

Index